THE
FUTURE
OF
DEMOCRACY

THE
FUTURE
OF
DEMOCRACY

Lessons from the Past and Present
To Guide us on our Path Forward

By Steve Zolno

REGENT PRESS
Berkeley, California

Cover photo: ErechteionTemple, Acropolis, Athens

Printed in the USA
REGENT PRESS
Berkeley, California
www.regentpress.net
regentpress@mindspring.com

To the Students, Faculty and Staff
of Shimer College

Where Democracy Thrives

Contents

Preface &
Acknowledgments

When I was in high school it seemed to me that something was missing in my education. My teachers were well-meaning and covered all the required topics. Sometimes they allowed students to express an opinion. But even then I was aware of being a product of an educational system that didn't prepare me to function in the real world.

I learned rote skills but not the relevance of those skills to my life or the world. I was taught to repeat the views of texts and teachers about history, literature and other subjects, but never was encouraged to come to my own conclusions. I had no idea about how the "facts" of science that I was forced to memorize related to a larger picture. I didn't learn to come up with creative solutions to problems.

In a few years I was expected to be an adult capable of making my own decisions, but I was not encouraged to develop thinking skills or my own values. I felt unprepared to be a responsible participant in the democracy that I soon was to inherit.

I was told that if I wanted to succeed – which meant having a good job, a house and a family – all I needed to do was find a college a lot like my high school. This option seemed less and less appealing as I approached graduation.

I began to wonder about some crucial areas that my education didn't address. If democracy is about respecting the rights of individuals, how do we bring that quality into our lives and the real world? If we have free choice, how do I avoid a clash between my freedom and that of others? In a democracy we can vote for the candidate of our choice, but how do we make that choice? What values should I expect candidates to represent to earn my vote? And perhaps most importantly, how do I clarify my own values?

I wondered what democracy really looks like. Is it rows of homes in the suburbs filled with families whose children play team sports that they support with car washes? Is it conflict in the streets between police and protesters who believe that the country is heading in the wrong direction? Or is democracy about getting the best job I can while ignoring the poverty and inequality around me?

I wasn't the only young person in the late 1960s who had doubts about the values that seemed to run our world. Youthful protestors filled the streets in the US, France and other countries. They objected to what they considered the shallow post-war world we inherited where material possessions were the driving force. But if there was an alternative, the protesters also didn't seem clear about what that might be.

I never received a satisfactory answer to my questions about the nature of democracy and how to make it a lived reality. And fifty years later, with my own child in school, it seems that not much progress has been made. People appear to be just as uncertain about what democracy really means and how to make it work. Thus this book was born.

It seems to me that the practice of democracy cannot be taught as a course to which we answer questions on tests. It mainly is imparted by the examples of parents and teachers who take a genuine interest in youth and show faith in the ability of young people to come to their own conclusions so as to become responsible citizens. In the world outside the home and classroom, democracy is best modeled by leaders who emphasize the importance of each individual and are themselves examples about how to make the world a better place. Democracy is based on a faith that people can participate in their own self-governance and make it work. Engagement with others toward common understanding and action are what best prepares us for this task.

In today's political climate – and perhaps in all political climates – there is a struggle between the best and the worst elements in humanity. By "best" I mean what has worked to serve and preserve the human race. The long-term success of any civilization depends on bringing the talents and abilities of the greatest number of people into play. This is best done in an environment that recognizes the dignity of every human being.

There are those who favor democracy and those who work against it in the families, schools, work situations, organizations, and governments that affect our daily lives. For those who believe in it, perhaps the most important question we should ask is: "What can we do to preserve and strengthen democracy amidst the forces that oppose it?"

For those of us fortunate enough to live under governments that we consider democratic, citizens vote for those who represent them. That is where participation ends for most of us. Around the time of national elections we start paying attention to the process of choosing our leaders. Yet we rarely demand that those who seek our votes show by word and deed how they intend to improve our world. Promising to change past or present practices is not enough.

The ability of governments to meet the needs of those they serve is based on developing and moving toward a shared vision, as well as working together on a path toward that vision. The vision of democracy is serving the needs of the greatest number of people possible. When we vote do we think about whether the views of candidates are in tune with democracy, or do we just cast our vote for those who seem the most aligned with our own views or most confident?

I intend to trace how the thread of democracy has worked its way into and out of the lives of people and civilizations through time – from the distant past to the present. I don't plan to reinvent the wheel, but hopefully to show how the wheel called democracy got rolling and how best to keep it moving forward as effectively as possible.

And as I will show, no matter how strong the forces of oppression have been, the wellsprings of human respect and dignity continually await an opportunity to re-emerge. But after these eruptions do occur, the result often is a return to the oppressive conditions they were intended to purge.

It is difficult to see the history we make as we create it. Stepping away and understanding the trends around us is a challenge. I am not the first to notice that history reveals its lessons in retrospect. Thus we might ask if there are any "grand themes" to history. This work can be seen as a view of the democratic element in our world over time and an exploration of its possible path forward.

Interspersed throughout Chapter I are mini-segments entitled "*The World of Wine*." My friends know that I am a wine enthusiast. I also appreciate well-made beer and spirits. That said, one might wonder how I ever got this book written. A little more seriously: wine has been considered a true hallmark of civilization and congeniality throughout much of human history. It contributes to the democratic element in social settings – for at least as long as the party lasts! I have given examples of the importance of wine as a part of our political and personal heritage through time.

My project never could have gotten rolling without the help of my mentors, editors and friends who have supported me and provided feedback on how I could state my views with greater clarity and precision. Where I failed in that goal I have only myself to blame. Those who have supported this process have my undying gratitude, including Terry Cullinane, Aron Dunlap, Steve Freedkin, Benjamin M. Friedman, Dennis Kaplan, Rob Katz, Ken Knabb, Robert Keohane, Ethel Murphy, Karen Ohlson, Deborah Pearl, Adina Sara, David Shiner, and Harold Stone.

I especially want to thank Professor Albert Dragstedt, who, for years has led our little study group in a rediscovery of the classics and their application to our times and lives.

Democracy:

- *A form of government in which people choose leaders by voting*
- *A country ruled by democracy*
- *An organization or situation in which everyone is treated equally and has equal rights*

— MERRIAM-WEBSTER DICTIONARY

Introduction

Why another book on democracy? Many works have been written about the democratic process from the time of the ancient Greeks to the present. Wherever, and in whatever form it has existed, the establishment of a democratic government always has been a response to conditions seen as oppressive. To succeed in the long-term, every attempt at democracy must include a clear and viable path forward. Yet little has been written about what is needed to sustain such a path – from the efforts of individuals to the actions of nations.

Governments are not the only forms in which democracy can take place. Our personal relationships, families, schools, organizations, and institutions also can be workshops for democracy. In these places it can be practiced that so that it eventually blossoms into full expression at the level of our nations. At its core, democracy is based on "the determination and longing to be treated with some degree of consideration."[1]

When primitive societies grew too large to be governed by consensus, members of tribes, states, and then nations were expected to follow the dictates of a ruler. Subjects often pushed back against oppression. Rarely, though, have truly democratic societies emerged as a direct result of revolution.

The first known democratic state, according to most historians, was Athens around 460 BCE. After the ancient Greeks there were elements of democracy in a number of political entities, including Rome that extended citizenship to conquered peoples. As we will see, there even was a degree of democracy among serfs in the Middle Ages. But the idea of democracy at the level of a nation wasn't resurrected until the approach of the "Enlightenment" beginning around 1700, when European writers began to question the absolute rule of monarchs. This laid the groundwork for both the American and French Revolutions by the end of the century.

Since that time democracy has been tried on all continents, at times with greater success than others. After its introduction in the United States it slowly spread to over 100 nations that considered themselves democratic. Types of democracy have been established around the world and many governments have democratic elements.[2] Democracy exists to varying degrees within many nations, but no system is exactly the same. The United States, for example, is considered a constitutional republic, Britain is a constitutional monarchy, while India is a parliamentary democracy.

Just as there are no individuals or groups of people exactly alike – with the same values and beliefs – there is no one model for democracy. The only standard by which any truly democratic institution must operate is that it continues to move toward government that benefits the largest number of individuals possible.

Voting is no guarantee of real democracy that assures the rights of all. Candidates, referendums, and propositions are limited to what is on the ballot, and in some countries voting options are pre-selected by those in power. Voting often leads to unforeseen results which fail to live up to promises or expectations. If voting results in the domination by some groups or individuals over others, the result no longer is democratic. Debates – where people line up on one side or another about issues or candidates – are not the same as real discussions about how to maintain democratic values.

Democracy, along with opposition to it, is found throughout our world. Yet nations are made of people, and to understand the progress and challenges of nations we must have insight into the human beings who make them up. There have been attempts to provide this insight from the time democracy began. Plato, Aristotle, John Locke, Jean-Jacques Rousseau, Voltaire and James Madison are among those who have written about how human ideals and inclinations affect our interactions and contribute to the success or failure of political institutions.

There is a common thread to the themes of these great thinkers: maintaining respect for the aspirations of the individual. For democracy to succeed there must be a commitment by those involved to creating and moving toward a common vision. And what is that vision? In democracy power resides in the people as a whole. This, of course, is more easily said than achieved. If democracy is government by the people it requires a faith among them that they can work together to pursue self-governance. The goal of a nation – or organization – that considers itself democratic must be that the rights of all participants are honored, with the possible exception of those who prove a danger to society itself.

In these pages we will discuss how genuine democratic elements within a country are likely to lead to a better future for its people. We will explore the ways that real democracy

– that which benefits the largest possible number of people – contributes to progress and growth. We will consider how quality human interactions – those in which all are respected – affect relationships and organizations, and what can be done to bring them into play. We will examine why the continuation of democracy is challenged everywhere it exists. And we will seek to understand how our views – and our actions based on them – move us closer to, or further from, a society that honors the rights of every individual.

Cooperation Based on Trust

There are specific ways by which our institutions and governments succeed or fail. Success depends on establishing and maintaining trust. Preserving trust must be an ongoing effort if human interactions are not to regress to inequality or tyranny. This requires a commitment to maintain respect for every individual. Only ongoing respectful communication can guarantee the trust needed for democratic interactions.

Cooperation based on trust is the most important tenet of every successful human interaction. It allows us to establish long-term connections as we create ongoing, non-threatening relationships. The cooperative pursuit of goals in our homes, schools, communities, nations, and international institutions benefits us all.

Trust is the 'glue' that binds us. It allows us to identify and promote mutual self-interest. Trust encourages effective communication to take place both within, and between, nations.[3]

The democratic process involves making agreements with others that all are expected to keep. By living in a democratic society we agree to follow laws that are made by elected representatives on our behalf. In well-functioning democracies we support each other in mutual self-interest; laws are made and enforced for the benefit of all. Trust is essential to maintaining agreements, even if it is a guarded trust, because it makes democratic interactions and governments possible. It encourages respect for human dignity and rights. It allows democracy to exist and – hopefully – to thrive.

Every family, organization, community, city and nation is made up of people whose customs and laws reflect their views about how they should interact. Within the family, there usually is a degree of trust that results in an ability to live and work together. As we participate in organizations such as businesses or governments, successful interactions also rely on trust. Our faith in the governments that so greatly affect our lives is based on whether we can trust those who run them. But as our myths, history, and experience tell us, trust easily can be betrayed and turned to distrust.

The Consequences of Distrust

The openness and trust of our early years yields to more caution as we mature. As children, our parents or teachers used criticism to redirect us from ideas or behaviors they considered inappropriate. We also felt betrayed when others seem to no longer to be worthy of our trust. Our world view changed as we internalized new values – based on what we were told and our experience – on our way to adulthood. Our values shaped our concepts of right and wrong and became our guides in determining who to trust and who not to trust.

Our assumptions about people became reflected in trusting some and distrusting or avoiding others. We become convinced that some people are to be treated warily or with hostility, often for good reason. We learned to fear them as a threat to our mental or physical well-being.

Our distrust often is based on an assumption that others are different from us. They have different backgrounds, different looks or a different outlook on life – creating a distance between "us" and "them."

Trust seems easy between allies who focus on a common enemy. But when rebellions overthrow tyranny, distrust often develops among those who replace the old order, sometimes with the same level of intensity once focused on the tyrant.

In our daily interactions we feel either connected to – or disconnected from – those we encounter. We tend to trust some people and distrust others. We vacillate between modes of trust and distrust throughout our lives, which becomes expressed in our relationships and political institutions. We interact positively with some and confront or avoid those we mistrust.

In both our personal and political lives we find ourselves aligned with those we believe are like us – or think like us – and separate from those who are different. We become certain about the correct views that people should hold to make the world a better place, and criticize those whose views we think could potentially destroy it. Our distrust for those who we think are different can become intense as we construct a mental wall between them and us. But that wall also cuts off our communication and ability to work with others.

Rebuilding Trust

Every group of individuals, large or small, becomes democratic when we interact respectfully to identify and move toward common goals.[4] What we call dialogue often really is disagreement or criticism that pits us against each other. But history shows us that when we use respectful dialogue we are more likely to identify and progress toward what we want to achieve. The reintroduction of respectful, democratic interactions can represent a radical departure from what has gone before. It can mark the beginning of a renewed sense of trust in working together toward a future of shared decision making and accomplishment.

Democracy has the potential to improve our lives by creating a more just world. Many use the term "democracy" to focus on individual preferences and their own needs, rather than on what benefits the whole. Terms such as "liberty" can refer to what works best to preserve individual rights, or on the intent by some to impose their will on others. If only considered to be rule of the majority, democracy has the potential, by those who pervert it, to crush individual liberties. At that point it no longer really is democracy. The direction of true democracy must be played out in respectful interactions by those whose lives are affected, with the interests of all kept in mind.

We only know our own limited concepts of ourselves, others and our world. The world beheld by each of us is different.[5] Our words—even when enlarged into phrases and sentences—only reflect a part of what we see and want to express. Communication is difficult, and often the most simplified phrases, although attractive for their brevity, only are limited reflections of the world around us or what we really think or feel. Miscommunication is common. Establishing common goals and reaching agreement on how best to work toward them is a continual challenge. But despite the obstacles inherent in communication, our choice always is whether to work toward greater trust between ourselves and others or to assume that others cannot be trusted.

It ultimately may be true that many people – and nations – are not worthy of our trust. But failing to try communication creates a foregone conclusion that reaching mutual goals is impossible. To create real communication we must be aware of the limitations of our perceptions and of human communication skills. Our judgments always are based on limited evidence and are inevitably incomplete. But understanding this brings greater humility to our interactions. It allows us to step back and consider with others what we might do as equals to mutually bring our world to a better place, rather than simply trying to impose our own views. This is the promise and challenge that real democracy holds.

The size of modern governments would never allow us to return to the "direct democracy" of Athens, where only a small percent of residents were allowed to participate. In our world it always will be a few representatives who determine if we are governed by democratic ideals. Thus it is essential to determine and express our views about whether those who represent us pursue the interests of only a narrow segment of the population or the broader interests of all.

When the interests of only a few are represented, the interests of those at all levels of society are negatively affected. When economies collapse all suffer the effects. Leaders who claim to understand and support democracy must represent the long-term interests of the population as a whole or they fail to represent any of us. We can bring democratic interactions to bear in our institutions, organizations, and personal lives. For society to move toward a more secure future for everyone, we must become better at clarifying those lessons from our past that can shine a light on the path before us.

In the following chapters we will (1) look at the origins of democracy, (2) consider the extent to which democracy – or its denial – affects our current world, and (3) discuss what is needed to maintain the benefits of democracy for our future.

Clarity about democratic ideals and their application to our lives and institutions is essential for those who want to live in a truly civilized world. The following chapters attempt to demonstrate how to create and maintain this clarity in every type of human interaction. As you read through these pages it will become clear how the themes of trust and distrust have shaped us and our cultures from the beginning and how they are likely to continue to shape our future. Practicing democracy may not make it perfect, but it increases our chances of making it possible.

Democratic vs. Egalitarian Societies

In addition to discussing democracy in governments, we will use the above third definition of democracy throughout this book: "An organization or situation in which everyone is treated equally and has equal rights." This can apply to families, schools, businesses, governments or any type of organization. It even can be brought into everyday interactions with others. The definition of egalitarianism is not quite the same: "A belief in human equality especially with respect to social, political, and economic affairs." A government can be egalitarian, but it only becomes democratic when everyone is treated equally. One person – or a few – can dominate in egalitarian situations, but truly democratic situations demand equal treatment and respect for all.

Endnotes

1   "Everywhere that the word *democracy* has fought its way forward across time and space, you can hear both these themes: the purposeful struggle to improve the practical circumstances of life, and to escape from arbitrary and often brutal coercion, but also the determination and longing to be treated with respect and some degree of consideration." *Democracy: A History*, Page 19

2   "It can be (and has been) adopted with some success on every continent, in societies with long and cruel experiences of arbitrary rule, cultures of great historic depth... in East and South and Southeast Asia, in Latin America...in Sub-Saharan Africa and even the Middle East." *Democracy: A History,* Page 181

3   "For...institutions to be morally acceptable, they must rest both on humane beliefs and substantial mutual trust." *Power and Governance in a Partially Globalized World,* Page 261

4   "Democracy is a way of personal life controlled not merely by faith in human nature in general but by faith in the capacity of human beings for intelligent judgment and action if proper conditions are furnished." From "Creative Democracy – The Task Before Us," by John Dewey. First Published in *John Dewey and the Promise of America*. Progressive Education Booklet No. 14, 1939, Page 230

5   "We are all the same, that is, human, in such a way that nobody is ever the same as anyone else who ever lived, lives or will live." *The Human Condition*, Page 8

"Man is born free, and everywhere he is in chains"
— Jean Jacques Rousseau in *The Social Contract*[1]

Chapter I

Democracy's Past

Origins

The promise of democracy is that it will provide us the freedom to make the major choices that affect our lives. Many also believe it is the political system that best maximizes the potential of every individual. But where did the idea of democracy come from, and why is it considered so important by so many?

Our intent is not just to review history, but to identify trends toward – and away from – the recognition of human dignity through time. We will consider whether institutions that call themselves democratic have brought the greatest benefit to the most people, and do our best to understand the nature of governments that are likely to create the greatest stability for those under their wing.

What we call history actually is a continuum of time that comes out of the past and moves through us on into the future. At some point our most ancient ancestors decided that they were separate entities with a conscious history and a place in their community. They no longer simply followed the instincts that flowed through them. They became aware of themselves and their actions. They began to believe that some actions were good and others were bad and shared these values among them. But perhaps most importantly, at some point they began to seek recognition from others as valid and worthwhile human beings.

Our ancestors had to struggle for food and shelter, but by joining forces to hunt and protect themselves their chances for survival improved. As our brains became larger over the course of countless generations we were better able to anticipate our needs and plan more effectively for the dangers we were to encounter.[2] And as the size of our social structures increased, more extensive rules and rituals were required to guide our interactions with our communities and world.[3]

Biologists tell us that evolution did not take a direct path from the beginnings of life to the present. Along the developmental route to the world we know, the branches of many species ended, with the survivors those best able to adapt to changing environments. But the majority became evolutionary dead ends.[4]

In East Africa a fossil was found of a human-like skull of a group that biologists named Sandlooper. They had a huge cranium that indicates a brain larger than current humans – nearly all we know about a race that lived perhaps 100,000 years ago. Most likely that brain provided an advantage for many generations, but for unknown reasons this species, like most, died out.[5] A possible lesson here is that even being a successful species for a while does not guarantee long-term survival. In the case of Sandlooper, a large brain may have been an advantage, but this was not enough to ensure indefinite continuation; it may have been a disadvantage in dealing with new environmental challenges.

In these pages we will refer to this quality as the "persistence of the past" – the continuation of characteristics, attitudes, or ideas that seemed successful for a time but no longer confer an advantage. Evolution and the march of time make outmoded habits, customs, and brains an impediment to continued functioning.

Most evolutionary biologists would agree with Darwin that changes over time to every life form always have been, and continue to be, ongoing, with no final forms, including our own.[6]

But what can we know about whether the earliest human societies had elements of democracy, since there are no witnesses to prehistory? Scientists use a number of methods to shed light on our origins. They glimpse at what human life probably was like from its earliest times primarily by: (1) studying and interpreting bones, pottery, jewelry, and other objects at archeological sites dating back before human record keeping, (2) observing people who live in primitive societies in our own time, (3) examining the social patterns of animals, and (4) describing the behaviors of young children.

As more sites are found that provide evidence of early habitation, the likely dates of human origins continually get pushed back. New discoveries regularly challenge current models. In Europe, the earliest traces of human habitation (*Homo erectus*) go back about 700,000 years, based on sites in present-day Hungary and Italy. *Homo erectus* was followed by *Homo sapiens* (modern humans), who migrated into the Near East 90,000 years ago and into Europe about 40,000 years ago.[7] The main migration paths out of Africa seem fairly well established, while the likely date of the earliest migration to the Americas continues to be moved earlier.[8]

The Pech Merle Cave in southwestern France, with art believed to be about 25,000 years old, presents an awe-inspiring spectacle to the visitor. After squeezing through a narrow entrance, a large opening appears. One is confronted with drawings of animals that clearly were a focal point in the lives of individuals long before the existence of written language. What appear to be bison and horse-like animals – some in color – convey a very different view of the world and way of life from our own. We can imagine a family or clan gathering in the cave by a fire for warmth and light and discussing the animals depicted there in the same way that a modern family gathers around a television. Did they use signs or verbal language? Did they relive the day's hunt, use the pictures to evoke the spirits of animals they wanted to capture, or tell stories based on the art before them? Was their cave art used in a ritual to help them practice and rehearse the hunt ahead?[9]

At some point after the gathering – perhaps the next day – an expedition took place. Decisions had to be made about what or where or how to hunt and who would participate. Was there a strong individual who assumed leadership or were more "democratic" methods used – a consensus or vote – to make essential decisions that would affect the group's survival? We can be fairly certain that once a strategy was determined, with or without the use of actual language as we know it, the hunting excursion was more likely to succeed if everyone was able to agree and work together using a common plan. And if the original plan failed, the ability to communicate and find an alternative strategy increased the possibility of success.

Of course we never will know with certainty if there was any type of democracy among our earliest ancestors. However, anthropologists have studied the myths of early people, as well as the decision making process of primitive societies from our own time, that provide a glimpse into what may have been the early decision making process. There tends to be greater democracy – group decision making or consensus – among smaller groups, with larger groups requiring greater specialization, particularly in choosing leaders.[10] Large societies had a greater division of tasks – including hunters and gatherers, makers of baskets, pottery, clothing and jewelry, healers, rule makers and enforcers. Trade began as goods were exchanged between societies that could not find or produce what they wanted.[11]

People in primitive societies in Africa and South America still travel and hunt in tribes, but all societies have moral codes that help them supersede their individual aggressions.[12] This makes it likely that rules for behavior were present in the earliest human societies to provide guidance to live together successfully. Being able to follow rules and rituals that govern encounters with each other and the outside world – at first oral, then written – would likely have increased their chances of survival. Rules enabled them to move beyond conflicts and work more effectively toward common goals. Rituals provided spiritual inspiration and practice in encounters with enemies – both human and animal. What remains uncertain is to what extent freedom and choice were considered important to early humans – including those who lived far before the dawn of civilization – or if these ideas are of more modern origin.[13]

An assumption of most ethologists (scientists who study animal behavior) is that observing animals sheds light on the origins of human interaction. This is based on the belief that we share common ancestors. An established "pecking order" – with leaders and followers assuming a hierarchy of roles – can avoid conflict while increasing efficiency for activities done by the group.[14] We know that primates often search for food in small groups, for example some chimps hunt together.[15] Many animals also communicate to warn others of their species about potential danger. Thus it seems likely that the species from which we evolved were able to cooperate toward common goals – an ability essential to the advent of democracy.

Studies of young children provide insights into early human behavior because they have had relatively little indoctrination into the ways of society. We often portray childhood as a time of freedom and innocence in our discussions and literature. Yet children are not really free because they depend on those around them for what they need to survive.

We are born into a family and society that hold expectations for us about how to act and what to believe, and most of us learn to live up to those expectations as we mature.[16] We imitate models that we see around us such as how to act as male or female members of society. We begin to identify with a particular race, nationality, religion, or economic group. We come to believe that those who belong to groups different from our own are separate from us by their nature, and we assume communication with them will be more difficult than with those who look and think like us.[17]

Although our personalities take years to develop, the expectations placed on us by our families and societies begin at conception. As we move toward adulthood these expectations become a part us. But as we go about our daily lives and interact with others and our world, we rarely give much thought to what has gone into shaping the person we have become.[18]

As every parent knows, each child is an individual with distinct talents, tastes, and personalities – even within the same family. Thus it seems that our behaviors and the choices we make are determined at least to some extent by our internal makeup as well as external influences.

Young children are infinitely creative. They continually come up with new and original ideas in their play and interactions but lose much of that creativity as they age. When they start school they may discover that they are talented at writing or math, athletics, or that they have natural mechanical skills. They begin to think of themselves as either leaders or followers. They believe themselves proficient in some areas and not others. The preferences and tastes they develop ultimately shape the direction of their lives and determine who they are seen to be by others and themselves.[19]

With the advent of adolescence, many children make choices that are different from the lessons they have been taught or the lifestyles they see around them. Although this might seem negative to parents, it may be a healthy trend that leads them to making original choices and moving their lives in a new – and possibly more viable – direction. But at what point do we at last choose a clear direction for ourselves and become adults who take responsibility for our own lives? When do we really make our own decisions, or are our actions as adults always determined by our backgrounds? And even if we live in a democracy, is it really possible to forge an independent path?

Regardless of whether we really are born "free," the person we become desires the freedom to make choices and determine her or his destiny. We want opportunities to develop and express our talents in a way that maximizes our control over our future. If not allowed to make these choices we are likely to believe ourselves oppressed.

To maximize our chance of being able to make the major choices that affect our lives we must live under a form of government that supports our right to make them, or at least one that does not interfere with that right. For thousands of years going back at least to the ancient Greeks – politicians, philosophers, historians, and ordinary citizens have debated how best to create a government that protects the ability of individuals to determine their own direction.[20]

If we believe democracy worth preserving, we must understand its origins to determine in what ways it has succeeded or failed to meet its lofty aspirations of greater freedom and choice for all. Once we compare what it has achieved with the ideals that we hold for it we hopefully can learn the lessons – and make the required adjustments – to keep it viable for ourselves and future generations.

Understanding why democracy is appealing to so many is essential to preserving it. Is the desire for freedom – and the ability to make choices that come with it – a part of human nature that goes back to our origins, or is it a relatively recent innovation in human thought? For those who value democracy, when and why did we decide that choice was important, and how did we begin to think it essential to participate in determining our own fate rather than simply submitting and allowing others – or our circumstances – to choose a direction for us? In this chapter I present an historical and geographical overview of societies through time, focusing on how elements of democracy have woven their way in and out of the structures of our civilizations.

From Prehistory to History

As our ancestors began their migration from the south through the north of Africa and beyond, they brought with them an ability to work together with others that allowed their primitive societies to progress. As societies developed around the world there were common patterns. There was a progression from more democratic governance in small groups to more specialization as societies grew larger and more authority was concentrated in the hands of rulers. Those who were ruled gradually had less contact with their rulers, who often gained god-like status. This usually was seen as the structure needed for survival of growing city-states and eventual countries. Rulers occasionally were overthrown, usually by those who already were in powerful positions. At this point the possibility of democratic government no longer was considered an option.

The first settlers of Egypt made the transition from the hunter-gatherer stage to agricultural civilization as early as 6000 BCE, aided by the fertile crescent of land provided by the annual flooding of the Nile. Beginning in what is known as the Predynastic Period, about 4000 BCE, archeologists have been able to determine that there was a fairly egalitarian civilization in

Egypt because there is little difference in the grave goods found in burial sites. This changed as an elite group developed about five hundred years later, as evidenced by more elaborate tombs. Communities grew larger and got into conflicts, which led to unification in about 3000 BCE. Kings eventually were all-powerful, which included being considered owners of the land. Human sacrifice was introduced as rulers began to take entire households with them into the afterlife.[21]

Peasants were tied to the land where they worked and taxes were collected as a portion of the land's produce. Labor was more akin to serfdom than slavery. Writing developed to keep records of taxes, workers, and product distribution, but only scribes who needed to keep records learned to write, perhaps 1-2% of the population. Art was encouraged and supervised by the state in the forms of ceramics, jewelry, goldsmithing, woodworking, painting and statuary.[22]

The great period of pyramid building began under Sneferu in the Fourth Dynasty, about 2600 BCE, followed by his son Khufu who built the largest pyramid at Giza. Construction methods – which used 2.5 million stones each weighing tons – still are a mystery to this day.[23] The Nile provided fertility that resulted in grain, fruit, oils and animal products that were sufficient in all but the most severe periods of drought. The Egyptian king was considered a god and only he could communicate with the other gods.

There is no generally accepted archeological evidence of the exodus of the Israelites from Egypt, but biblical scholars peg this account at about 1450 BCE.[24] Around this time the Pharaoh Akhenaton replaced the pantheon of Egyptian gods with the one Sun God, Aten.[25] He ordered the traditional idols to be destroyed. Worship of this One God replaced the hierarchy of priests – with their many gods – who had shared in ruling over Egypt. After the death of Akhenaton the priests removed his temples and Egypt

The World of Wine

Wine was an essential part of the culture of the Egyptians.

There is clear evidence of grapes having been planted and wine having been made in the Nile Valley from about the fourth millennium BCE. A colorful mural from the tomb of Nakht in Thebes from the fifteenth century BCE depicts harvesters picking ripe grapes from an arboretum.

— *Wine*, Page 14

returned to its traditional political and religious divisions.

Perhaps most importantly for the origins of democracy, the concept of the One God represented the idea of a single creator of everything, and thus a god accessible to everyone. It might be that the remaining practitioners of direct worship of the One God were forced from Egypt at this time or left of their own will. The account of the Israelites' liberation from slavery is perhaps the oldest in western culture that affirms the intrinsic value of human beings – one that has affected the course of history to this day.

This idea of One God – and the unacceptability of worshiping idols – was the most essential teaching of Moses to the Israelites. But, according to the Hebrew Torah (which later became part of the Bible), on their journey out of Egypt, they resumed their idol worship when Moses was out of sight.[26] The book of Exodus tells us that the Israelites were left wandering through Sinai for forty years before reaching their promised land of Canaan (today's Israel, Jordan, Syria and Lebanon) because of their failure to follow God's commands.[27]

The concept of the One God still is affirmed by the daily

Jewish prayer, the Shema:

> *Hear, O Israel*
> *The Lord God is one Lord*
> *And you shall love the Lord your God with all your heart*
> *And with all your soul*
> *And with all your might.*[28]

When they reached the Promised Land, the Israelites were told to destroy other cities completely – including Jericho[29] and that of the Midianites.[30] This is one of the earliest examples of one race being denied their own humanity and then turning around and doing the same to another. There are of course many similar examples throughout history – up to our own day – of those who claim the superiority of their own race and deny the validity of others.

Long-term settlements became possible with the advent of agriculture, which allowed previously nomadic groups to remain in one place, vastly expanding the number of people who could be fed.[31] It could be argued that agriculture was the greatest invention of all time. Clearly it had to be developed via a series of other innovations, including the plow, which was used throughout the ancient world, and the domestication of animals and plants. It seems likely that there was an element of cooperation and freedom in this development, because – as we will discuss – great inventions rarely are developed in a tyrannical state. Inventiveness requires long-term experimentation plus confidence and trust between individuals to yield viable results. Such an environment is rare under the distrust imposed by tyranny. In China, for example, innovations such as the voyages to discover new trade routes, or even the invention of the clock, were aborted due to lack of governmental interest in improving the lives of people.[32]

Hammurabi, King of Babylon in the eighteenth century BCE, formulated the first comprehensive code of law that has survived.

The World of Wine

Wine is a part of the weekly Shabbat ceremony in Jewish Homes on Friday night, which marks the beginning of the Sabbath. Wine also is included during the annual Passover Seder, as well as at other holidays. (The Passover Seder was the setting of the Last Supper by Jesus and his disciplines.) Jews are commanded by the Torah to keep Shabbat (the seventh day) as a day of prayer and rest, because that is the day that God rested from creating the universe. The Fourth Commandment states: "Remember the Sabbath day, to keep it holy."

The prayer used before drinking the cup of wine:

בָּרוּךְ אַתָה יְיָ אֱלֹהֵינוּ מֶלֶךְ הָעוֹלָם בּוֹרֵא פְּרִי הַגָּפֶן

Blessed are You, Lord our God, King of the universe,
who creates the fruit of the vine.

It was written on a large stone and contains 282 laws, including "an eye for eye," later reflected in the Hebrew Bible. This area of what is now the Mideast was called the Fertile Crescent due to the seasonal rainfall that allowed the development of agriculture. There was frequent warfare between the groups inhabiting the area. The inhabitants of what is present-day Syria and Palestine were known as Canaanites starting about 1600 BCE.[33]

The Jewish community in Palestine was divided between those who assimilated the lifestyle of their hosts and those who wanted to maintain a separate existence and engaged in rebellion that always was put down brutally. According to the Hebrew Bible[34] Jerusalem was destroyed after three rebellions against the Persians in about 600 BCE. They were allowed to return under

Cyrus in 537 BCE. A Jewish rebellion against the Romans under Titus was put down in 70 CE, and after a revolt in 135 CE the Jews were expelled from the area.[35]

The earliest known Greek civilization goes back to the Minoans on the island of Crete starting about 2000 BCE, although evidence of human habitation there begins 5000 years earlier. Their religion was centered on the Earth Goddess and sacrifice of animals and children in times of danger. They engaged in trade with other Greek city states and societies as far away as Egypt and Palestine, but yielded to the Mycenaean culture from the mainland around 1600 BCE.[36]

Early Greek city states were ruled by kings with loyal followers. One of the great mythical heroes of the ancient Greek world was Ulysses, otherwise known as Odysseus.[37] He is a key figure in both the Iliad and Odyssey of Homer, who was revered as the chronicler of these two epics that revolve around the Trojan War, believed to have occurred about 1200 BCE. Homer, who may have been a composite figure, wrote down these oral traditions hundreds of years after the actual events.[38] They were the most pervasive myths of the Greeks at the time of Plato and Aristotle in the fourth century BCE and influenced hundreds of plays (most of them lost) by the tragic playwrights of that time, including Aeschylus, Sophocles, and Euripides. They provided the everyday entertainment of the Greeks in addition to shaping their myths and history.

The Iliad tells most of the story of the expedition to Troy by about 1000 ships under the leadership of King Agamemnon of Mycenae.[39] The goal was to retrieve the legendary beauty Helen, who left her husband Menelaus (Agamemnon's brother), to run off with Paris, prince of Troy. The Odyssey follows Ulysses home after this war of ten years and on further adventures. In these myths and the plays based on them there is little reference to democracy. There were clear consequences for the losers of these wars – and not much had changed by the time of Thucydides, who wrote a history of the Peloponnesian war in which Athens was ultimately defeated by Sparta in 405 BCE. The pattern in most of these wars was that the winners shared the spoils of the cities that were defeated. The men were killed or enslaved and the women and children became the property of the victors.[40]

Solon was the legendary giver of the laws that led to Athenian democracy. In about 570 BCE he reformed aristocratic rule and created a system that provided shared governance among a greater number of land owners. He reversed the slide toward tyranny in which the wealthiest aristocrats took away the property and liberty of farmers and others who had become indebted to them.[41]

According to legend the Olympic Games began in 776 BCE, and were held every four years.[42] The competitions included racing, boxing, wrestling and horse racing. The extensive site of Olympia still can be visited, including the housing area for athletes who spent months traveling from the cities they represented throughout the Greek world, and the stadium where the foot race took place on the second of five days of competition.

Delphi, high in the hills northwest of Athens, was the religious center of ancient Greece. Those in search of answers to life's problems – personal or political – made the pilgrimage and awaited the wisdom of the Oracle, sometimes for months, which often was delivered in vague terms that made interpretation uncertain.

The Athenians practiced a form of participatory democracy that was very different from the style of representative government found in modern democracies. Those who were allowed to participate – about 10% of the population – voted on major state decisions such as whether to go to war and also were required to participate in juries by lottery.[43] It was an Athenian jury that voted in 399 BCE to execute Socrates.

In 431 BCE, when a war began between Athens and Sparta, each engaged a large group of city states to fight on their side. Athens was led by Pericles, who evoked the spirit of democracy as perhaps has not been done as effectively until Lincoln's Gettysburg Address. Pericles' Funeral Oration – as related by Thucydides – gave an account of Athenian democracy at the battle site where the bodies of many still awaited removal:

Our constitution does not copy the laws of neighboring states; we are rather a pattern to others than imitators ourselves. Its administration favors the many instead of the few; this is why it is called a democracy. If we look to the laws, they afford equal justice to all in their private differences; if no social standing, advancement in public life falls to reputation for capacity, class considerations not being allowed to interfere with merit; nor again does poverty bar the way, if a man is able to serve the state, he is not hindered by the obscurity of his condition.[44]

This "equal justice to all" actually applied only to the ten percent of persons who were citizens.

The Athenians and Spartans both voted on whether to enter the war against each other.[45] Athens was the largest and most influential democracy of its time, but engaged in increasing subjugation of other city states who were members of its "alliance" – even some that wished to remain independent.

The Peloponnesian war increased in intensity over the course of twenty-seven years, and according to Thucydides, both the Athenians and Spartans provided severe punishments for "allies" who sought to remain independent.[46] With the defeat of Athens ended the first great experiment with democracy we know of – an idea that, according to many scholars, was not revived in practice for nearly two thousand years. But Athens was a direct democracy rather than the representative model that we have today. The vast majority of the population was made up of slaves, women and children who were ineligible to vote or participate in government. And as we shall see, there have been elements of democracy in many states since that time, although most have not been called by that name.

Socrates – as portrayed by his pupil Plato – championed the idea of questioning all that we think we know about others, the world, and ourselves. He taught that as we rid ourselves of pre-conceptions we arrive at a greater sense of truth.[47] Plato's pupil Aristotle pioneered what today we might call the "scientific method," or "empiricism," which advocated using actual obser-vation to establish our concepts of the world rather than relying solely on beliefs or logic.

About a century after the Peloponnesian war, Alexander ("the Great") of Macedonia (north of Athens) rose to power. He forged the first Western empire that spanned from North Africa to India. He marched with 10,000 or more men across thousands of miles, recruiting more along his path who were fascinated by his leg-end. He overthrew the Persian Empire and was welcomed by the Egyptians in 332 BCE because of the oppression of the Persians. In Egypt he established his new city, Alexandria, which replaced Athens as the most important cultural center of the ancient world. Alexandria had the greatest library and museum of its time, and had many of the great thinkers of the era among its residents, including Galen, the renowned physician, and the mathematician Euclid who laid the foundations for geometry.[48] Alexander's sud-den death in 323 BCE at the age of 33, perhaps from influenza, caused a battle for succession among his generals, with Egypt being taken over by Alexander's friend and general, Ptolemy I.[49] One legacy of Alexander was that so large a geographical area could be united under one rule – soon to be imitated by Rome.

At around the time that the Greeks were moving from pre-history to written history, a well-documented civilization already

The World of Wine

The Greeks were well-known for their consumption of wine at lengthy philosophical seminars, as portrayed by Plato, and at their feasts at which Bacchus, the god of good living, was invoked.

From Plato's Symposium:

Socrates took his seat . . . and had his meal. . . . When dinner was over, they poured a libation to the god, sang a hymn, and — in short — followed the whole ritual. Then they turned their attention to drinking. At that point, Pausanias addressed the group: "Well gentlemen, how can we arrange to drink less tonight? To be honest, I still have a terrible hangover from yesterday, and I could really use a break. I dare say most of you could, too, since you were also part of the celebration. So let's try not to overdo it."

The Museum of Wine in Art at Château Mouton-Rothschild near Bordeaux, France, houses a magnificent Greek wine vessel from about 500 BCE that features mythical figures in black on gold, including Pan, god of music, playing his pipe.

was aging in China, which was on its third dynasty. Traditional Chinese history tells us that there was a gradual transition from a tribal society based on clans, from about 5000 BCE, to a state-level society, with the establishment of the Xia Dynasty in 2000 BCE, although modern archeological evidence doesn't always match this narrative. This yielded to the Shang Dynasty starting in about 1600 BCE, which practiced writing, had walled cities and horse-drawn carriages. Although this system has been compared with feudalism, it was centrally governed, and eventually yielded to the Zhou Dynasty, starting in about 1000 BCE, which lasted through the time of classical Greece, to 256 BCE. Rulers sought to shift allegiance from the more democratic clan to the less democratic state, and provided severe punishments for those who resisted the new order. Their dynastic system included burying hundreds of "companions" with the elite in their tombs.[50]

Although China was more egalitarian in its tribal stages, throughout the long history of Chinese dynasties there is no record of efforts to provide decision-making power to anyone other than those at the top. Their system was fused to ancestor worship – honoring the past and those who ruled with the authority of ancient tradition. However, challengers occasionally did overcome those in authority and establish their own dynasties, mainly through war, but tribal groups generally were absorbed into the dominant dynasty. For most of its history, Chinese law was mainly a list of punishments for prescribed infractions.[51]

Toward the end of the Zhou dynasty, there was a move toward greater democratization during the Warring States period (481-221 BCE), in which Chinese historians tell us that over one million people were killed. With the elimination of many of the elite, military and civic promotions needed to be based more on merit than lineage.[52]

Confucius, who died in 479 BCE, was a scholar who had only a handful of followers at his death. But his reputation based on the sayings attributed to him grew over the centuries and affected the Chinese view of duty and order: "I transmit but do not innovate. I am truthful in what I say and devoted to antiquity." His teachings emphasized the importance of sons obeying fathers and wives obeying husbands.[53] Central to his ideas is that peace of mind comes from accepting traditions and one's situation in life.

The absolutism of Chinese emperors left no room for the development of democratic incentives. In an effort to suppress the idea of education for the masses – particularly traditional Confucian teachings – Qin Xi-huang in 213 BCE ordered the burning of all books and the execution of 460 scholars who refused to give them up. Despite continual rebellion under the next dynasty – the Han – the nobles who rebelled never were successful in overcoming absolute central power or in sharing government decisions as eventually happened in Western democracies.

The controlling Chinese aristocrats slowly became wealthier over the next four hundred years. Money lending increased these disparities by creating debt for the poor. Eventually the nobility avoided paying taxes or participating in the state to the extent that it collapsed. We will see the same patterns among the elite in Europe. It wasn't until the eleventh century that centralized power included an administrative system that allowed promotion within the government based on ability rather than patrimony.[54]

The claim to legitimacy of Chinese rulers throughout history was based on the "Mandate of Heaven," similar to the Divine Right of Kings that was eventually overthrown in Europe.[55] The treachery between kin was probably more extreme than Shakespeare could have imagined, and would have provided grist for many great plays if only the Elizabethans had known of the excesses of these ancient dynasties.[56]

In the Western hemisphere, Peru's first inhabitants arrived as early as 10,000 BCE, and sophisticated societies arose there around 3,000 BCE. The Peruvians raised and wore cotton long before Europeans even knew of it.[57] In Mexico, the Olmec civilization flourished nearly as far back as that of the Chinese, as evidenced by the calendars they created. Starting in about 1800 BCE they were able to live in cities due to their independent discovery of farming; they developed writing and mathematics, and practiced human sacrifice. The Mayan civilization began about 1000 BCE and expanded to cover much of what is now Mexico and

The World of Wine

Wine production in China is believed to go back 5,000 years. From about 1,700 to 900 BCE the guang was used for ceremonial purposes. The guang was a bronze or iron pouring container with a rounded base. Its top and pouring spout were in the shape of an animal. It was used to pour rice wine at banquets and was enclosed in the graves of individuals of high status. *Christie's Auction Catalogue,* September 16, 2010

Guatemala, nearly covering the Yucatan Peninsula with cities.[58]

The Mayan civilization disappeared in about 900 CE, probably as a result of overuse of the environment, drought and perpetual conflict with neighbors.[59] As one drives through the Yucatan today it is apparent that only a fraction of the settlements that once covered that peninsula is excavated, and that there are countless more cities buried under vine forests yet to be uncovered.

In 1927, archeologists discovered a spear point between two bison ribs near Folsom, New Mexico pointing to the possibility that Pleistocene man had lived in the Americas over 12,000 years ago. A number of human tools – such as axes and spear heads – also were found not long afterwards in nearby Clovis that clearly established the existence of an early settlement of at least the same age.[65]

Rome began its slow ascent – well before the civilization of the Greeks had peaked – as a village of huts in the eighth century BCE, and eventually ruled an empire that united most of what is now Europe. Many areas that succumbed to Rome's rule previously had been dominated by local tribal states, while those areas that Rome failed to conquer remained tribal. In northern Britain the Picts fended off Roman domination via fierce warfare.

According to legend, the Etruscans who ruled Rome were ousted by a popular rebellion in 509 BCE.[61] The Roman Senate – still before written records – elected two Praetors, who had to agree on any decrees, as joint heads of state for terms of one year. The Senate had 300 members appointed for life, and they themselves voted on their replacements, which created a growing aristocracy and caused the majority of Roman people to withdraw from civic life. The army was composed primarily of the common people (the plebs), which led to the election of Tribunes to represent them, but the Tribunes also became powerful which again created an imbalance of power.[62]

Rome began the practice of allowing defeated towns to become a part of Roman life and customs – often as citizens or allies – so that its influence began to quickly expand. Citizenship was a privilege that could be earned by individuals from all walks of life, freed slaves included.[63] Rome also severely persecuted toward those who opposed it – including Jews and Christians.

Via a network of excellent roads and settlements populated by their citizens, Rome effectively established a partnership with those in its area of influence by rewarding those who supported it with increased security and a vast trading network. This provided a greater range of goods than would be otherwise possible and was an effective means of creating a loyal following among those willing to cooperate with Roman rule.[64] The first known securities market was organized in Rome due to the great wealth that was brought in by its vast trading network. It had the prerequisites for an equity market, including transferable capital, available credit, and people willing to take risk.[65]

For most of the next century there was a contest for power between the aristocrats and groups representing the bulk of the population. Caesar was immensely popular after he conquered

Gaul (now France). He then led his troops to war against the Senate and Pompey, who was then Consul of Rome, which he won in 48 BCE, establishing himself as dictator for life, but soon was assassinated.

After Caesar's assassination in 45 BCE Rome no longer was a republic, and became an empire under Caesar's nephew Augustus in 31 BCE. Its territory – expanded to a total of 6.5 million square miles – included lands from North Africa at its southern limits to the Middle East, and north to Britain. This empire was relatively stable until the third century when it was beset by economic crisis and attacks from Germanic tribes and the Persian Empire.[66]

Rome included an opportunity for citizenship for many who were willing to become players in the greatest and most civilized society yet known. Though not a democracy in the sense we use the word today, Rome had many democratic elements that included a greater number of citizens than any civilization to that time. Ancient Rome provided a broader citizen base than any state before it, which marks a major advance in democracy's progess.

The difference in lifestyle and political outlook between the West and East had been noted as early as Hippocrates (c460-c370 BCE), who stated that the Westerners were aggressive and liberty-loving while those from the East were more wise but peace-loving.[67]

Early Christians spread throughout the ancient world, amidst much persecution, after the conversion of Paul in about 33 CE.[68] Paul, who previously persecuted Christians, describes his conversion in the Christian Bible:

For you have heard of my previous life in Judaism, how I persecuted the Church of God violently and tried to destroy it; and I advanced in Judaism beyond many of my own age among my people, so extremely zealous was I for the traditions of my fathers. But He

The World of Wine

Wines were produced by the Etruscans in Central Italy from at least the eighth century BCE. The Romans produced and exported wine to large areas of what is now Europe. Bacchanalian revelry in the early Roman republic resulted in such debauchery that it was outlawed, but not to great effect since the revelers often were the law makers. By the thirteenth and fourteenth centuries Italian wine was exported by merchants at considerable profit.

There is almost no region untouched by vineyards in Italy. The quality control system that was introduced in 1963 helped to standardize a market that was often confusing for consumers and sometimes fraudulent. The most famous and sought-after Italian wines are those in Tuscany, which produces Chianti and Brunello di Montalcino from sangiovese grapes, and the Piedmont region which produces long-lived Barolo and Barbaresco from nebbiolo grapes. A more recent addition is the Super Tuscans, made from Bordeaux grapes such as cabernet sauvignon. *Wine*, Pages 334-35

who had set me apart before I was born, and had called me through His grace, was pleased to reveal his Son to me, in order that I might preach Him among the Gentiles.[69]

In 313 CE, the Emperor Constantine, a new convert to Christianity, gave freedom of worship to Christians. He renamed Byzantium as Constantinople – at a meeting point of Europe and Asia – in 330 CE. Christianity became the official religion of the empire in 380 under Theodosius. After his death it was divided into its western and eastern divisions which stand today as the

Roman and Eastern Churches.[70]

Soon Rome, like much of Europe, was invaded numerous times by marauding tribes. The Middle Ages – with its well-known decline – began at this time. But Roman law, administered by judges who aimed at some degree of fairness and equal treatment, generally remained in place, rather than rule only by the local nobles or kings.[71] In many ways, Christendom filled in to provide moral guidance throughout Europe as the influence of Rome waned.[72]

The writings of Saint Augustine (354-430) did much to cement the reputation of Christianity in the West. His *Confessions,* which tell of his conversion, convinced many that the Kingdom of God was more worthy of devotion than attention to earthly matters.[73]

Boethius (484-520), a member of the Roman aristocracy, continued to copy the works of Aristotle and other Greeks, ensuring their survival. The distillation of known information, which led to a spread – and thus democratization – of knowledge, was collected and distributed by the encyclopedists of the day.[74]

The Roman calendar was still in use in the West until the sixth century, when the monk Dionysius the Little determined that, in a Christian world, the calendar should be dated from the birth of Jesus. He established the seven-day week to reflect the time it took to create the world. Church bells began to mark the hour of the day, allowing villagers to organize their activities in sync with Church worship and each other.[75]

Pope Gregory (c. 540- 604), who also was a general, defended much of what was left of the Roman Empire in an attempt to introduce religious and humanitarian ideas. He sent representatives throughout Europe to convert pagans wherever possible. In addition to his many reforms he was responsible for Gregorian Chant.[76]

For much of the first millennium there were no clear countries with borders in what eventually was called Europe, but a collection of settlements that were periodically invaded and changed governance, depending on the success of the latest invaders.[77] Christendom continued to be split between the Eastern and Western Churches.[78]

The central administration of the Romans yielded to fiefdoms throughout what eventually became Western Europe, and for most people there was little communication with the world beyond their immediate vicinity. Most of the needs of the lords and serfs of the estates were produced locally. The Roman roads, which had been solid and straight to allow the movement of troops, deteriorated into dirt paths that discouraged communication and commerce.[79] Eventually landlords needed to introduce small reforms in their contracts with their serfs because of a shrinking labor market.

Feudalism provided a degree of protection from the waves of barbarian marauders and an opportunity for a relatively stable life. It was based on a contract between the lord and tenant – protection in exchange for services such as working the land. A breach of contract by feudal lords led to occasional revolts among peasants.[80]

Within the family, the Church forbade marriage between close relatives and committed married couples to continue their vows for a lifetime. The Church also encouraged the contribution of property to itself of those who died without heirs, which added to its immense wealth. One-third of the farmland in France was in Church hands at the end of the seventh century.[81]

England, like the rest of Europe after the fall of Rome, was at first divided into self-governing tribes. Households were grouped into villages with the king at the head of such tribes as Angles, Saxons, Jutes and Celts. They were governed by tribal laws, with compensation due to the injured based on the nature of the injury.

Germany also had similar tribal law in place which included

retaliation not just against the perpetrator but against the criminal's family. The introduction of Christianity provided greater equality and morality via models of saints who taught compassion and equality rather than retribution, although clearly that model often was not followed. The conversion of the pagans in Eastern Europe was not complete until 1417.[82]

The third major monotheistic religion, Islam, was founded by the Prophet Muhammad after his revelation and vision of the One God in the year 610 near Mecca, in Saudi Arabia. At first he was persecuted and ridiculed by believers in the traditional gods who were members of the local nomadic tribes. But by 628 he was able to march with 10,000 followers on Mecca in a primarily peaceful takeover of that city during which idols were smashed by him and his followers. By his death in 632, most of the Arabian Peninsula had been converted to Islam, some via war and some by peaceful means.[83] A series of civil wars followed Muhammad's death to determine the leadership of the new religion which divided his followers into the eventual Shiites (followers of Muhammad's cousin Ali) and Sunnis (followers of the caliph Mu'awiya, who administered the first, or Caliphate dynasty from 661-750). The enmity between these divisions has lasted to this day.

The Qur'an exhorts Muhammad's followers to use war in an attempt to spread his vision, but it also includes passages that deny superiority to any race and encourages believers to avoid violence and to treat women respectfully.[84] Early Islam had no actual codes of law but was administered under the guidance of the Qur'an.[85]

The followers of Muhammad spread his religion – mainly by force – at a rapid pace through much of the Middle East, North Africa, the Orient, and Spain within the next 100 years. Muslim armies moving northward from Iberia (modern Spain) into Gaul only were stopped from conquering Europe by Charles Martel at Poitiers in 732.[86] But once established, the huge areas under

The World of Wine

Germany is the world's northernmost quality wine producing region.

Wines in Germany were made in Roman times with extensive plantings near the Mosel and Rhine rivers. Monasteries developed wines for sacramental purposes starting about three hundred years later. Over time, economic fluctuations and phylloxera, a louse that destroys vineyard stock, greatly reduced the wine-making capacity of the area.

Germany is known mainly for its long-lived white wines, usually made from Reisling, which come in various levels of sweetness. Kabinett is the driest, with Spatlese and Auslese (select harvest) coming next. A greater level of sweetness is found in Beerenauslese (second harvest), from hand picked grapes that stay on the vine until almost consumed by rot, and Trockenbeerenauslese (dried berries), which is rare and expensive. The famous Eiswein is made from grapes that stay on the vine until frozen. *Wine,* Page 446-47

Muslim rule were tolerant of Christians and Jews who they considered "people of the book," although Muslim teaching is that Islam has superseded those religions.[87]

Between the fourth and seventh centuries the scrolls used by scribes to pass on human knowledge and history were gradually replaced by the codex, a small book or manuscript which was much easier to read and copy. The codex was copied onto animal skins and still very expensive, but it resulted in knowledge being more available to those who could read (still a small minority).[88]

The ruler who united most of the lands that eventually became Europe was Charlemagne (c742-814), who engaged in continual and brutal wars to Christianize Europe. The pagan Saxons were given a choice to convert or die, with up to 4,000 being killed in one day.[89] He established a unified currency and code of laws in addition to having his counselors reform writing to make it more accessible. Charlemagne's efforts to establish rule by law throughout his realm – rather than by the whim of local lords – was a step in the direction of democratization. The serfs also won their emancipation under Charlemagne.[90] He had himself crowned emperor of the Holy Roman Empire in 799 by Pope Leo III and spread education and literacy among young knights.

In 910 the great abbey of Cluny was established in southern Burgundy, which attempted to overcome many of the previous abuses that made monks and peasants vulnerable to the whims of wealthy patrons. Cluny's influence – an attempt to return to the Christian principles of godliness and justice – spread throughout Europe and dominated Western culture for over 200 years. It led to a resurgence of religious practice – including care for the poor and the encouragement of religious art. The monasteries under the Clunaic influence also served as the inns of Europe for the travelers of their time.[91]

In 987, Hugh Capet took over the Carolingian Dynasty of Charlemagne, which became centered in Paris, and lasted over three hundred years. As of the year 1000, Europe still was composed of a number of small kingdoms with no real nations as we know them.[92] However, during the next three hundred years many areas were converted to Christianity, including what is now Bulgaria, Bohemia, Poland, Hungary, parts of Scandinavia, and Western Russia. Yet this area remained largely feudal and ineffectively governed, especially after incursions by the Mongols.[93]

After the Muslims conquered North Africa in the eighth century, they developed trade routes using camels traveling a thousand miles south. The two most profitable commodities were

The World of Wine

Charlemagne was the owner of many vineyards and a connoisseur of fine wine. One of his favorite vineyards was Corton in Burgundy, which produced a great red wine, or Grand Cru, made of pinot noir. According to legend, Charlemagne's wife was upset that her husband's beard bore a perennial red wine stain. So Charlemagne had an area of the vineyard torn out and replanted with white grapes. To this day, *Corton Charlemagne*, made from Chardonnay, is considered one of the great white wines of the world.

gold and slaves. Seasonal rains in the highlands of Sudan – south of Egypt – had allowed the development of agriculture to flourish since the third century BCE. The *Ghana*, or local king, and his subjects practiced paganism and idol worship.[94] Many natives of the area eventually converted to Islam.

The religion of India is largely based on the Vedas that were composed beginning in the second millennium BCE. As with many scriptures, they were passed on orally until they were written down around 1000 CE. The idea upon which they are based – the unity between all creatures and things – ultimately is a democratic principle. No one can be considered superior to others, as all are part of the essential energy flow of the universe. It was the responsibility of each king to uphold this principle as the basis of justice in his rulings with his subjects. Thus a spiritual view dominated the politics of India as well as the everyday lives of its people. A downside was that occupations were static within families for generations because individual advancement was not seen as being as important as unity with the cosmic whole.[95]

There also was a warrior class in early India made up of aristo-crats and professional soldiers. The Bhagavad-Gita, one of the most holy Sanskrit texts, was written in the fifth century BCE. It portrays a conversation between the warrior Arjuna and his charioteer – the god Krishna – as they are about to go into battle. The main teaching of this text is to have one's actions guided by the principle of unity with God – or Dharma – as opposed to individual gain or even the victory of one's tribe or nation. It is fair to say that it differs consid-erably from any Western battle text. It preaches equality based on unity with the Divine. *Yoga* – in this context – means practice that leads to the experience of that divine unity.

The man who sees me in everything
and everything within me
will not be lost to me, nor
will I ever be lost to him.

He who is rooted in oneness
realizes that I am
in every being; wherever
he goes, he remains in me.
When he sees all beings as equal
in suffering or in joy
because they are like himself,
that man has grown perfect in yoga.

Ashoka, one of the most famous leaders of early India who lived in the third century BCE, began to extend his rule via harsh warfare and slaughter. He became a pacifist after converting to Buddhism, and his empire crumbled under his descendants. The Gupta dynasty (320-480) was able to unite much of Northern India, and forced numerous tribes under the domination of one umbrella. But defeated rulers were allowed to stay in place which created a weak state vulnerable to attack. By 515, India was over-whelmed by invasions by the Huns and regressed into a collection of weak and smaller states.

Villages in ancient India operated independently and were not dependent on a larger state. The Brahmins (religious leaders) promoted a religion that emphasized the ephemeral quality of life and therefore did not promote literacy, and this view still limits mobility for the poorest classes. The king only was considered a legitimate ruler if he followed the laws outlined in the scriptures, as interpreted by the Brahmins, and revolts would take place when kings became too autocratic.[96]

Of course these practices prevented India from establishing a strong, central state. The Indian bureaucracies were totally based on birth privilege and not on merit – there was no way for lower castes to advance themselves. There also was no attempt to standardize laws and practices – such as weights and measures – throughout the country until British rule in the nineteenth century.[97]

Beginning in the tenth century, India experienced a series of invasions that imposed the values of other cultures, such as the Muslims and eventually the British, who while imposing colonialism, introduced the concept of democracy. The Muslim influence lingers on today in Northern India and Pakistan, which is a Muslim state, but the Muslim conquerors did not impose the type of central administration that is seen in China and the West. The British occupation, however, imposed a unity of administration, language and custom that lingers to the present. India remains unstable in many ways, with the allegiances among its citizens being largely to their own region rather than the state, which has impeded the building of modern transportation and communication systems.[98]

At the end of the seventh century the first Heavenly Sovereign, Jito, ruled in Japan. A Buddhist theocracy developed with the Sovereign as head of state.[99]

The World of Wine

Wine drinking in Japan goes back at least 2,000 years.

A funeral ceremony is described by a Chinese envoy to Japan in the first century:

At death they use a coffin with no outer sealing box. Earth is built up like a mound. They observe more than ten days of obsequies, during which time they do not eat meat. The chief mourner wails, and others sing, dance, and drink sake. After interment the family assembles to go into water for purification.

Sake still is used in Japan in many types of ceremonies – weddings, wakes, New Year celebrations, and to mark an occasion like a business arrangement or new home.

A Concise History of Japan, Page 20

The Second Millennium

The Second Millennium – but a bleep in the total time of human existence – produced the greatest progress toward democratic institutions and government of any period, but also has generated the greatest number of wars and casualties.

As this period opened, the western world began to emerge from what many historians consider its darkest period and seemed on the verge of becoming a more civilized society. There was progress toward a greater appreciation of the talents and abilities of the individual, yet persecutions of those who did not fit the mainstream were rampant despite growing proclamations of humanism. As populations expanded, lands became more settled which led to the gradual creation of national borders.

We began to live in larger and more organized societies with more elaborate rules and laws. Yet our tendency toward aggression remained unconquered – in both individuals and nations – as we repeatedly attempted to expand our influence and borders at the expense of others. We promoted models of behavior that preached tolerance, yet were forced to live with the results of the intolerance we practiced.

The democratic ideal – government guided by the recognition of the value of each individual – became established to the greatest extent in Western Europe during this period then spread to the New World, with less democratic influence the further one goes east. That said, there continued to be conflicting elements between greater and lesser degrees of democracy in every region on earth.

1000-1500

In Western Europe the millennium opened with a myriad of skirmishes and minor wars between fiefdoms that sent out their knights in battle against each other, although rarely in as chivalrous a manner as later portrayed in romances such as those of Chrétien de Troyes in his stories of the Knights of the Round Table.[100] Such ideals – about how to treat others with respect, particularly women – would establish rules of behavior and influence readers for centuries.

Christianity was founded upon principles of forgiveness[101] and non-judgment.[102] But once it had become the established religion in Europe it faced down numerous "heresies" that it believed challenged its absolute position as the representative of God on Earth. One reason for protests against the Church was that sacraments – and thus salvation – often were sold by priests who accumulated considerable wealth.[103]

An attempt to free the Church from political influence came about under Pope Gregory VII, starting in 1073, who declared that he had the ultimate authority on earth, including the ability to depose kings.[104] He forbade the marriage of priests and outlawed the sale of Church offices. He separated the spiritual from the secular worlds, but with that opened new possibilities for the establishment of secular rule.

After the year 1000, what historians call "the rule of law" – a legal system where those who make the laws also are subject to them – became more firmly established in the West. Genuine rule of law is largely tied to economic growth and human creativity. States where people feel oppressed are less likely to create the trust needed for a robust economy. Rule of law also allows individuals to go about their daily lives – including holding and transferring property – without interference from government, except when they are challenged through legitimate governmental channels based on laws.

Many Western nations, if not actually democratic, witnessed progress toward recognition of the validity – and value – of individual human beings during this period, which moved the world in the direction of democracy. Some religious leaders, such as Francis of Assisi, were able to exert influence on the men and women of their time and subsequent times by inspiring them – via word and action – to acknowledge the holy aspect of God's creation, including human beings, and thus treat each other with greater compassion:

Where there is charity and wisdom, there is neither fear nor ignorance. Where there is patience and humility, there is neither anger nor vexation. Where there is poverty and joy, there is neither greed nor avarice. Where there is peace and meditation, there is neither anxiety nor doubt.[105]

The Crusades began at the end of the eleventh century in an attempt to reverse Muslim successes in conquering much of the Middle East, Northern Africa, and the Iberian Peninsula – and to drive what the Pope considered infidels out of the Holy Land. Their stated intent was to spread the Christian principles of charity and compassion, but they practiced extreme violence, including the slaughter of those who got in their way including many Jews, Muslims and Christians. The first Crusade captured Jerusalem in 1099, but it was recaptured in 1187 by Saladin, the Muslim leader who commanded armies throughout the Middle East. Although the Crusades were not successful at reclaiming the Holy Land, working together toward a common cause increased the identification of many with the idea of a unified Europe.[106]

Louis IX (later Saint Louis) of France went on two Crusades, financing the first by taking land from Jews. His grandson, Philip IV (le Bel) established an independent Papacy starting with Clement V in Avignon in 1309 after a tax dispute with Boniface VIII of Rome.[107] Philip also was the first to convene the Estates General in 1302, ostensibly an advisory body, composed of Clergy, Nobility and Commoners, but actually a means by which the king raised revenue. The Estates General met only periodically and when called.[108]

By the twelfth century the Church established a central canon law and moral authority that superseded the laws of many governments. In the Eastern Church, bishops continued to be chosen by rulers, which had the effect of localizing the laws.[109]

English common law developed slowly after the conquest by William I of Normandy in 1066. William and subsequent kings traveled about the country enforcing laws that were intended to be fairly administered throughout the realm. Eventually a circuit of judges was trained to enforce these laws as equitably as possible.[110]

England had been organized into shires before 1066. The

shire reeve (sheriff) became the ruler of each shire, as well as representative of the king. All freemen were required to attend meetings to discuss local issues, particularly grievances, in an effort to resolve them. This was a much more egalitarian model than existed in the rest of Europe at the time. A system called the hundreds (each composed of a hundred farm estates) led to the establishment of the jury system. Eventually royal courts replaced local jurisdictions.[111]

Henry II, great-grandson of William, reigned 1154-89 and brought effective rule to England after a series of weak monarchs. His descendants – the Plantagenet dynasty – lasted two hundred more years. He traveled throughout his empire to maintain and administer justice and expand English common law.[112]

In Europe and the West, despite high birth mortality rates, women began to marry later and have fewer children than in other parts of the world. More were in the work force. Although western countries were far from totally democratic, women often were recognized for attributes other than just child-bearing. Women in England were allowed to hold and dispose of property.[113]

Education, for those who received it, was mainly the domain of the Church, which meant a considerable dose of religion along with writing and history.[114] The center of European theological studies was Paris. Peter Abelard, in the twelfth century, taught the use of "ceaseless questioning," via Aristotle, to approach God, and that an accurate description of God is beyond us because of the limits of language.[115] Thomas Aquinas maintained, in the thirteenth century, that the existence of God can be apprehended by a mystical understanding that transcends reason: "And just as the soul exists wholly everywhere in the body, so God exists wholly in each and every thing."[116]

Europe's economy still was primarily agricultural, although poverty became less prevalent as the era of serfdom ended. When pilgrims came to town for religious feast days, they also brought their wares to market. The large Gothic cathedrals with their spires and transepts reaching up to the heavens presented a respite from the routine labors of everyday life. They provided a glimpse of the holy for those who were awe-struck by the magnificent architecture that – along with the rituals performed within – represented God on earth.[117]

Along with a greater acknowledgement of people's needs, a gradual increase in democratization took place. In many towns laws were administered by jurists who presided over disputes. Town lords ruled, but greater liberties were granted and exercises in self-governance were introduced, such as in the town of Nimes in France, where the count agreed to the election of counsels in 1198. Examples in England include the granting of "customs" – similar to a constitution – by Henry I to Newcastle-upon-Tyne, and the granting of "royal privilege" to London in 1155.[118]

In Eastern Europe, Hungary became a Christian nation in the twelfth century, as did Poland and Bohemia. Eastern Europe in general became a Christian region, although the borders between countries there would not be stabilized for centuries.

The Mendicant orders – including the Franciscans founded by Saint Francis in 1206 – were determined to return to the original teachings of Jesus. They renounced the worldly wealth that had become common among monks and were determined to live on alms. But as often happens when inspirational movements evolve to become the established tradition, the mendicants became the chief prosecutors of heretics under the Inquisition.[119]

The Normans established settlements in the north of France – the region still called Normandy – and then conquered parts of the Italian peninsula. A descendent of the Normans, Frederick II, established a kingdom early in the 1200's in Palermo where a multicultural community of Christians, Jews and Muslims led to increased general prosperity.[120]

This was a relatively peaceful period in Western Europe, which encouraged the expansion of trade and improved prosperity throughout the region, from Italy to Spain to Germany, as well as areas outside the Christian realm, such as the Muslim lands in the south and Slavic tribes in Scandinavia. Southern England and Northern France specialized in textile production. Roads were still poor and taxes were imposed by local lords to pass through their lands, so trade was still far from "free." Many bridges were built in this period, and rivers were used to transport goods wherever possible, including the Po, the Rhone and the Mosel. Sea trade was the slowest but cheapest means of transportation. The lack of a single currency also inhibited the expansion of trade, which gave rise to a class of merchants that arranged international loans. Taxes on sales transactions often were avoided by the wealthiest classes, which increased the financial distance between the wealthy and poor.[121]

In the 1200s an appreciation of human nature and reason − thus humanism − was beginning to be practiced in many newly established universities. This was the beginning of people thinking of themselves as having been created in the image of a Savior who God sent to earth and who suffered in the same way as people do. This was reflected in the art of the time in numerous paintings of the Crucifixion.[122] Individual learning and growth in skills were beginning to be emphasized during this period, but laughter and joy also were encouraged, partly due to the teachings of Saint Francis. The appreciation and promotion of the individual who had a purpose in the present world − not just the world of salvation − had begun.[123]

The Magna Carta of 1215 gave notice to kings in England that they could not simply confiscate land, although this would still be done by some, such as Henry VIII, under the pretense of enforcing laws. This eventually meant that to wage war a king would need to levy a tax, and was the beginning of the need for kings to work collaboratively with their subjects.[124] In 1265, a new type of Parliament began meeting at Westminster, composed not just of nobles but of knights and burgesses of local boroughs. This legislative body was the foundation of the House of Commons.[125]

Knowledge based on experiment and discovery – not just belief – began to be developed. Chemistry began to replace alchemy and astronomy began to replace astrology. Roger Bacon initiated the "scientific method" by introducing optical and chemical experiments at Oxford and Paris, but Bacon ran afoul of religious authorities and was forbidden to continue his work. William of Ockham developed the idea that knowledge only should be based on observation and described in the briefest and clearest way possible – thus "Ockham's razor."[126]

Yet for hundreds of years the western world still was not free of belief in magic and superstition. Enlightened ideas did not penetrate to all levels of the population. Religious beliefs – including that of "original sin" – continued to supersede belief in science, and block its path at many turns.[127]

Ancient writings – particularly those of Aristotle – that had been preserved by Arabic scholars were passed on in the late twelfth century.[128] The need for improved record keeping due to the expansion of trade led to the establishment of schools that emphasized mathematical skills. A pioneer in this field was Leonardo Fibonacci, who traveled on business throughout Southern Europe in the early 1200s and used symbols that were originated by the Hindus and then passed on by the Arabs – what we now call Arabic numerals – starting with 0 and going up to 9, without which modern math would be impossible.[129]

During the Middle Ages there were a number of revolts, led mainly by relatively well-off peasants – not the poorest – who believed that their rights and economic conditions were being threatened. In the cities, where many peasants had migrated, there was discontent due to increasing poverty, poor living conditions, and taxes, which led to trade unions and revolts from the 1200s up until the time of the French Revolution.[130]

A generally growing prosperity allowed Europeans to begin reaching out to the rest of the world. The Venetian Polo brothers traveled and traded with Ceylon, the Mongols and possibly China. Merchants from Venice, Genoa and Catalan set out to import spices, with over a hundred mentioned in the chronicles of the time. They were used for medicinal purposes, embalming the dead, and of course for preserving and enhancing food. Citrus fruits and cane sugar also were imported which led to a higher standard of living.[131]

A more urban Europe emerged, centered around towns. People benefited from the trade that increasingly took place at the town centers, and more children benefited from schools that provided an education in basic skills.[132] Universities flourished in such places as Bologna, Naples, Paris, Oxford, Cambridge, Lisbon and Salamanca, at first under the local bishops but eventually more independently of the Church. Their earlier teachings were influenced by Aristotle, who emphasized reason and inquiry over faith.[133]

Book formats were revised and became more user-friendly. They began including chapters and indexes and were more widely available, thus leading to a broader democratization of knowledge. Parchment eventually was replaced by paper at a fraction of the cost. For the first time books were read by individuals for pleasure; one did not have to be of the noble classes in order to learn. Women were allowed to read devotional books. Encyclopedias also developed as compendiums of the state of knowledge.[134]

Towns became the dwelling places of freemen – those freed

from the encumbrances of feudal serfdom. Towns also reflected a concern for cleanliness – not always fulfilled – with the streets being paved, rubbish and waste water having a means of disposal. The few largest cities had populations of about 200,000, but the bulk of Western Europeans lived in small towns. There was as yet no appreciation of things natural; the woods were a place to be feared, but the beauty of the creation of towns was generally admired. Agricultural surpluses allowed more peasants to move to the towns as general prosperity grew amidst the increase in skilled craftsmen who could ply their trades in leather, clothing, barbering, metal working, jewelry, baked goods, meats, cheeses, spices, and medicines. Inns began to provide drink and food and a bed for travelers.[135] Thus the needs of the average person were increasingly addressed.

In England, local taxes were collected and used for creating town improvements such as roads and walls. This was a time of relative equality in which most town-dwellers were expected to contribute to civic expenses. The town was more democratic than the feudal model, although there was considerable inequality between classes – such as merchants and craftsmen – which grew throughout the Middle Ages. Nevertheless, the townspeople benefited from an economic flow that included an egalitarian encounter in the marketplace where many had something to trade in exchange for something they needed or wanted.[136] Despite many abuses, there was a growing sense of belief that the government and its laws were fair, including an increasing sense of national spirit.[137]

Efforts at greater equality were not seen in most other European countries at the time, such as France, where the laws and courts continued to favor the local lords. This led to growing resentment among peasants that eventually exploded in the French Revolution. The area that became France was much less unified, as the King only had the ability to govern the area around Paris until later expansion; there was little unity of national spirit – or even language.

Jews in many Italian cities were confined to separate areas beginning in the eleventh century. Many magistrates insisted on this segregation due to Jewish customs and religious laws that also required living separately from Gentiles. In Venice, the Jewish area was called *Il Ghetto*. In Poland-Lithuania, cities such as Warsaw excluded Jews from the central town. They were forced to live on settlements on the outskirts, called *shtetlin*, or townlets. Jews were not allowed to reside in Russia in the late eighteenth century unless they converted to Christianity, but when that country took over parts of Poland in 1791 under Catherine "the Great" Jews were forced to live in what was called the "Pale of Settlement" – mainly Poland, Lithuania, White Russia, and Ukraine.[138]

The fourteenth century was marked by a series of natural disasters, including the Great Famine (1314-22), due to poor harvests resulting from cold and wet conditions, contributing to a rise in crime and theft, and the Black Death (1348-49), one of many plagues that killed millions in Europe. The plagues challenged the religious beliefs of those who wondered how the wrath of God could strike good people and sinners alike. Many thought that Judgment Day was imminent. They prepared for it by self-flagellation (in case they were the guilty ones) and the killing of Jews, who were less affected by plague, possibly due to stricter hygiene practices.[139] Many Jews fled to Poland, which became their main sanctuary in Europe.[140]

In that time of plagues, art and books called *Danses Macabre* reflected the realization that death could strike at any time, with poems and artwork describing how people of any walk of life could be snatched from life. Some of this even was placed on the tombs and walls of cemeteries.[141]

Let's go forward, gentle Merchant
And don't bother to weigh
The merchandise they are asking for.
It's madness to think about that anymore.
You must think about your soul.
Time goes by, hour after hour,
And all we can do is to use it well.
Merit and good conduct last. [142]

Throughout the century wars continually devastated the populations of Europe. Men and women no longer were safe even in castles due to the introduction of gunpowder and cannons from China. Horses began to be used in warfare.[143] The long-term enmity between France and England had begun, and much of the territory that we now call France was periodically under the control of England. Roving bands of warriors raided villages, inflicting rape and murder, decimating the population.[144]

In Russia, the town that later became Moscow was settled in 1146. Novgorod, an independent municipality in the far north that was ruled by an assembly of free citizens, lasted for centuries. It extended its influence in many directions and repulsed a number of invasions, including one by Sweden in 1240, under the leadership of the legendary Alexander Nevsky.[145] It eventually lost its wars – and independence – to Moscow in 1478, when Ivan III slaughtered its population.

The Ottoman Empire – a Muslim state named after its early leader Osman in 1302 – became more advanced than any European state due to its extensive ability to organize its vast expanse. The Ottoman Turks conquered much of the former Greek world starting in 1353, and then massacred the "flower of European chivalry" – members of the last Crusade – in 1396.[146]

The Ottomans captured Constantinople (now Istanbul), the

center of Eastern Christendom, in 1453 – which had resisted onslaughts from Barbarians and others for a thousand years – by adopting the use of the new technology of gunpowder and cannons. This sent fear throughout the Christian world.[147] By the 1500s the Ottoman Empire ranged from Western Asia to Europe, including North Africa, the Middle East, Eastern Europe and Western Russia.

Nationalism – identification with a country rather than a region – slowly increased. Leaders inspired their troops by oratorical, as well as military, skills. A major victory for the English was the Battle of Agincourt (in Northern France) under Henry V in 1415, later immortalized by Shakespeare who created a speech summarizing Henry's inspiring words:

> *From this day to the ending of the world,*
> *But we in it shall be remembered –*
> *We few, we happy few, we band of brothers;*
> *For he to-day that sheds his blood with me*
> *Shall be my brother; be he ne'er so vile,*
> *This day shall gentle his condition;*
> *And gentlemen in England now-a-bed*
> *Shall think themselves accurs'd they were not here.*
> **— Henry V, Act 4, Scene 3**

Joan of Arc, who has become a symbol of insurrection in the face of oppression, was nineteen when, inspired by a vision, she managed to rally French troops against the English toward the end of the Hundred Years War. Although eventually caught and burned at the stake in 1431, she was the inspiration for the eventual expulsion of the English from French soil. By the end of the fifteenth century, France began to emerge as a more centralized monarchy, with roughly the borders of the modern state.[148]

In Western Europe wealthy merchants financed the

construction of churches with elaborate religious artwork and hospices for the poor. This was encouraged by the Church in such places as Siena and Beaune for those wishing to guarantee their soul's salvation.

The invention of movable type by Johannes Gutenberg in 1450 eventually allowed the diffusion of information and ideas to the common people. The printing of books developed slowly as they still were costly to produce. Mainly religious works were printed at first.[149] By 1500, 40,000 books would be printed in France alone.[150]

The period between the fifteenth and nineteenth centuries in Western Europe was that of the greatest state building, gradually moving from rule by localized kings to larger administrative and tax systems that encouraged residents to think of themselves as members of nations rather than of their region. Wars needed to be financed almost continuously throughout this period, but wars that took place between nations also were instruments of state building.[151]

The Renaissance bloomed in Florence under the influence of the Medici family, who controlled the city from 1434 and who were great patrons of the arts. They restored churches, as well as building a hospital in Jerusalem, while advocating for the use of popular language to replace Latin. Though they ruled as despots, the Medici supported the creative potential of talented artists and craftsmen and spread education to the masses through the creation of libraries. The Renaissance then slowly spread to most of the rest of Western Europe.[152]

Because of its emphasis on fine art and churches, Italy was one of the world's first tourist destinations. Nevertheless, the Italian states engaged in interminable wars up until unification in the 1800s.[153] Within states there were ongoing feuds between families, including much treachery and even poisoning, as so poignantly portrayed by Shakespeare in *Romeo and Juliet*.[154]

In 1492 Spain expelled the Moors from their last stronghold

in Granada, and compelled the Jews to convert to Catholicism or leave the country. The Sultan sent ships from Constantinople to collect Jews who wanted to continue living under tolerant Muslim rule.[155] As every Western school child knows, this also was the year of the first sailing of Christopher Columbus in an attempt to circumnavigate the globe; he landed in what he thought were the islands off India.

By the end of the fifteenth century gold and other precious metals were in great demand to meet expanding monetary needs. Early expeditions to Africa failed, but eventually gold was discovered in Sudan, south of Egypt. In 1444, an expedition of six Portuguese ships under Henry the Navigator sailed to islands off the coast of western Africa and seized 235 men, women and children, separating families and causing great distress among those captured. A court chronicler described the scene:

Some held their heads low, their faces bathed in tears. . . some groaned very piteously, looking toward the heavens fixedly and crying aloud, as if they were calling on the father of the universe to help them; others struck their faces with their hands and threw themselves on the ground.[156]

Thus began the slave trade that would be an economic boon for some and ruin the lives of many others for the next four hundred years.

After many attempts by the Portuguese to sail from Europe to the Orient by working their way around Africa, Vasco de Gama navigated his way to India beginning in 1497.[157] Another Portuguese sailor, Fernando Magellan sailed to the Spice Islands in 1521 after going around South America, and his crew returned via the Indian Ocean after he was killed during the voyage. This proved that the world was round after all.[158] The Middle Ages came to an end in Europe with an expanding horizon of the world.

At the end of the fifteenth century China was an advanced and powerful nation, but did not expand its influence beyond its own borders. The Ming Dynasty, which was in power from 1368 until 1644, was the first to establish legitimate examinations for civil service positions, putting aside favoritism toward family and associates.[159]

After successfully dominating and decimating the populations of the Americas and Africa, the European powers set their sights on Japan. The Portuguese arrived in the mid-sixteenth century. The rumored riches of Japan tempted the Europeans, but though embroiled in disputes between competing warlords, the Japanese were fierce warriors, well-organized and hard to conquer. Thus missionaries were sent to conquer their souls, but they were expelled in 1587 due to their competition with the established Buddhist and Shinto worship. Rather than being subjugated, the Japanese adopted foreign technology. They imported gunpowder from China, eventually became manufacturers and exporters of muskets, and became adept at manufacturing lenses for scientific exploration. They adapted the potato for their own use, and exported silver for profit.[160]

In 1853, Commodore Perry of the US arrived in Tokyo, and the feudal lords realized that they needed to give up their traditional sword and archery warfare if they were not to end up a Western colony like China. The American influence caused the Japanese to adopt American ways, such as a more centralized government and a modern educational system.[161] In 1858, the country was opened to outside trade by a treaty with the US. In the 1880s Japan began producing textiles, particularly cotton, which became its main export.[162]

While Europe was beginning the second millennium, the Western Hemisphere was populated by numerous civilizations in both the North and South. Anthropologists vary in their views of the earliest societies in America before the arrival of Columbus, but evidence keeps pushing the dates further back. Thanks to recent archeological research, a view that currently is gaining ground is that there may have been a series of migrations going back as long as 40,000 years or longer. Some researchers also believe that many of the areas that were found thinly populated upon the arrival of Europeans had hosted highly complex civilizations that had been decimated by the advance of smallpox before Europeans even set eye on them.[163]

The native tribes of what became the Northeastern United States were successful at agriculture and engaged in long-distance trade. They were admired by the Europeans who first saw them in the sixteenth century as exceedingly healthy, strong and clean, probably due to an excellent diet, especially in comparison with the arriving Europeans who lived on rations and rarely bathed. Observers reported seeing large settlements. In the late 1600s, after a series of Indian wars in Massachusetts, the victorious Europeans sold thousands of natives into slavery which was a common practice throughout the colonies.[164]

In 1370 the Aztecs founded Teotihuacán in Mexico and operated a succession of federations into the fifteenth century.[165] The native populations of Mexico developed advanced agricultural techniques, which included the cultivation of maize, tomatoes, squash, beans and avocadoes. When Columbus introduced maize to Europe, it became a staple in many countries, including its use for polenta in Italy. Research shows that these New World societies – with populations in the hundreds of thousands – also engaged in long distance trade with each other. Their culture included the use of mathematics and astronomy to mark the seasons. They also engaged in devastating wars with each other much like the Europeans.[166]

By the late 1400s the Incas of Peru ruled an area larger than any large European state of the day. As they conquered other populations, they moved them from their lands and forced them into work camps to build roads and other projects. They built palaces and temples made of stones that fit together without mortar. This impressed the Europeans who were not capable of a similar feat. They also eliminated hunger in their dominions.[167]

1500-2000

During this period most of the world began to throw off old prejudices and beliefs that had slowed much of the progress of human knowledge, beginning with the West. This led to continual new insights based on observation and exploration. The theories of Copernicus, around 1514, and the examination of the cosmos by Galileo by telescope 100 years later, although suppressed by the Inquisition, broke the news that the earth — and thus humanity — no longer was the center of the universe.

Human dignity became a greater consideration in philosophy, religion, and the creation of governments. There was a trend toward more democratic principles that recognized the potential of people to self-govern, and treated them less as perpetual children incapable of governing themselves.

As Aristotle had speculated in his *Politics* (c 335 BCE): "The soul has naturally two elements, a ruling and a ruled; and each of these has a different virtue, one belonging to the rational and ruling element, the other to the irrational and subject element."[168] As our rational minds slowly opened to gaining new insights about the world we still managed to keep our minds closed — for the most part — to people we decided were different from us in belief or background. This led to the greatest amount of persecutions and deaths by war and genocide in history, despite our increasing belief in ourselves as rational beings. During the last century of the Second Millennium, our rational self went to the moon and back, while our irrational self remained in the Dark Ages.

Advancing technologies pointed the way to a better life for the average person, yet technology also was used to create a new level of destructiveness that superseded the greatest cataclysms of the past. It provided a means for us to impose an unprecedented wave of inhumanity upon ourselves.

After the early 1500s there was a considerable increase in agricultural production in Europe due to clearing more land for production and the introduction of buckwheat and maize from Mexico, which created more reliable crops and lessened incidents of poor harvests that would cause mass starvation.[169]

The Protestant Reformation began in Germany in 1517, with an attack on the corruptions of the Church by Martin Luther, whose pamphlets were aided by wide distribution resulting from the printing press. Afterwards there would be devastating wars between Catholics and Protestants throughout Europe for five hundred years. The gap between royalty and commoners also grew during this period exemplified by, for example, the Chateau of Chambord built on the Loire by Henri II and Catherine de Medici with 440 rooms. At the peak of the struggle between the Catholic monarchs and Protestants (called Huguenots in France), Catherine ordered the Saint Bartholomew's Eve Massacre in 1572 in which 25,000 Protestants were killed throughout the country.

Catherine's son Henri IV ruled France with a firm hand from 1589, but with an eye and ear for what would benefit all economic levels of the country's population. He promoted religious tolerance, art, crafts, agriculture and manufacturing, constructed roads and bridges, and remodeled Paris for the enjoyment of his subjects by building public squares, such as the Place de Vosges.[170] He issued the Edict of Nantes in 1598 providing greater freedoms for Protestants.[171]

The Reformation that began under Luther spread throughout Northern Europe as more people could read what the Bible said for themselves. This contributed to a growing concept that people had a right to come to their own beliefs and no longer needed to depend on the Church for their religious ideas. Luther's writings backed the doctrine of "justification by faith," as opposed to "justification by works."[172]

In England, King Henry VIII, who desired a male heir, sought a divorce from his first wife, Catherine of Aragon, which was denied by the Pope. Henry then attacked the Church and confiscated its property. The Act of Supremacy, passed in 1534, ended papal authority in England, making the King the head of the English Church. He executed any churchmen standing in his way, including Thomas More, author of *Utopia*, who eventually became a Catholic saint. Henry's second wife, Ann Boleyn, had already given birth to Elizabeth, the future Queen, in 1533, but Henry divorced and executed her as he continued to seek a male heir, working his way through six wives, including Jane Seymour, who died soon after bearing the son he so greatly wanted.[173] Edward VI assumed the thrown at age seven but died at fifteen.

What many consider the "Golden Age" of England began under Elizabeth I, daughter of Henry VIII and Ann Boleyn, who was crowned Queen of England in 1558, at the age of 25. The Catholic bishops claimed that Elizabeth was not qualified to rule due to being a Protestant, and of questionable birth. Nonetheless, she sought to walk the fine line of religious tolerance and became perhaps the most popular of all British monarchs. She never married, but had four successive "favorites."

The rule of law in England slid back precipitously under the reign of the Stuarts in the early 1600s. The country became more authoritarian and corrupt as these monarchs insisted on the divine right of kings. The purchase of offices – which was common on the continent – threatened to overthrow the democratic direction of the country. Charles I used the court system to go after his own enemies. He tried to impose English religious liturgy on Scotland in 1637 which led to war.[174] He dissolved Parliament in 1629 in a dispute over religious issues and the raising of taxes. This led to a decade-long civil war that resulted in Charles' beheading. Abuses of power under the "Protectorate" of Oliver Cromwell that followed led to the Restoration under Charles II in 1660. But his pro-Catholic sympathies – in a land that was primarily Protestant – resulted in the Glorious Revolution and the install-ment of William of Orange as king in 1689.[175]

The Glorious Revolution established an equitable system for taxes. Although taxes increased, they were seen by the English public as being required to fund two expensive wars with France and Spain. But the increase in taxes did not stifle the English economy, which continued to expand – instead war may have contributed to an expansion. Wars required taxation and orga-nization and therefore tended to make the state stronger. By the nineteenth century a few of England's neighbors in Northern Europe also created similar tax systems that stimulated their economies.[176] Thus taxes, even in those times, became a way to enable the government to make purchases that create employ-ment and benefit all levels of society.

One possible reason for the relative stability of England was that, in comparison with its neighbors, it was somewhat isolated. Although it was vulnerable to attacks from the Continent and Scandinavian tribes through much of its history, its shape as an island encouraged the English to think of themselves as a unified whole earlier than the rest of Europe.

The essays of Michel de Montaigne had a humanizing influ-ence on science and education in France.[177] In his "Essay on the Education of Children" he proposed that learning the skills most needed in life should precede training in specific disciplines: "After having taught him what will make him more wise and good, you may then entertain him with the elements of logic, physics, geometry, rhetoric, and the science which he shall then himself most incline to, his judgment being beforehand formed and fit to choose, he will quickly make his own." Rene Descartes brought about a revolution in thought by emphasizing the responsibility of the individual in determining her or his views, rather than depending on the Church to define one's role. His famous statement: "I think, therefore I am," first appeared in 1637 in his *Discourse on Method*.[178]

In 1513, Niccolo Machiavelli published *The Prince*. Despite Machiavelli's reputation as a backer of tyranny, his advice often was positive. For example, his recommendations include: "A prince should also demonstrate that he supports talent by supporting men of ability and by honoring those who excel in each craft."[179]

In the early 1500s Spain, under Charles V, had the largest empire in the world. Despite a considerable influx of gold from the New World, expenses greatly outstripped income due to wars with countries throughout Europe. Charles forced tax increases through the Cortes, the Spanish Parliament. An uprising ensued which further weakened the government.[180] Under Philip II, who became King in 1556, and his successors, Spain's dominance faded during the remainder of the century, punctuated by the defeat of the Spanish Armada in 1588 by England, which ruled the seas and trade routes thereafter. His persecution of minority regions and religions and his backing of the Inquisition caused rebellion and general discontent.[181]

Spain expanded its influence into the New World with Cortes destroying the Aztec empire in Mexico in 1521 and Pizarro devastating the Incas in Peru in 1533. In Bolivia and Mexico, Spanish rulers lived off the extracts from the mines which were worked

The World of Wine

Mexico was the first country in Latin America to produce wine after Cortes sent for grape cuttings from Spain in 1522. The biggest Latin American producer now is Argentina, followed by Chile and Brazil. Wine also is produced in Uruguay, Peru, Bolivia, Ecuador, and Venezuela.

Argentina's Mendoza region may be the most famous wine producing area in South America. It also is a popular tourist destination, with the snow-capped mountain chain of the Andes in the background. It is known for its Malbec wine, well-priced and popular throughout the world and its Cabernet Sauvignon, both of which have their origins in Southwest France. Argentine wines are generally attractive and usually ready to drink when relatively young. Wine, Pages 840-42.

by indigenous tribes that essentially were slaves.[182] Upon the death from smallpox of thousands of natives who were expected to be used as forced laborers, the colonial economy collapsed and the Spaniards began importing slaves from Africa.[183] After the settlement of Mexico, Spain continued exploring and settling northward into what is now California, Arizona, and Colorado. The Portuguese overcame the Dutch to settle Brazil. Russia established settlements in Alaska as far south as Fort Ross in California[184]

When Peter, who became known as "the Great," assumed the Russian throne in 1672, he moved the capitol to Saint Petersburg and imposed modern innovations. He also drafted the entire aristocracy into lifelong service in the army. In exchange for military service, the nobles were exempted from taxes and given land grants.

Peter also was known for his enthusiastic torture of his enemies.[185] Many Russian nobles owned large numbers of serfs, thousands in some cases. Peter's autocratic methods, however, made it impossible for Russia to operate effectively after his death due to a lack of trained administrators who could make independent decisions.[186]

Catherine, also known as "the Great," assumed the Russian throne in 1762. A friend and correspondent of Voltaire, she expanded Peter's building program but brought further suppression on the serfs, particularly after the French Revolution of 1789.[187] She continued the Russian expansion in the direction of Sweden-Finland and Poland-Lithuania.[188] Her grandson, Alexander I, flirted with the idea of a constitutional monarchy and led Russia in its successful repulsion of Napoleon in 1812, which left 600,000 men to die in the snow after the unsuccessful siege of Moscow.[189] Tsar Alexander II freed the serfs, but was assassinated in 1881, which drove the Russian monarchy to establish yet greater repressions.[190]

The first settlements in North America were in Montreal, under Jacques Cartier of France in 1536, and Saint Augustine, by Pedro Menendez of Spain in 1565, following the destruction of a colony of Huguenots. Menendez's settlement was destroyed in turn by a larger group of Huguenots a few years later. Thus the enmities of the Continent were transferred to the New World from the beginning.[191]

The trade routes to the Americas expanded exponentially in a little over 100 years. By 1600, 200 ships per year sailed between New York and Spain. Many products from the New World quickly became popular such as pepper, coffee, cocoa, sugar and tobacco. This trade had a profound impact on the wealth and health of Western Europe.[192] As the English became dominant in the New World they settled Jamestown in Virginia in 1607, followed by settlements in Maryland, the Carolinas, New York and New Jersey.[193]

The Pilgrims, a group of about 100 Protestants, sailed for what is now Massachusetts in 1620. They claimed to follow the teachings of John Winthrop, who spoke of a "city upon a hill" with equality for all under a God who loves his creation. However, the actual model that they perpetrated was the opposite of democracy: strict rules and punishments were imposed by those who claimed to represent Christian love.[194] They imposed the same religious intolerance they had left Europe to escape.

The French soon got in on the game in the future United States. In 1682 they established Louisiana, named after Louis XIV, which eventually was sold under financial stress by Napoleon to the US under President Thomas Jefferson in 1803.[195] The Louisiana Purchase included areas from the Gulf of Mexico north to Canada, which nearly doubled the territory of the United States.[196]

In the early 1700s a coalition of six northeast tribes formed an alliance to work together for their mutual benefit. They created an oral constitution called the Great Law of Peace by which they all were bound. The tribes – which were headed by women – agreed that all major decisions would be made by consensus, which in many cases took a long time, but avoided war. When matters of the greatest importance were being decided the will of the people was sought. For the most part, individuals in native societies valued their freedom. They did not understand or see the need for the strict laws and customs of the Europeans who soon moved in. Because of the egalitarian nature of their society, they were unable to get used to the idea that any person was superior to any other as the Europeans tried to teach them.[197]

In 1648 The Treaty of Westphalia created an agreement between European countries that had been struggling against each other for over thirty years. Much of Europe had been devastated – in Germany villages and farms were in ruins and the population was substantially reduced. The Treaty established an uneasy peace between France, Germany, Austria, the Swiss, the Dutch, Spanish and Italians, and attempted to guarantee religious toleration between Catholics and Protestants. This treaty laid the foundation for the resumption of trade that started Europe on a path to greater prosperity.[198]

Louis XIV, the "Sun King," consolidated the monarchy in France as it never was before or afterwards. After assuming the throne in 1638, he made the aristocracy totally dependent on himself at Versailles, the largest palace in France. His rigorous routine included long days of meetings with ministers to plan the details of administering his kingdom. Despite his absolute hand, he believed himself a father to his country and usually endeavored to treat all his subjects fairly. Louis expanded the country's influence abroad, increased trade, and promoted art and music in a way that had not previously been done. He also engaged in wars that left the treasury broke by his death. When he revoked the Edict of Nantes in 1685, he drove out 200,000 Protestants who had been an essential part of the economic backbone of the country.[199]

Under Louis, there were divisions between "estates" – aristocracy, bourgeoisie, and peasants – who barely considered themselves a part of the same country. Government offices were sold to the highest bidder by an administration that continually was strapped for cash. Enforcement of government tax policies was rigged for the elite who thought it beneath them to pay taxes that therefore fell on the peasants. The king was not dependent on the Parliament to make laws – he could force through any laws he considered important.[200]

During the reign of Louis XV, there was a general increase in prosperity due to improvements in industries such as coal-mining, metalworking, and textiles, and a new network of roads was begun. Trade with colonies such as Guadeloupe and Martinique brought a degree of success from sugar and the slave trade. But

France already was functioning under weakened economic conditions – including war with an England that dominated the seas – that were to place a burden on the next monarch, Louis XVI, and contribute to his downfall.

In 1651 Thomas Hobbes wrote that human life in the state of nature is filled with chaos and anxiety – it is "nasty, brutal and short." He claimed that states exist to bring greater stability to human existence.[201] In the late 1600s and 1700s, John Locke,[202] Jean-Jacques Rousseau,[203] and Voltaire[204]– members of the European "Enlightenment" – declared that freedom is our natural condition, but we sacrifice much of it to enter into a "social contract" that provides mutual protections and allows us to live together in a more peaceful and stable society.[205]

According to these writers, governments and laws exist to provide better security than we would have in our natural condition where – as individuals, families and tribes – we would need to struggle continually for survival. They believed that when states achieve their purpose they create a system that provides us with more control over our lives than we would have without it. Locke and Rousseau also held that when a state becomes oppressive we have the right to replace it with another that is capable of providing more freedom and choice. At about the same time, the theories of Isaac Newton on the nature of the universe led to a new faith in science as a route to understanding.[206]

Throughout Europe in the early 1700s, there was a growing wealthy professional and commercial class, as well as an artisan class, but also an increase of poverty in the cities. In England, the Enclosure Movement took land that had been worked by peasants.[207]

In 1707, the Act of Union was signed by England and Scotland, creating a united Parliament and free trade between the two countries, while England assumed Scotland's debts. But the birth of Great Britain did not end the rebellions of the high-landers who wanted an independent Scotland. This culminated in the Battle of Culloden Moor in 1746, in which over 1,000 were killed. After this the Gaelic language was forbidden as well as Highland dress, followed by the Clearances over the next 100 years which decimated the Highland culture.[208] Ireland, where both Protestants and Catholics were persecuted, was omitted from the Act of Union. It remained a nation apart which did not participate in England's legislative or industrial progress. Ireland eventually was forced into the United Kingdom through the second Act of Union in 1801.[209]

The Industrial Revolution, roughly corresponding to the period 1700-1850, saw greatly increased production on farm land from inventions such as horse-drawn plows and reapers. This led to an improved food supply and population gains. The need for less people to work the land resulted in an enlarged labor pool, which eventually migrated to the cities to participate in increasingly mechanized manufacturing, made possible at first by steam engines and later by coal. The appearance of factories to produce cloth and clothing contributed to a grim landscape saturated with grit. Factory workers were numbed by long hours and repetitive work.[210]

1776 saw the publication of Adam Smith's *The Wealth of Nations,* a turning point in the history of economics, and his famous summary of the "theory of capital," later known as capitalism. Smith believed that the "invisible hand" of the economic market would function best to provide general prosperity if left largely untouched. The division of labor, Smith argued, would create more efficient manufacturing and farming, and thus greater prosperity for all.[211] Yet he also was concerned with justice. In the days before the great revolutions of America and France, he held that it was up to the monarchs to maintain justice for all in their realm. He describes: "The second duty of the

The World of Wine

In April 1663, the famous London diarist Samuel Pepys tasted a wine that inspired him to write a long description in his diary. He had drunk "a sort of French wine called Ho-Bryan" that had a "good and most particular taste." He was referring to Chateau Haut-Brion in Bordeaux, later recognized as one of the Grand Cru (great vineyards) in the Classification of 1855.

References in documents referring to Haut-Brion go back to 1435. Haut-Brion, and Bordeaux wines in general, had their origins in the middle ages when it was discovered that the gravelly/clay soils of the region produced, in good years, magnificent long-lived wines made of the blends best suited to the region: Cabernet Sauvignon, Merlot, Petit Verdot, and Cabernet Franc. At that time there was not the same concept of France that we have today. The Bordeaux region, in the Southwest, was part of Aquitaine and ruled by English kings. The main "road" between Bordeaux and Britain was the sea route; overland travel was much more difficult and likely to result in spoilage. *Haut-Brion,* Pages 2-4

---

sovereign, that of protecting, as far as possible, every member of society from the oppression of every other member."[212]

The American Revolution, which started in 1775, was instigated by the British colonies on the East Coast of North America that considered themselves overtaxed and underrepresented as British citizens. No betting person would have considered the rebelling thirteen colonies to have a chance against the most powerful empire of the time. Many in Parliament spoke out against the oppression they saw as being foisted upon the Americans.[213]

George Washington, who previously fought for the British in the Indian Wars, took charge of the disorganized revolutionary forces, perhaps 20,000 in total, eventually called the Continental Army. At first, the colonists expressed the view that they only were fighting to maintain their rights as English citizens.[214] Because of a shortage of enlistees, Washington was glad to lead a mixed army that included blacks, Indians, young and old.[215] Washington always was aware that his authority derived from the Continental Congress, a group of representatives of the thirteen colonies that met in Philadelphia.

In January of 1776, the British under General William Howe were besieged in Boston by Washington's troops. The British were short of supplies, but the Continental Army was suffering through a cold winter with low morale and little money; perhaps 9,000 troops went home at the end of their enlistment on January 1, and not all were replaced. After collecting and securing cannons from upper New York, Washington began the bombardment of the entrenched British troops on March 2 from Dorchester Heights in Cambridge, and the British, along with thousands of Loyalists, were forced to evacuate. For not only the Continental soldiers, but for much of the population of New England, this was a turning point in morale.[216]

From there Washington's troops made haste for New York, which was essential to defend, politically and strategically, and they plunged into constructing fortifications.[217] Washington had about 7,000 troops in comparison to 30,000 for the British including mercenaries, more than the city of New York, when their armada arrived on June 29.

On July 2, the Congress in Philadelphia voted to terminate ties with Britain. The Declaration of Independence, completed on July 4 after many drafts by Thomas Jefferson, contains the most famous words in the annals of democracy:

We hold these truths to be self-evident, that all men are created equal, that they are endowed by their Creator with certain unalienable Rights, that among these are Life, Liberty and the pursuit of Happiness. That to secure these rights, Governments are instituted among Men, deriving their just powers from the consent of the governed. That whenever any Form of Government becomes destructive of these ends, it is the Right of the People to alter or to abolish it, and to institute new Government, laying its foundation on such principles and organizing its powers in such form, as to them shall seem most likely to affect their Safety and Happiness.[218]

In February of that year, an English immigrant named Thomas Paine, who had failed at business to that point, published a fiery booklet, *Common Sense*. In the spirit of other Enlightenment authors, he wrote that government, when poorly managed, brings suffering to those who are governed. By implication, the British government incited rebellion in the Colonies by ignoring their needs:

Society in every state is a blessing, but government even it its best is but a necessary evil; in its worst state an intolerable one; for when we suffer, or are exposed to the same miseries by a government, which we might expect in a country without government, our calamity is heightened by reflecting that we furnish the means by which we suffer.[219]

With the onset of winter, Howe decided to rest his exhausted men for the winter in northern New Jersey and New York, as was typical for "civilized" armies. 1,550 Hessian mercenaries and some British troops were encamped across the river in Trenton, New Jersey. Washington had about 6,000 men left who could fight; about 1500 were incapacitated due to the cold. Nevertheless, Washington planned an attack which would cross the Delaware on Christmas night and then march north to attack the enemy force. All night, boats were loaded with cannons and horses, but a major storm struck while they were waiting to cross. Two men froze to death on the march. The attack, which was planned to begin before dawn, was not able to begin until 8AM, which eliminated the element of surprise. But the Hessian force and the British soldiers were defeated. This was the beginning of the reversal of the course of the war that lasted for another six and a half years, but as news of the rebellion's success spread, help came in from France, Spain and the Netherlands.[220]

British ships commonly attacked New England towns during the war just to incite fear. In the summer of 1777, Benedict Arnold, a popular leader, led his troops to a victory over General John Burgoyne at Saratoga. This began turning the tide and brought the French more fully into the war. Arnold later became a British spy. Captain John Paul Jones, an American of Scottish descent supported by the French, attacked the British mainland and engaged in battles with British ships in their own waters. In 1778 the British offered the Americans a reconciliation agreement, but lacking full recognition of American independence, it was turned down.[221]

In 1781, Louis XVI committed much of his navy to aid the American cause, which allowed the conflict to end in two more years. A combined American and French force, led by Washington and Lafayette, descended on Chesapeake Bay by land and sea in the Battle of Yorktown in October. General Cornwallis surrendered, and the fate of America was in its own hands after that point.[222]

According to Joseph Ellis, "Based on what we now know about the military history of the American Revolution, if the British commanders had prosecuted the war more vigorously in its earliest stages, the Continental Army might well have been destroyed at the start and the movement for American independence nipped in the bud. The signers of the Declaration of

Independence would then have been hunted down, tried, and executed for treason, and American history would have flowed forward in a wholly different direction."[223]

The Articles of Confederation, written by Congress in the early stages of the war and later confirmed by the states, allowed states maximum autonomy without forcing them into a union. The results were distressing to founders such as John Adams and James Madison, who realized that thirteen sets of laws and customs that often were incompatible created an ungovernable entity.

In 1787 a committee was assembled to create an acceptable replacement for the Articles. The most prominent members were Benjamin Franklin, Alexander Hamilton, and James Madison. They agreed that sovereignty did not reside with the government or states; the founding principle was that the authority for government was "We the People." Beyond that, nearly everything else was decided after a long-argued process, with continual reference to that same founding principle. Yet they did work out a compromise that lasted, known as the US Constitution, which has been amended only twenty-seven times to date. The first ten amendments were included from the beginning as the Bill of Rights.[224]

Blacks and Indians had served nobly in the Revolutionary War and there were nearly 700,000 slaves. So were blacks or Indians to be included in the definition of "The People," and if so, how? Many of the leading authors of the eventual Constitution were slaveholders, including Washington and Madison.[225] One "compromise" that was reached, but later changed, was to not count Indians toward congressional representation and to count just "three fifths of all other Persons." (US Constitution, Article I, Section 2) Thus slave ownership actually increased the representational power of the southern states in Congress. Another compromise was the continuation of the slave trade until 1808, which put off this contentious issue for thirty years. (Article I, Section 9)[226]

As Joseph Ellis states, "the debate was not resolved so much as built into the fabric of our national identity."[227] America's oldest tradition is to work together in good faith toward a common understanding and course of action so that our institutions can continue to thrive. An example was a compromise in which the southern states allowed the Federal Government to assume the states' war debt in exchange for locating the Capitol in the South.[228]

George Washington, who had become US President by unanimous choice in 1789 and continued for two terms to 1796, declined a third term for fear of turning the office of President into a monarchy. In his Farewell Address, Washington warned of the dangers of allegiance to political parties rather than to the principles of the US founding, advice we might well heed today:

There is an opinion that parties in free countries are useful checks upon the administration of the government and serve to keep alive the spirit of liberty. This within certain limits is probably true; and in governments of a monarchical cast, patriotism may look with indulgence, if not with favor, upon the spirit of party. But in those of the popular character, in governments purely elective, it is a spirit not to be encouraged. From their natural tendency, it is certain there will always be enough of that spirit for every salutary purpose. And there being constant danger of excess, the effort ought to be by force of public opinion, to mitigate and assuage it. A fire not to be quenched, it demands a uniform vigilance to prevent its bursting into a flame, lest, instead of warming, it should consume.[229]

Slavery dominated debate in Congress and the rest of the young country. The assumption that the United States was founded on egalitarian principles ensured that the debate would continue. The economy of the South was based on cotton, and the economy of the North based on industry, so a slavery based economy was harder for some to give up than others. In 1782, Virginia passed a law allowing slave owners to free their slaves if they decided to, which resulted in 12,000 being freed. Jefferson, in *Notes on the State of Virginia*, suggested a proposal that would free all slaves after the year 1800. Gouverneur Morris of New York, a signer of the Constitution, stated that slavery was a curse, and that slave owners should be compensated by Congress for its dissolution. The issue was not resolved until the country broke in two in 1865.[230]

Edmund Burke, known as the founder of conservatism in England, supported the American Revolution due to British incursions on the liberty of the colonists, such as the imposition of the Stamp Act.[231] But he opposed the excesses of the French Revolution.[232] He saw change as being essential to the continuation of society: "'A state without the means of some change is without the means of its conservation.'"[233]

In France, political opposition came from the nobles who had a hold on Parliament. While there was much agreement about what was wrong with their society, there was little agreement about what system should replace it, a problem that led to instability in France for long after its revolution.[234]

Louis XVI assumed the throne in 1754. He was a timid man easily influenced by his ministers. At first his popularity was boosted by his support of the American Revolution, but the ideals of the Declaration of Independence did not encourage his subjects to support him. Due to a need for funds partly brought on by a poor harvest, and after the land-holding clergy refused his request to raise taxes, the king was forced to convene the Estates General for the first time in 175 years in May 1789. At this meeting the Third Estate (those others than the nobles and clergy) made demands for equality inspired by the new American nation. When the king locked them out, some took over a tennis court and made an oath not to leave until a new constitution was put in place. On July 14 the crowd stormed the Bastille, a small prison, to obtain arms in a battle against the king's troops, and the French Revolution had begun. When Louis fled in 1791, he was brought back to face trial, and the fate of the French monarchy was sealed.[235]

Since the French Revolution took place in the largest and most powerful European country, it immediately aroused the monarchies of surrounding countries to suppress it. Meanwhile, the Constituent Assembly worked for the next two years to set up a constitutional monarchy on the order of Britain. Lafayette had just returned from aiding the American Revolution – he was joined by the likes of Danton, Robespierre and Marat. They wrote the Declaration of the Rights of Man and Citizen, which later would become a model for the United Nation's Universal Declaration of Human Rights. They abolished the Three Estates and replaced them with the American model of the Executive, Legislative, and Judicial branches of government. France introduced suffrage for all men in 1792 – still excluding women – and the number of eligible voters jumped from 250,000 to about nine million. The working day was reduced to ten hours and slavery was abolished in the colonies. The lands of the Church – about eight percent of the country – were sold off.[236] Despite the promises of universal freedom contained in the Declaration, the terror that followed, and the despotism that followed that, deprived many not only of their liberties but their lives.

After the trial and execution of Louis in 1792, an alarmed coalition of powers including England, Prussia, Russia, Spain, Austria, Sardinia, and Naples united against the Revolution while a civil war raged within the country. At this point the leaders of the new Republic began executing revolutionary leaders and established a dictatorship. A conscription of 600,000 men was called which successfully challenged the invading armies. Robespierre, who had come to represent the absolutism that he had worked to overcome, met the guillotine in July of 1794.[237]

Despite a promising beginning that was supported by advocates of democracy in Britain and the US, the French Revolution devolved into a terror that devoured itself. It had been largely inspired by the Enlightenment writers that spurred the American insurrection, but like many revolutions it became obsessed with tearing out its disease without prescribing a cure. There was no generally agreed way forward – no commitment to creating a vision for the country to replace its dysfunction. And so the dysfunction changed from one form to another and yet to another with no end in sight.

Napoleon Bonaparte impressed his officers with his skills as a member of the artillery in the battle against Italy. He initiated a coup and had himself declared Emperor of France in 1804. Over the next ten years his empire was to include present-day Austria, Italy, Germany, and the Netherlands, but when he tried to replace the king of Spain a rebellion weakened him. He then lost a half million soldiers in his invasion of Russia in 1812. He was forced to abdicate in 1814, was exiled, then returned, and then was defeated once again by the British at Waterloo in 1815, after which we was exiled again and died at age fifty-two on the remote island of Saint Helena. A dichotomy between populism and autocracy has remained France's legacy ever since.[238]

The revolution of 1830 was caused by the autocratic policies of Charles X, who was forced to flee, and who was succeeded by Louis-Philippe, an ex-revolutionary. He, in turn, was forced out by the 1848 revolution which featured the student barricades described by Victor Hugo in *Les Miserables*:

The barricade St. Antoine was monstrous; it was three stories high and seven hundred feet long. It barred from one corner to the other the vast mouth of the Fauborg, that is to say, three streets. . . . Merely from seeing it, you felt an immense agonizing suffering that had reached that extreme moment when distress rushes to catastrophe.

The Second Republic of 1848 gave way, by 1852, to the Second Empire under Louis Napoleon, nephew of Napoleon Bonaparte, who ruled as Napoleon III. The French economy grew during his reign: he encouraged more industry to develop and stayed in power longer than any French leader after the Revolution. He also was responsible for a modernization of Parisian boulevards by Baron Haussmann and major parks. He attacked Prussia (Germany) in an attempt to match the glory of his uncle with an outmoded and undertrained army, which led to defeat and the end of the Second Empire in 1870.[239]

Nationalism spread, starting in Europe, and then to America, but it took a long time for individuals to learn to identify with a nation rather than their local interests. The French began to think of themselves as one country as they went to war with the rest of Europe under Napoleon. Britain was forged from England and Scotland. Nationalism also took hold in those countries they fought. Americans, who were about one-half originally opposed to their Revolution, gradually began to think of themselves united. National anthems and holidays strengthened that process. Ideas of racial identify – including those of an Aryan, Caucasian or Slavic race, were introduced in Europe in the late 1800s which increased national unity. This led to movements to expel minorities. Separatist movements by those who preferred to identify with their region rather than a country ran counter to nationalism.[240]

The census of 1790 shows a total of just under four million inhabitants of the United States. About twenty percent were slaves, with only two New England states having none. Acts for the gradual abolition of slavery were in place in many northern states. Slavery was abolished in Russia in 1723, in England 1807, and in France 1815. Russian abolished serfdom in 1861.

John Adams, Vice President under Washington, was elected the second US President in 1796 after competing with Jefferson. It took months for the Electoral College results to come in. Adams, an aggressive personality, once was close friends with Jefferson, but criticized his endorsement of the French Revolution (Jefferson later changed his mind) as well as his elaborate lifestyle and debt. Jefferson refused a spot on the new cabinet. Political parties already had formed, with Adams at the head of the Federalists and Jefferson leading the opposing Democratic-Republicans (later the Democrats).[241]

Jefferson then defeated Adams in the election of 1800. Trust had eroded between the two former friends to the point that they stopped speaking after 1797 and only began corresponding again in 1813.[242] They both died on the 50th anniversary of the Declaration of Independence, July 4, 1826. Adam's last words were "Jefferson still lives," but Jefferson actually just had died.

In the early 1800s the expanding white population and westward migration increased the pressure on indigenous Americans, forcing them into a smaller area of land. For most of them even the idea of land ownership was foreign. Andrew Jackson, a notorious Indian fighter, was elected US President in 1828. He ignored the order of the US Supreme Court under John Marshall that the Cherokees could not be removed from their lands in Georgia. Nearly all Native tribes east of the Mississippi were made to leave. The Cherokees were submitted to a forced march, the "Trail of Tears," from their ancestral home in Georgia to Oklahoma. Out of the 16,000 who were forced to take that march in the middle of winter, about half died.[243]

The early 1800's saw the birth of Romanticism in Europe and the US which put aside the rationalism of the Enlightenment and evoked identification with a spiritual side of humanity outside

The World of Wine

In 1774, Thomas Jefferson had wine grapes planted on his estate in Monticello, Virginia. This didn't work out well due to poor weather and the distraction of the upcoming Revolutionary war.

He served as America's Foreign Minister to Paris from 1784-89. Always the entertainer and bon vivant, Jefferson took two tours of European wine country beginning in 1785. He visited all major wine areas in France, plus some in Northern Italy and Germany. He sent back cases of great Bordeaux chateaux, such as Lafite and Yquem, which he later used for entertainment at the White House and his Virginia estate. At that time wines that now sell for hundreds of dollars per bottle sold for about one dollar, a lot of money for a drink at the time.

Jefferson died $10,000 in debt, over one million of today's wine dollars, which made it impossible for his slaves to be freed at his death as was his wish. Perhaps there's a cautionary tale here for those who like to collect wine. See *Passions: The Wines and Travels of Thomas Jefferson*

the influence of religion.[244] Immanuel Kant, in his *Critique of Pure Reason* disputed the idea that reason can necessarily lead to truth, showing that both sides of any argument can be made to seem valid. Thus there must be an *a priori* knowledge, or understanding that precedes logic. Kant claimed that this essential knowledge is the understanding with which every human being is born.[245] Kant still is influential, often referred to by scientists and philosophers to this day.

A movement toward independence in Mexico was sparked in 1810 by a priest, Miguel Hidalgo, when he joined wealthy revolutionaries to overthrow their Spanish rulers. The desperately hungry peasants erupted in favor of the revolution, which moved quickly from Guanajuato to Mexico City. The royalists eventually were able to crush the revolutionary forces. Resistance resumed about one year later under another priest, Jose Maria Morelos, who had greater leadership skills. After a two year struggle independence was declared on November 6, 1813, but this rebellion also was crushed.[246]

After years of revolutionary struggle Benito Juarez was elected Mexico's first civilian president in 1861. But he inherited a bankrupt treasury and was unable to repay the governments of France, Spain and Britain. France imposed a constitutional monarchy under Napoleon III, which angered the US until overthrown in 1867. Juarez resumed civilian power that abolished the privileges of the Church and reduced the influence of wealthy landholders. His policies mainly benefited the middle class, while the Indians and lower classes, who were required to pay the most taxes, remained in poverty.[247]

In 1810 in New Granada (later Columbia, Ecuador, and Panama), an attempt to seize power was sparked by the white minority. A radical group, the Patriotic Society of Caracas, under Simon Bolivar and Francisco de Miranda, wealthy landowners, sought to sever ties with Spain, which would be to their great economic advantage. Non-whites, however, were kept out of all positions of power. This group soon began to trade independently with the US and Britain. Bolivar gained power in 1815, but decided that the American model of democracy never could work in South America due to the disorganization he had seen as the result of revolutionary movements. He and Jose de San Martin, a Spanish ex-commander, fought to set up independent governments in South America. Bolivar succeeded in establishing local governments in separate areas in the vast territory of South America by avoiding direct confrontation with Spanish forces.[248]

In 1830, Alexis de Tocqueville – who was frustrated with the lack of democracy in his native France – visited the United States and observed the effects of that noble experiment, which he related in his classic: *Democracy in America*. The idea of equality was foreign to most Europeans, who were accustomed to a society based on privilege and birth, but Tocqueville was impressed by the level of equality and community spirit he observed.[249] He admired the efficiency of government and the American education system, but he was concerned that the political system was vulnerable to corruption because government officials were dependent on their pay, unlike in France.[250] He was surprised by the inability of Americans to understand and discuss their own democratic system.[251] He also was saddened by the plight of African and Native Americans, which he saw as a blight upon an otherwise well-functioning democracy, and foresaw that even the abolition of slavery would not remove strife between races.[252] His insights still are cited today for their continued relevance.

Ireland experienced a potato famine from 1845-49, caused by a fungus that destroyed the staple of the Irish diet. In the previous 60 years Ireland had experienced a 300 percent population explosion. The depletion of the food supply that had sustained the poor caused massive migrations, especially to the United States.[253]

Revolutions took place in a number of European countries in 1848, including Austria, Prussia and Italy, due to difficult economic times and the growing resentment of the middle and working classes that they were not equal partners in the economy. Most were brutally suppressed. However, some monarchs realized that revolutionary ferment was a sign of the times – likely for the future as well – and they took the initiative to allow popular reforms. Russia remained the country most resistant to instituting change.[254]

In England, Charles Darwin ignited a revolution in our understanding of the nature of life when he published *The Origin of Species* in 1859. Darwin disrupted the entire framework of our knowledge of the natural world by claiming that all species slowly came into being by the process of "natural selection" that still is going on all around us, but too slowly for us to observe. The backlash against his theories from religious fundamentalists still rages to this day. In the same year John Stuart Mill published *On Liberty*. He warned against the tyranny of the majority and argued that the only reason that force can be justified by individuals is for self-protection.[255]

In the US, the abolitionist movement that began in the early 1800s met stiff opposition. An abolitionist newspaper writer in Illinois was killed by a mob in 1837, and those opposing abolition engaged in attacks on the Philadelphia homes of blacks in 1842.[256]

The growing clouds of civil war that had been building since the country's inception burst open after shots were fired at a boat bringing troop reinforcements to Fort Sumter in Charleston Harbor, South Carolina, on January 8, 1861. Mississippi was the first state to secede from the Union later that month. After his inauguration, Abraham Lincoln called for 75,000 volunteers to serve for 90 days, but later regretted the promise of a time limit as the war dragged on. The Confederates, under Jefferson Davis, issued a conscription for all white males between 18 and 35.[257]

Lincoln, who was sworn in on March 4, 1861, was the first Republican President. He won the nomination at his party's convention on the third ballot. Lincoln assembled his cabinet from a "team of rivals" which had previously opposed him. William Seward became Secretary of State, Salmon Chase Secretary of the Treasury, and Edward Bates Attorney General. Many other cabinet members were from the opposing Democratic Party.[258] Lincoln's oath of office was administered by Roger Taney, Chief Justice of the Supreme Court, who had issued the 1857 Dred Scott decision declaring that slaves could not be citizens and that the government could not regulate slavery in territories that were added after the founding.

The Civil War's first battle, which became known as Bull Run, took place near Manassas, Virginia, with about 35,000 men on each side in July 1861. Realizing that war actually is bloody, a number of Union troops reminded their commanders that their three month enlistment was over and began heading home.[259]

The war slogged on for four more years, with tremendous losses on both sides, a total of about 600,000, the most ever lost in a war in which Americans fought. Lincoln needed to replace numerous mediocre generals which likely prolonged the conflict. He lost a son and had to deal with a wife who was mentally unstable. Yet he showed immense patience and compassion at most times, even for his enemies.

Lincoln met with Frederick Douglass, an advocate for civil rights, a number of times at the White House. Douglass helped recruit soldiers for the Union cause, although he was distressed that Lincoln did not call for the emancipation of slaves earlier in the war. Lincoln had run on a platform of only limiting slavery in new territories, but issued the Emancipation Proclamation on January 1, 1863, when it seemed likely that the North would win the war. The total number of Negroes (as they were then called) in the US army was 186,000. They played an important part in securing a victory.[260]

The turning point was the Battle of Gettysburg in July 1863. The Confederates decided that they needed to challenge the Union forces on their own turf. The Union Army only knew that Lee's forces were moving north, but not their destination, which they feared might be Washington. After an intense exchange, the battle, and eventually the war, was won by Union forces.[261]

The combatants would forever be memorialized by the words of Lincoln – much like those of Pericles 2300 years before – in an address he had scratched on the back of an envelope on his train ride to the event. It extended and deepened the concept of liberty of the American founders:

It is rather for us to be here dedicated to the great task remaining before us – that from these honored dead we take increased devotion to that cause for which they gave the last full measure of devotion – that we here highly resolve that these dead shall not have died in vain – that this nation, under God, shall have a new birth of freedom – and that government of the people, by the people, for the people, shall not perish from the earth.

General Lee surrendered to General Grant in a congenial and civil ceremony at Appomattox, Virginia, on April 10, 1865.[262]

Lincoln was assassinated by John Wilkes Booth, a Southern activist and actor familiar with Ford's Theater where he shot Lincoln on April 15, 1865. An attempt also was made on Seward's life. The rest of the cabinet gathered at the boarding house across the street and waited for the end, which came the next morning. Stanton's tribute is the one most remembered: "Now he belongs to the ages."[263]

The Civil Rights Act of 1866 passed by Congress and signed by President Andrew Johnson outlawed slavery, but that was just the beginning of 100 years of segregation and obstacles to civil rights such as employment discrimination and voting obstruction that effected not only blacks but indigenous Americans.

In 1890, a group of 350 Sioux under Sitting Bull walked to the Pine Ridge Reservation in South Dakota in sub-freezing temperatures to surrender. This was fourteen years after a group of

Dakotas had killed George Custer and most of his troops at the Little Big Horn. Some of the troops overseeing the surrender had served with Custer. One of the Sioux resisted giving up his gun, and immediately three hundred Sioux were annihilated by the repeating guns that were trained on their camp.[264]

Otto von Bismarck, "the Iron Chancellor," who had forged Prussia into a powerful state, defeated France in 1870. Antagonism between monarchists and republicans ended with the founding of the Third French Republic, with a constitution that created a strong President, similar to France's government to this day. The President can hire or dismiss the Prime Minister or Parliament at will, but then must contend with a newly elected Parliament that may or may not support his policies. Freedom of the press was introduced as was the right to divorce, which the Church opposed. Boys and girls began to attend school together in classes that no longer were dominated by religious teaching. France also expanded its colonies in Africa and Asia during this time.[265]

In Western Europe growing industrialization brought a growing horde of workers to the towns which often were unprepared for them. Families lived in hovels; children worked long hours in factories alongside their parents. Cholera epidemics remained a problem until greater sanitation was introduced by building new sewer systems. After this, birthrates increased and death rates decreased. Basic literacy was required to function and hold jobs in the urban environment and more schools opened. In the universities, new disciplines developed to help understand and guide society's transformation, including economics, ethnography, anthropology, linguistics and sociology.[266] The spread of education led to a diminishment of ignorance among the masses and a growing democratization of knowledge.

In Africa, the 1800s combined European imperialism with a desire to convert the natives to Christianity. The interior was not known by Westerners until explored by missionaries in the mid-1800s. David Livingstone, who had a difficult time finding converts and was legendarily lost for years, traveled extensively in Africa from 1841 to 1856. He covered over 2500 miles and named a mile-wide falls he discovered after Queen Victoria (now in Zimbabwe). He brought back accounts of nations that spoke a profusion of languages and convinced the European powers, particularly the British, to colonize the interior.[267] Only Abyssinia (later Ethiopia) was able to maintain its independence. The Suez Canal, a joint French-Egyptian enterprise that linked the Mediterranean to the Red Sea, avoiding the need to sail around Africa, was started in 1859 and completed in 10 years.[268]

In 1888, the British fought an "uprising" in Sudan. Twenty-three-year-old Winston Churchill, a correspondent for the London *Morning Post* and an army officer, reported on the war. The British faced about 50,000 Sudanese troops with antiquated weapons and massacred over 10,000 by using the newly perfected Maxim machine gun.[269] At the southern end of the African Continent another war was caused by the discovery of gold and the desire of the British to move aside the Boers, or Dutch settlers, to get what they considered their share, which they did by destroying their farms and moving them into concentration camps.[270]

The US also tried its hand at imperialism via the Spanish American War of 1898. After the sinking of the USS Maine in Havana's harbor, the US intervened to support the wars of independence of Cuba and the Philippines from Spain. In the ensuing Treaty of Paris, the US took control of the Philippines, Guam, Puerto Rico and Cuba.[271]

Theodore Roosevelt, US President from 1901 to 1909, had served in the Spanish-American war. He fought to end the stranglehold of large trusts on the economy and was an environmentalist who established national parks and monuments. He also

was an ardent imperialist. In his 1909 speech, "The Expansion of
the White Races," his belief in the doctrine of "manifest destiny"
was clear:

*There is one feature in the expansion of the peoples of white, or
European, blood during the past four centuries which should never
be lost sight of, especially by those who denounce such expansion on
moral grounds. On the whole, the movement has been fraught with
lasting benefit to most of the peoples already dwelling in the lands over
which the expansion took place.*[272]

In China, there was political chaos from the time of its initial
revolution, led by Sun Yat-sen in 1911, to the 1949 takeover by
the Communists under Mao Zedong. A series of warlords and
generals ruled alternately or consecutively, with the most stable
administration of the period being under Chiang Kai-shek, who
was forced to Taiwan by the Communists.[273]

The early twentieth century hosted some of the greatest trans-
formations in human thought and lifestyle. Light bulbs replaced
kerosene lamps, automobiles replaced horses, and machines with
wings fulfilled the perennial human dream of flying. Picasso
attempted to combine all perspectives of a subject in one view,
Freud explored the depths of the human mind, and Einstein
overthrew everything we thought we knew about our universe.
All of these results – and many more – represented the result of
revolutionary thought nurtured in the bosom of Western democracy. Western nations were troubled by developing threats to the
democratic process in many parts of the world – as they still are
– but they supported a freedom of spirit that exceeded anything
up until that time.

Socialism became a movement in much of Europe in the
1800s. It was rooted in the theory of a society where resources
were shared, rather than a belief in competition. Workers

demonstrated for better pay and working conditions. Unions were developed in Britain, France and Germany. Karl Marx and Freidrich Engels published the Communist Manifesto in 1848 which advocated "The proletariat (working people) organized as the ruling class," eventually leading to "an association in which the free development of each is the condition for the free development of all."[274] The German Social Democratic Party, which still is in existence, was established in 1890.

In Russia, where a type of communism would eventually take hold, people became disillusioned with the "loving father" image of the Tsar. An underground movement of educated revolutionaries started in the 1870s to educate Russian workers about human rights and Marxist ideology. Even though Alexander II had freed the serfs, there was severe suppression following his assassination in 1881. In 1905, a march by Saint Petersburg workers and their families was fired upon with hundreds of casualties. The suppression of the subsequent revolution led to greater resentment among the population and to their eventual support of the next revolution.[275]

During the late 1800's Mexico, Argentina and Chile enjoyed considerable political stability and economic progress. But Mexico still failed to establish a stable constitutional system of rule of law. Its president, Porfiro Diaz, only paid lip service to the 1857 constitution. His main interest – and way of staying in power – was to cater to the wealthy interest groups that always had been the scions of society. His ability to balance Mexico's many interest groups depended on him and not the rule of law. A decline in living standards and a general discontent led to a revolution that began 1910. Heroes such as "Poncho" Villa and Emiliano Zapata led popular insurgencies, but in 1913 Victoriano Huerta took the reins of government and reestablished the old order.[276]

During the early 1900s, Argentina experienced a level of

prosperity and political stability similar to that of the US and Europe. It produced an excess of meat and grain that it exported. But its fundamental structure, which favored the elite and kept the rest of the population in check, remained in place. The poor – some of them immigrants from Europe – lived and worked in the cities. Eventually trade unions gained power and were radicalized, inspiring a series of strikes in 1919. The president tried to put popular reforms in place by increasing public spending, but run-away inflation disrupted the economy. Juan Peron assumed the presidency in 1946 on a popular program of promoting substantial social and economic benefits. But by 1949 Argentina was in severe economic crisis due to a drop in export earnings, with inflation at 33 percent. To save the economy, Peron opened up the country to foreign investors, such as Standard Oil, who gained rights to oil production in Patagonia, a pristine area in the south. As public discontent increased, Peron limited democratic rights and expression, persecuting the opposition. His relationship with the Church and military deteriorated, leading to civil war and to his overthrow and escape to Paraguay in 1955.[277]

Oil was first discovered in Persia (now Iran) around 1900, which was the only Middle East producer into the 1930s. After World War I it became clear that there also was oil in the ground near Mosul (currently in Iraq), which was developed jointly by Britain and France. When the US found out about this oil, it insisted that it be included in the planning and production, which ultimately was shared by British, American, and French companies.[278] Oil later played an important part in the foreign policies of these nations.

In 1907, a group of 400 women who adopted the term "suffragettes" marched on Parliament Square in London. They were confronted by a guard of police on horseback, causing panic and chaos, with about two dozen sentenced to jail for terms of up to twenty-one days. Their cause went beyond the vote to insisting on equal pay in the workplace for women and public pensions. The leader of this movement was Emily Pankhurst, who when widowed at forty, began to work at the registry of births and deaths where she found the records of many illegitimate births to poor women who had been raped or seduced by older male relatives. Mrs. Pankhurst, as she was known, and her three daughters led the movement for women's equality in England by giving talks to increasingly large crowds throughout the country and using confrontational techniques, such as interrupting meetings of Parliament with shouts of "votes for women," gradually leading to violent action and property destruction. In this period before the First World War, men who were not property holders also were denied the right to vote in England.[279] American women fought for that right during the same period and won it in the state of New York in 1917, and then nationally in 1920 by the Nineteenth Amendment to the US Constitution. British women had to wait until 1928.

A group of students and intellectuals known as the Young Turks materialized at the turn of the century and organized a rebellion in 1908 to establish a more egalitarian government, but struggled among themselves for years for control of the Ottoman Empire. In 1915, the Ottomans, fearful that their Armenian population was forming an alliance with Russia against them, decided to forcibly expel the Armenian population living in the eastern part of Turkey. Over one million are thought to have died in that massacre.[280]

World War I

During the early 1900s, tensions were running high in all European nations that had formed two main alliances: the first composed of England, France and Russia; the second made up of Germany, Italy and Austria. Militarism and national pride were the themes of the day. When a Bosnian nationalist student assassinated Archduke Franz Ferdinand of Austria-Hungary on a visit to Sarajevo in June of 1914 the First World War was sparked. Austria declared war on Serbia, followed by declarations by Germany on Russia and France. The British, like much of Europe, were unprepared for war, but in August they issued an ultimatum to Germany to stop their invasion of Belgium, and once unanswered, reluctantly entered the hostilities.[281]

War fever gripped the populations of both sides. Twenty million men were called up in a war that everyone expected to be short, but that lasted four years as men on both sides of the Western Front lined up and annihilated each other with little progress in either direction. The Eastern front involved confrontations between the Russians and Romanians against the Germans. The Ottomans joined the struggle on the side of Germany. Soldiers were mowed down as they were stalled in trenches; families were decimated as the cream of European youth never returned home. This "war to end all wars" was by far the most costly in history to that point.[282]

The United States, trying to remain neutral, lost 128 lives in the 1915 sinking of the Lusitania by a German submarine, making it clear that the Atlantic would no longer be safe. Germany also was caught trying to recruit Mexico to its cause. Thus the US entered the fray in 1917. In that same year, the British defeated the Ottoman Empire in the Middle East after their assaults on the Suez Canal in Egypt and Palestine. These areas became "protectorates" under British control until the next major war.[283]

In the last half of the nineteenth century, there had been a steady migration of Jews from Eastern Europe to settle in Palestine due to increased persecution. "Political Zionism" was founded by Theodore Herzl, an Austrian journalist and agnostic Jew who wrote an influential book, *The Jewish State*, in 1896. In 1917, a letter was published from the British Foreign Secretary Arthur Balfour to Lord Rothschild, a British Zionist, stating the intent of the British Government to create a "National Home for the Jewish people [but]... nothing shall be done which may prejudice the civil and religious rights of existing non-Jewish communities in Palestine." This became known as the Balfour Declaration.[284]

After an initially successful offensive by the Germans in 1918, British tanks began to push back quickly and decisively in August, which broke the will of the Germans to press on. They offered an armistice to President Woodrow Wilson in October. The Kaiser was exiled and sought refuge in the Netherlands.[285]

The total war losses on both sides of over eight million soldiers and perhaps twelve million civilians, with many more incapacitated, stifled the growth and economy of those nations for years. Then the flu epidemic of 1917-1918 killed off more than the war – about fifty million worldwide – which further stunned an already shocked world.[286]

At Versailles on June 28, 1919, a "peace" treaty was signed by all major parties to the First World War, with only the victors present at negotiations. President Wilson pushed for a strong international government that would allow for a peaceful resolution of disagreements. He was progressive in many ways, including backing the vote for women, abolishing child labor, promoting anti-trust laws, and creating an eight-hour work day for railroad workers. His Fourteen Points included disarmament, free trade, and self-determination for colonies who had been under the thumb of the largest nations. His plan never was supported by the European victors who were bent on revenge. But Wilson also was a southerner who segregated the civil service in the US.[287]

The reparations exacted by the European victors of World War I were impossible for Germany to pay. The League of

Nations – which the US Congress refused to join – was unable to enforce any of the treaties that were signed. There were a number of attempts to form a union of states in Europe after the war, such as the Locarno Pact of 1925, and non-aggression pacts, such as the Kellogg-Briand Pact of 1928, none of which were effective.[288]

Territories in the Mideast were divided among France, which received Syria and what would become Lebanon, and Britain, which oversaw Palestine, Jordan, and Iraq. The population of Palestine swelled with the immigration of 60,000 Jews because of anti-Semitism in Germany and Austria. This caused violent confrontations with the Palestinians who had lived there for generations.[289]

The Turkish War of Independence was fought in 1919–22. In 1920 Turkey won a victory over the occupying Allies which had defeated the Ottoman Empire. Kemal Pasha, one of the Young Turks, later took the name Ataturk and became the first president of the new Turkey. They then defeated the Greek forces during the Greco-Turkish war and expelled the Greeks. Persons of Turkish descent were expelled from Greece at the same time.[290] Turkish law became based on that of Western democracies when Ataturk established a secular state that included free education and the right for women to vote. Turkey became a republic in 1923.[291]

The Russian revolution of 1917 had caused the withdrawal of the Russian army from World War I and eased the burden on the Germans temporarily. The February Revolution began with demonstrations in Petrograd that ended with the abdication of Tsar Nicholas II. A second revolution in October ended with the Bolsheviks in power, headed by Vladimir Lenin. A civil war followed, pitting Reds (Bolsheviks), supported primarily by urban workers, against Whites, including most of the upper and educated classes. Peasants were reluctant warriors, but their support led to the ultimate victory of the Reds. Nationalists in many regions also fought for independence. Ukraine, in the south, was occupied by the Germans. Kiev changed hands repeatedly. Bolsheviks undertook a number of extreme measures to control the economy and hold on to power. When it appeared that the royal family would fall into the hands of the Whites they were executed.

Lenin died in 1924 following a series of strokes. After a power struggle at the top levels of the Communist Party, Joseph Stalin was in command by the end of the decade. The country embarked on a ruthless campaign of industrialization and agricultural collectivization in the 1930s. Agricultural production dropped precipitously due to farmers being deprived of incentives, with famine as the result. Industrialization forged ahead, with increased production of steel, coal, and chemicals. The Russian Church was outlawed and replaced with the cult of Stalin. Priests were killed and churches closed. "Enemies of the State," most of them chosen randomly by Stalin, were rounded up, made to confess, and shipped to the Gulag, where few survived. In the Ukraine, Stalin forcibly confiscated the food supply in an act of genocide, causing the deaths of millions.[292] Many European Communists still thought well of the reforms of Stalin; word of his Terror was effectively suppressed.

After the First World War there was a broad-based movement among the Egyptians to remove the British protectorate and establish independence. Student and worker strikers, Christians and Muslims, men and women leaders all united in demonstrations to expel the British. Having no real choice, the British Cabinet terminated the Egyptian protectorate in 1922, but retained a right to protect Egypt against any future foreign invasion to protect the Suez Canal. A new constitution was put into place the next year. The Muslim Brotherhood, which was opposed to all secular political parties, was founded in 1928.[293] When the Prime Minister suspended the constitution in 1929 there were student riots to restore it.

After the world entered the most serious economic downturn of the century, the Germans were able to improve their situation by increasing industrial output. The person who led this resurgence was the man whose name – for most of the world – has become synonymous with evil.[294]

The Great Depression

Throughout history there have been many financial bubbles that burst, plunging much of the world into a downturn. Financial markets were poorly regulated until the world-wide Great Depression that followed the Wall Street Crash of 1929, with market downturns of varying severity occurring commonly in the United States and Europe. These usually correlated with boom and bust cycles based on wars, over-speculation, easy credit, trade wars, or inflation. Financial cycles in the United States occurred on an average of every 29 months from 1854 to 1945.[295]

The origin of stock and bond markets goes back to Roman times when groups of investors began trading in the Forum. In the Italy of the 1300s, the government borrowed money for municipal projects by issuing transferable bonds. Shares in the Dutch East India Company were immensely popular in the 1600s, attracting investors from all over Europe as their prices mounted, bringing in a 30 percent return in its early years.[296] Speculators at first received substantial returns from the South Sea and Mississippi companies in England and France, but over-enthusiastic investing resulted in escalating prices that could not be sustained by returns. A common result was a huge bubble that caused markets to crash and created a financial panic throughout

Europe. England enacted the Bubble Act in 1720 in an attempt to curb over-speculation.[297]

In the United States, the first major market collapse occurred in 1787. The original exchange was held in coffee houses until 1792, after which an agreement was signed stabilizing trading practices. This eventually resulted in the establishment of the New York Stock Exchange in 1817. The first stock issues were conservatively based on insurance companies and banks.[298]

The 1920s were a time of general prosperity that fueled market speculation, although there were growing income disparities during that period. People of moderate means were able to invest as "investment trusts," the precursor to mutual funds, were introduced.[299]

The Great Depression did not come on as quickly as commonly believed. The US market moved up and down violently in late October 1929, losing one third of its value, but was propped up by a number of bankers buying shares. The market climbed back and temporarily rose during a rally in early 1930. After that, market averages continued to drop as more banks, unable to meet their debts and cover depositors' accounts, went out of business. Those who could withdraw their funds did so, taking money out of circulation, which further hurt the economy.

Unemployment in the US during the Depression climbed from 4.3 million in 1930 to 12 million in 1932, a full 25% of the work force. The Reconstruction Finance Corporation, created by Congress under President Hoover, pumped $500 million into the economy at the top – banks, mortgage companies, insurance firms, and railroads. It stopped some bankruptcies, but the funds had little impact on those who needed it most.[300]

By 1932, the United States was in a full depression, followed by much of Europe. "Hoovervilles" – encampments of the homeless – developed in every major American city. The political fallout in that year's election resulted in the removal of Republicans from the White House and both houses of Congress. The Republicans were seen as advocates of free market government that allowed those at the top to dominate, leaving "the grounds" for those at the bottom. Small investors lost everything, while the wealthiest continued to have enough to continue their lifestyles largely uninterrupted, helped by dropping prices of consumer goods.[301]

The Glass-Steagall Act, passed by Congress in 1933, outlawed bankers from speculating recklessly with "other people's money," which also was the title of a book written by Louis Brandeis. His ideas greatly influenced the legislation. The second piece of legislation to come out of the crisis was the Securities and Exchange Act of 1934, which required stock exchanges to register with a new commission.[302]

The "New Deal" under Franklin Roosevelt made only a small dent in the slump, but may have prevented things from getting even worse. At first Roosevelt stumbled, cutting salaries for government employees when what was needed was economic stimulation. The 1933 Civilian Conservation Corps was instituted to give work to young men and the Tennessee Valley Authority created dams, electricity and jobs; the Federal Emergency Relief Act provided $500 million in direct aid to cities and states; the National Industrial Recovery Act reformed industry and labor unions, regulated work hours, and outlawed child labor, but it was declared unconstitutional by the Supreme Court in 1935; the Work Projects Administration provided billions in funds for reforestation, flood control, rural electrification, water works, sewage plants, slum clearance, and student scholarships; the Agricultural Adjustment Act provided subsidies for threatened farmers whose yields surpassed consumption due to the economic slump.[303]

European countries tried to put up a financial wall to keep the US contagion from sinking their economies. Loans for foreign exchange in Germany became restricted to only those that were "essential." In France, the Leftist Popular Front government introduced new measures limiting speculation in foreign countries. In England, John Maynard Keynes, one of the most prominent economists of the day, introduced a nationalistic approach to prevent "economic entanglements between nations." No markets were permitted in the Soviet Union.[304]

The Roosevelt Administration negotiated a trade deal that – between 1933 and 1938 – involved sixteen nations and lowered trade barriers to improve their economies in the face of the threat posed by the rise of Hitler. This was part of the Good Neighbor policy, a strategy that solidified relations between the U.S and its neighbors before and after World War II.[305]

The Depression hit Germany especially hard at first. Hitler became Chancellor in 1933 through democratic means, but soon his government passed a resolution granting him dictatorial powers to deal with the "Red Plot." He quickly destroyed his rivals and withdrew from the League of Nations. He managed to blame the Jews for both the evils of Russian communism and American capitalism.[306] The Aryans – although undefined – were the superior race, or "culture bearers," while the Jews – and other representatives of cultural impurity – were the enemies.[307] The Nazis introduced euthanasia for those with disabilities to maintain this purity.

The Jewish communities in Austria and Poland had experienced considerable prosperity and integration into their societies as late as the mid-1930s, but concern about anti-Semitic trends in Germany was growing among them. "There were Jewish film stars, Jewish boxing championships, Jewish woman MPs, Jewish millionaires."[308] This all crumbled with the Nazi annexation of Austria and its invasion of Poland.

As usual, there was division within France between the

wars. The presidency of France changed hands on an average of once per year as the struggle between the right and left nearly consumed a barely functioning government. The French Communist Party was believed by many to be directed by the Soviets. They were opposed by the Radicals, republicans who believed in small government, and ultra-conservative groups funded by millionaires such as Francois Coty, the perfume manufacturer, and Pierre Taittinger of Champagne fame, who blamed minority groups for all of Europe's woes, including the Jewish refugees coming from Germany. And then there was a series of strikes carried out by workers who believed their interests to be underrepresented.[309]

In 1936 a difficult coalition was assembled to run the French government under Leon Blum, who received enough tepid support from all sides to prevent anarchy. He worked out agreements that increased wages, created a forty hour work week and two week paid vacation, appointed women to his cabinet, and extended school enrollment up to the age of fourteen.[310]

In the midst of all this European turmoil, a civil war broke out in Spain in 1936, followed by an attempted coup by General Francisco Franco against the Spanish Republic. This became a European struggle with the Germans and Italians supporting Franco, and the Soviets supporting the Republicans. The International Brigades from around the world were composed of about 50,000 foreign fighters on the side of the Republic, including Ernest Hemingway, who immortalized the struggle in his novel *For Whom the Bell Tolls*. The British stayed neutral. Although the sympathies of Blum were with the Republic, he could not act without jeopardizing his delicate coalition. Franco prevailed to install a brutal dictatorship, with the execution of at least 130,000 of his enemies, that lasted until his death in 1975.[311]

Despite being given the right to vote by the Fifteenth

Amendment in 1870, many US blacks still were blocked from voting. Segregation and job discrimination continued. Beginning in about 1915, blacks began to move north, a movement which continued into the 1970s. There were some gains made after the official overturn of segregation in *Brown vs. Board of Education* by the US Supreme Court, but opportunities for blacks still were greatly limited. Amidst lynching and threats from the Ku Klux Klan, they sought greater equality and opportunity in the North.[312]

World War II

The beginning of the series of events that led directly to the Second World War was the signing of the Munich pact of 1938 that allowed the annexation of the Sudetenland, the German-speaking area of Czechoslovakia. More than half the people in England and France, the countries that signed the pact with Germany, favored it. Further pacts, including one between Stalin and Hitler in 1939, encouraged the Germans to annex more territory.[313] It was with at least one eye closed that the eventual Allies encouraged the aggressions of Germany and overlooked its substantial arms build-up, while much of Europe, including France, had a military system that had not been updated since the end of the previous war.

In Italy, Mussolini, the founder of fascism, ruled legally as Prime Minister from 1922 and established a dictatorship in 1925. In the 1930s he began to impose his will abroad, hoping to establish a new Roman Empire. In 1935, he used the excuse of a border skirmish between Italian holdings in Africa to attack Ethiopia. He later sent troops to Spain and Albania, and joined the Rome-Berlin Axis in May of 1939.[314]

Ethiopia, also called Abyssinia, in Northeastern Africa, was a highly developed country under European influence with schools, hospitals, churches, and a railway. Under Emperor Haile Selassie the country developed a parliament. Mussolini, having failed in his attempts at influence, attacked Ethiopia in 1935 with 100,000 troops, using aerial bombardment and mustard gas, killing thousands of Ethiopians. Haile Selassie appealed to the League of Nations to no avail, as the European powers still hoped to avoid another war. He ended up in exile in England.[315]

In September 1939 the Germans attacked Poland, which resulted in declarations of war by Britain and France. Despite this, the British and French were slow to attack as they weren't really ready for war. The Germans and Soviets split Poland between them. 150,000 Polish Jews were immediately shot or put into concentration camps, the rest of the two million consigned to ghettos that were run buy Jewish councils. On the Soviet side, a random assortment of 1-2 million "enemies of the state" was sent to the Arctic camps or into exile.[316]

Many Germans opposed the war at first, having recalled the horrors of the previous one. William Shirer, an American correspondent in Berlin, reported back: "There is no excitement here. . . no hurrahs, no wild cheering, no throwing of flowers. . . . It is a far grimmer German people that we see here tonight than we saw last night or the day before."[317]

In April 1940, Germany invaded Norway, and then easily overran France in May. British and French troops – a total of 338,000 – were evacuated from Dunkirk across the English Channel by an assortment of naval and private ships at the end of May.[318] General Charles de Gaulle, the eventual French President, retreated to London and began radio broadcasts to his fellow citizens encouraging them to fight on. The occupation – other than the humiliation of having a foreign ruler on their soil – was difficult for the French: there was a curfew that was punishable by death if violated and there were 1.5 million French soldiers in prison, which inhibited any resistance. There were heavy costs, including the annexation of Alsace and Lorraine by Germany and the occupation of the industrial north as well as the Atlantic seaboard, Lyon (France's second city), and the Mediterranean port of Marseille. Only the poor areas in between were left on their own as Hitler wanted to limit his expenditure of resources to save them for Britain and the Soviets. A puppet government was set up in Vichy in the south. Trade unions and strikes were outlawed. Gypsies, Communists, Freemasons, and of course Jews were outlawed from public office and commercial activity.[319]

De Gaulle made the leaders of England nervous with his arrogance and aloof communication as he broadcast poorly heard speeches across the English Channel to encourage his country-men. Both Churchill and Roosevelt distrusted him, although he was able to convince Churchill to name him leader of Free France soon after escaping to England. He wasn't willing to guarantee democratic freedoms to France in the event that he did become president after the war. Meanwhile, over 200 resistance organiza-tions would be set up in France.[320]

The French played their part by rounding up over 80,000 Jews for the Germans to deport to concentration camps under the direction of the Vichy police and Marshal Petain, a hero of World War I. After Romania, Vichy France was the most will-ing of Hitler's partners in the genocide.[321] Adolf Eichmann held a conference near Berlin in January 1942 to arrange logistics for the extermination of the European Jews. Resistance groups formed when Jews realized what awaited them. The Warsaw Ghetto uprising of April 1943 lasted three weeks and ended with the sui-cide of its final defenders. The outside world, for the most part, either didn't know or ignored the immensity of the extermina-tion during the war, at last realizing its extent with the liberation of the camps in 1945.[322]

Italy entered the war in June 1940 on the side of Germany. Although Mussolini and the Italians disliked Hitler and Germany, they wanted to be on the side of the eventual victors and share in the spoils. However, Mussolini confided that he didn't really want to engage in fighting that might kill Italians.[323]

Prime Minister Winston Churchill had the task of convincing his country that resistance to the Germans was worthwhile. Anticipating the attack that would soon come, he gave the most famous speech of his career to Parliament:

Let us therefore brace ourselves to our duties and so bear ourselves that, if the British Empire and Commonwealth last for a thousand years, men will still say: "This was their finest hour."[324]

The German air assault on England began in July 1940, with the intent of preparing for a ground invasion. The city of Coventry was destroyed by Luftwaffe bombers; great sections of London were set on fire.[325] The Royal Air Force (RAF), though ultimately unable to defeat the Luftwaffe in the air, kept the English Channel from being dominated by the Germans and minimized damage. Churchill did all he could to convince the US to enter the war, but the majority in Congress still hoped to avoid involvement. In August of 1941, Roosevelt told reporters that he would go to Maine in his yacht *Potomac* for a fishing trip, keeping the real purpose of his trip secret even from his wife Eleanor. Roosevelt was transferred to the Cruiser Augusta off Newfoundland for his first meeting with Churchill.[326]

That summer the British attacked Italian forces that held parts of Africa, beginning with Libya. The Italians, never up for a fight, had to be forced into battle by their commanders. Many of the British advances were temporarily reversed by the Germans in 1941 under the leadership of the legendary Erwin Rommel.[327]

In June 1941 Hitler broke his pact with Stalin and invaded

the Soviet Union, surprising and destroying much of their force on the ground. Their rapid expansion brought them quickly to the gates of Moscow. In Ukraine and Poland, Nazi soldiers engaged in random arrests and murders, stiffening the resistance. The population of Ukraine was decimated, with a loss of nine million in three years.[328] By July Stalin was willing to sign the Mutual Assistance Pact with Britain. This required Churchill to close his eyes to the fact that the Soviets were at the same time killing millions of their own.[329]

The Russians lost an estimated 25-30 million in the war, including civilian and military deaths. Their experience of enormous loss united them. An outstanding story of suffering – and courage – emerged from Leningrad (Saint Petersburg before and after) where, in a thousand-day siege that began September 8, 1941, 1.2 to 3 million civilians died of bombing or starvation, according to varying estimates. Amidst scenes of dead lining the streets and people cutting off parts of themselves to avoid starvation, Dmitri Shostakovich managed to write his Seventh Symphony, a rallying march that was performed in that city by 15 surviving orchestra members out of 100 in August of 1942.

In a letter written by a resident at that time, the siege was described in excruciating detail:

> *With every day that passes, life in Leningrad gets worse. People are beginning to swell up because they are eating patties made from mustard. Flour dust, which used to be used for making wallpaper paste, cannot be bought for love or money. Our beloved Leningrad has turned into a heap of dirt and corpses. Trams have long since ceased to run, there is no light, no fuel, the water is frozen, the rubbish isn't cleared. . . . And most important, we're tormented by hunger.[330]*

On December 7, 1941, six Japanese carriers launched bombers and fighters in an attack on Pearl Harbor in Hawaii. 2403

Americans were killed; 149 planes destroyed; six battleships were destroyed or left resting on the bottom of the harbor. Many American possessions and allies were attacked and quickly conquered throughout the Pacific. The attack drove American isolationists into concert with the rest of the nation as Congress declared war on Japan on December 8, followed by a Declaration of War on Germany and Italy two days later. [331]

The balance of air power did not begin to reverse until the massive allied bombing of German defenses in 1942. For the rest of the war, overwhelming numbers of Soviet soldiers were marched to their slaughter but eventually defeated the superior German military establishment. As the Red Army moved into Germany in 1944, it extracted revenge by executing entire villages.[332]

The "Big Three" Allied leaders – Churchill, Stalin and Roosevelt – met in Tehran at the end of 1943 to establish their strategy for the rest of the war, and then met again in Yalta toward the end of the hostilities. They agreed to divide Germany into four zones and discussed the prosecution of war criminals. The Soviets led the siege of Berlin with a vengeance and characteristic disregard for the lives of even their own soldiers.[333]

Following D-Day on the beaches of Normandy in June 1944, General Eisenhower swept the Germans out of France from west to east, supported by a large French resistance. De Gaulle returned triumphant to Paris in August, exclaiming that the French alone were responsible for the country's liberation. About 100,000 French collaborators were executed or otherwise punished. De Gaulle upheld the myth that those who collaborated with the Germans were a fringe minority and that the French Republic had always remained free from German influence. This state of denial lasted over fifty years, when President Jacques Chirac apologized for France's role in the deportation of the Jews.[334] Roosevelt had died in April of 1945 and was succeeded by Harry Truman.

The World of Wine

On May 4, 1945, Sergeant Bernard de Nonancourt, a tank commander in the Second French Armored Division, participated in an invasion of Germany which marked the retreat of the Axis forces and signaled the coming end of World War II. The town of Berchtesgaden in the Bavarian Alps was not far from the Berghof (mountain farm) which Hitler had built, and where during the war he had spent more time than in Berlin with mistress Eva Braun and his dog.

At the Eagle's Nest, a nearby retreat higher in the mountains which Hitler avoided due to elevation sensitivity, the French army discovered a cache of wine behind a steel door that contained cases upon cases of great wines that German troops had stolen. It contained a half million bottles from the best vintages, neatly stacked and nearly filling the cave with wines from Champagne, Lafite-Rothschild, Mouton-Rothschild, Yquem, and Romanee-Conti, among other French greats. Enough to make a connoisseur swoon. *Wine and War,* Pages 1-2

The war in Europe was declared over with VE day on May 8.

But the war in the Pacific still raged on. In February of 1945, three US Marine divisions attacked the tiny island of Iwo Jima, 700 miles south of Japan. The battle took six weeks due to the determination of the Japanese to hold on at any cost. The Americans prevailed after over 7,000 deaths, but this battle became a symbol of the turning of the tide in the Pacific. On April 1, the Allies launched an attack on Okinawa in a prelude to the long completion of a war that was prolonged only by Japanese resistance.[335]

Japanese rulers wished to end the war by the summer of 1945, but their generals knew that the results of surrender would not be favorable to them, so they were determined to fight on at any cost. That cost was the near-destruction of the cities of Hiroshima and Nagasaki by atomic bombs dropped by the Boeing Superfortress Bomber B29 *Enola Gay* on August 6, killing over 100,000 people, after which Japan surrendered unconditionally.[336]

The Fourth French Republic (1946-58), hobbled together under de Gaulle was even more unwieldy than the previous two republics. It included twenty-six coalition governments, and lasted only eleven years. There were continual strikes in protests against low wages and rising prices. The Fourth Republic had a new prime minister on the average of every six months. But strides in benefits were made: a social security system and votes for women were approved.

Italy also struggled for stability after the war. The contrast between the prosperous north and relatively poor south made Italy seem like the two countries it had been before its unification in 1871. Corruption caused by the Mafia in the south is still a factor in modern Italian life.[337]

The Nuremburg War Crimes Tribunal began in November 1945. It was the preference of the victors that an attempt be made to use the rule of law in trying what the Allies considered war crimes rather than just executing those they held responsible. The records of the Nazi party operatives were used against them, including plans for death camps, medical experiments, and other atrocities. Verdicts ranged from not guilty to long prison sentences to hanging for ten of the defendants.[338]

In 1963, Hannah Arendt attended the trial of Adolf Eichmann, who had been smuggled from Argentina to Jerusalem. He was accused of masterminding the murder of six million Jews. Her book, *Eichmann in Jerusalem* – subtitled *The Banality of Evil* – came out of her report, which was originally written for the *New*

Yorker magazine. She speculated on the nature of evil itself, and whether justice ever can make up for the greatest of evils.

The prosecution attempted to base its case on "anti-Semitism throughout history," but this brought up the issue of whether anti-Semitism itself is a crime, and how Eichmann could be prosecuted when he claimed: "With the killing of the Jews I had nothing to do. I never killed a Jew, or a non-Jew, for that matter." [339] Arendt portrayed Eichmann as essentially going along with what he was told to do, never thinking about the evil for which he was responsible. "The longer one listened to him, the more obvious it became that his inability to speak was closely connected with his inability to think. . . from the standpoint of someone else." [340] About 80,000 "mentally incompetent" people were euthanized before protest – especially from the Catholic Church – put a stop to this policy. [341] The Jewish leaders worked with the Nazis to organize their victims, having them fill out forms so that the killing could proceed in an orderly manner, and provided the lists of those to be loaded onto trains. The larger question that Arendt asks is whether unquestioning compliance with the evil in society is something that can be avoided. [342]

Financial aid to Greece and Turkey was provided under the Truman Doctrine beginning in 1947, with the intent of "containment" of communism. The Marshall Plan was instituted in 1948 and ran for four years with the establishment of the Organization for Economic Cooperation. It jump-started the economies of the previous combatants with over $13 billion in development funds. Britain, France and Germany were the largest recipients, but the Soviets blocked it in its sphere of influence. Germany experienced a rapid economic recovery as a result. [343] Japan's economy also recovered quickly with American help. [344]

NATO (North Atlantic Treaty Organization) was founded by nine European countries plus the US and Canada in 1949. Its mission was to show strength and counter the Soviet threat or any other threat as needed. As of this writing it has twenty-eight member states.[345]

The western colonial powers lost many of their holdings after World War II. India gained its independence from Britain in 1947. Mohandas Gandhi, who inspired resistance to British rule by non-violent protests, claimed that one of his main influences was the Bhagavad-Gita, which teaches peace of mind above all. India remains the type of democracy where personal ties to obtain and stay in office dominate the system rather than advancement based on merit. This often keeps the best qualified people and ideas from being considered.[346] Pakistan was created in the north from areas that were primarily Muslim; it left the British Commonwealth in 1973.

After the war, Britain wanted to be free of needing to negotiate the perennial conflict in Palestine between Arab and Jewish groups and referred the issue to the UN, where the General Assembly voted in November 1947 to partition Palestine into Jewish and Palestinian states. When Britain announced that they would be leaving Palestine in May of 1948 David Ben-Gurion declared a Jewish State. Egypt, Jordan, Iraq, Syria, and Lebanon converged on Israel and were driven back. The Israelis invaded Sinai but were stopped from taking the Suez Canal by warnings from the British.[347]

Gamal Nasser, who led the 1952 overthrow of the monarchy, became President of Egypt in 1956. All political parties were banned after an attempt by the Arab Brotherhood to assassinate him. He negotiated the British withdrawal and then nationalized the Suez Canal. The United States refused him arms because of his opposition to Israel, so he obtained them from the Soviet Union. He received the help of the Soviets in construction of the Aswan High Dam to control the annual flooding of the Nile.

In 1961, he nationalized most of the country's large companies and regulated the others in his first five-year plan. About half of Egyptians were literate by the time of his death, a huge increase.[348]

In May 1967, Nasser moved his forces into Sinai behind UN troops, which provoked Israel to prepare for war. Israel struck first on June 5, taking the entire West Bank from Jordan, the Golan Heights from Syria, and was threatening to overtake the Suez Canal, only to be stopped by a UN ceasefire agreement on June 8.[349] On the sixth of October 1973, the Arab allies launched a surprise attack on Israel on Yom Kipper, the holiest day of the year for Jews, which Israel won again.

Under Anwar Sadat new laws were enacted in Egypt in 1974 to reopen industry to private entrepreneurs and encourage foreign investment. In 1977, Sadat spoke to the Israeli Knesset after negotiations conducted under Henry Kissinger and then President Jimmy Carter, offering recognition of Israel. Negotiations began for the withdrawal of Israel from Sinai and mutual recognition between the countries.

Sadat was assassinated in 1981 at a military parade.[350] Hosni Mubarak immediately assumed the presidency under a declaration of a national state of emergency which he never lifted. He conducted an investigation into the death of Sadat, jailing two thousand militants. He agreed to joint military operations and training with the United States, which resulted in billions of dollars in aid. Mubarak's biggest challenge was dealing with religious extremists, particularly the Arab Brotherhood.[351]

The Middle East still remains in turmoil with civil wars in Syria and Libya. A military government is in place in Egypt, and there is considerable instability in Afghanistan and Iraq. The US remains a key protagonist in the area, having supported Egypt and Israel and opposed dictatorships in Iran and Syria. The US continues to be involved in trying to forge peace efforts between

Israel and its neighbors and to end the oppression of some governments, but this only has succeeded minimally so far.

After the Second World War the Communist regime continued governing the Soviet Union. In addition to repairing the wartime damage and dealing with the great loss of life, economic plans for industry and agriculture resumed. Production often failed to meet targets, which forced a large increase in imports. An "Iron Curtain" cordoned off the Soviet controlled Eastern Bloc from the West.

The Soviet Bloc claimed to be a Communist state, but it never fit the model of communism proposed by Marx. In *The Communist Manifesto*, Marx predicted that communism would rise voluntarily as workers overthrew their chains in industrial nations and establish a temporary state leading to a peaceful transition toward human equality.[352] The Soviet Union was neither largely industrial nor voluntarily created. It was established under a dictatorial government in which there was no evolution toward equality. Every major government move had to be approved by the Party's Central Committee which destroyed autonomy and did not allow for timely decisions. Individual incentives were removed. Thus both industry and farms failed to meet needs and projections. This forced a large increase in importation of materials and grain.[353] Millions of people who dared to challenge the authority of Lenin or Stalin were murdered as enemies of the state.[354]

Colonialism went into its final throes in the 1950s. The French colony in Algeria rebelled in 1958. This sparked violent protests in Paris. It led to a near coup by the Army and establishment of the Fifth Republic, which gave de Gaulle near dictatorial powers. To his credit, he allowed the colonies in North Africa to vote on staying under France or becoming independent.[355] France eventually set all of its African colonies free. The Belgian Congo, many times larger than Belgium itself, exploded into civil war in

1960, as did the Portuguese holding of Angola in 1975.[356]

Despite continued political turmoil in the period after the Second World War, France was able to establish a period of general prosperity for the next thirty years. The population increased by 30 percent and life expectancy improved by nearly ten years for both men and women, due largely to accessible medical services and increased incomes. The country became more industrialized – even its farms became more productive – and exports increased substantially. West Germany and Japan – its previous enemies – also saw substantial rises in the standard of living, as did the United States, while Britain lagged behind. France's enrollment in universities more than doubled, while four million immigrants from Southern Europe and North Africa arrived to take jobs that the French were unable to fill or found distasteful. Tenements rose in the suburbs to accommodate this influx that eventually were to become areas of extreme discontent.[357]

The 1960s was a period of general prosperity in the US, Europe and Japan, but most of Latin America stagnated as farms were not able to provide enough food to support the quickly growing population, and much had to be imported. Cities, though industrializing, were not able to absorb enough rural poor. Government agencies did not support increased food production or create an export policy that would improve the economy.[358] Despite claims to support democracy based on the US model, governments throughout the region continued to serve mainly the elite, with policies that neglected to bring greater economic equality to those in need.

In Cuba, a student revolution led to the installation of Fulgencio Batista in 1933. Under Batista there were general elections and a constitution that guaranteed universal suffrage and labor rights, a minimum wage and an eight-hour day. But the corrupt forces that dominated Latin America infected Batista's

Cuba, and a group of students led by Fidel Castro attacked an army barracks in 1953. After a two-year imprisonment, Castro trained in Mexico and then led another resurrection in 1959. He came to power amidst general popular support. Castro at first allowed political compromises that he thought were needed to strengthen his position, but then took absolute power, executing Batista's officials and suspending all constitutional liberties in the name of the revolution. Many previous supporters of Castro who opposed him were suppressed or left Cuba for Miami.[359] The US was threatened by the specter of communism at its back door. But recently these former enemies have begun re-establishing diplomatic and economic ties.

Starting in the 1950s in the US, blacks began demonstrating peaceably against southern segregation by staging a bus boycott in Montgomery Alabama after Rosa Parks was arrested for sitting in the front of a bus in 1955. This was followed by "sit-ins" at lunch counters that refused to serve blacks. Their main leader was Martin Luther King, who had studied the non-violent philosophy – and successes – of Gandhi. King led the March on Washington for Jobs and Freedom in 1963, at which over 200,000 heard speeches laying out hope for a better future, including his "I Have a Dream" speech. He was assassinated in 1968.[360]

Cesar Chavez was a union organizer and leader who dedicated his life to improving pay and working conditions for farm workers in the Central Valley of California. With his lifelong working partner, Dolores Huerta, he led numerous marches and strikes, as well as participating in hunger strikes beginning in the 1950s. He founded the National Farmworkers Association in 1962 (later the United Farm Workers). In 1968 he led a successful boycott of table grapes, which eventually yielded major concessions from grape growers. He also called attention to the dangers of pesticides on grapes to farm workers and consumers. His efforts were backed by Robert Kennedy and Jesse Jackson, who had marched with Martin Luther King. Chavez died in 1993, with his numerous hunger strikes possibly contributing to his death.

In the late 1960s France, England, the United States and many other countries were subjected to a period of youthful protest. Many were upset by what they saw as a world run by materialism and militarism that led to continued wars in places like Vietnam. They were expected to join the military and participate in the suppression of populations for which they saw no justification. No longer willing to accept what they considered the thoughtless conformity of their parents' post-war world, many teenagers and those in their 20's lashed out against what was, in their view, an "establishment" of complacency and lack of ideals. Protest songs of Bob Dylan, the Beatles, and other musicians sparked a youth revolution. The "Summer of Love" in San Francisco's Haight-Ashbury took place in 1967 to express the ideas of community and trust over competition. In Paris in May of 1968 student discontent with consumerism and the irrelevance of their studies to their lives led to rioting in the streets and a battle with police. De Gaulle dissolved the National Assembly and called for new elections, after which he emerged even stronger. Police also attacked youthful protestors at the Democratic convention in Chicago that summer.

The era saw the Space Race between the US and USSR. The Soviets launched Sputnik in 1958. Yuri Gargarin was the first man in space in 1961. But in 1969, the US put a man on the moon. The hope of intercepting nuclear weapons launched from rockets led to the announcement of the "Star Wars" program by Ronald Reagan in 1983.

The constitution of France that had been drafted during the crisis of 1958 gave the President, de Gaulle, powers that were unprecedented in modern times. The President was supposed to yield to the Prime Minister in matters of foreign affairs, but de

Gaulle was enabled by the constitution to dismiss Parliament and call for new elections to get his way, which he often threatened to do. For later presidents, there was a challenge to working under a system that was undemocratic in many ways.

Georges Pompidou, a prominent banker, was determined to operate the presidency in a more positive manner than his predecessor during his term, which lasted from 1969 to his death in 1974. He worked to maintain working relationships with the United States, Britain, the Soviet Union and the former French colonies in Africa. He responded to a growing feminist movement by granting equal custody rights to women, but followed de Gaulle's tradition of supporting Arab states in the 1973 Israeli war, at least partly to maintain the flow of oil to his country.[361]

Valery Giscard d'Estaing went out of his way to make the Presidency more informal, even having breakfast at the Presidential Palace with trash collectors and middle class families. The voting age was reduced from 21 to 18 under his presidency, but inflation and a sagging economy – made worse by the Iranian revolution and a steep rise in oil prices – caused him to lose the 1981 election to Francois Mitterand, a Socialist who opposed the death penalty and fought for prison reform. Improved social benefits were funded by increases in taxes on businesses, but unemployment nevertheless rose substantially.

Jacques Chirac, a conservative whose presidency began in 1995, re-privatized many of the industries that had been nationalized under Mitterand. Chirac moved back in a conservative direction by lowering taxes in an attempt to reduce unemployment, a policy that failed, but his Prime Minster, Lionel Jospin, a socialist, introduced the 35-hour work week and a job creation program for youth that did reduce unemployment. Periodic scandals involved politicians from all points on the political spectrum. This resulted in laws limiting political donations.[362]

In Britain, as in much of the world, galloping inflation was caused by quickly rising oil prices in the 1970s. Jobs were threatened by the weak economy. There was violence between the immigrant worker community and police. A civil war raged in Northern Ireland, with revolutionary Irish Republican Party (Sinn Fein) extremists attacking British officials. Britain entered the European Union in 1973 with the hope that expanding trade would boost its economy. Long miners' and teachers' strikes further challenged the economy. Margaret Thatcher, one of the most conservative Prime Ministers of the twentieth century, served from 1979 to 1990. She used tax cuts and deregulation of industry in an attempt to stimulate the economy. She introduced spending cuts in education and housing and she signed an agreement with Francois Mitterand of France to build a tunnel under the English Channel in 1986. She was forced from office by disagreements within her own party, but the economy did improve toward the end of her term.[363]

Thatcher was succeeded by John Major who served from 1990-97 and led the country during the first Gulf War in 1991. Tony Blair became Prime Minister in 1997 and attained a remarkable diplomatic achievement when Sinn Fein and Unionist leaders in Northern Ireland signed an historic peace agreement in April 1998.[364] Blair then led Great Britain into the twenty-first century (see Chapter II).

What some historians call a wave of democratization swept across much of the world beginning in the 1970s, starting with Spain, Portugal and Turkey, and then spreading to much of Africa, Asia and Latin America.[365]

Mikhail Gorbachev, the last Soviet leader, seeing his country suffering from political rigidity and economic stagnation, implemented the policy of *glasnost* in the mid 1980s, signaling increased government transparency. Poland was the first to give way to democratic demonstrations. After banning the Solidarity union, with its members imprisoned, the failing Polish Government later turned to the union leader, Lech Walesa, to organize a political party and participate in elections during which his candidates swept in every region. After that followed a chain of Communist government collapses, including Hungary, Czechoslovakia, and a bloody overthrow of the dictatorial Ceausescus in Romania. The Berlin Wall was demolished as a popular sport after the collapse of the East Berlin government in 1989. In 1991, the Ukraine opted for independence by a 91 percent vote.[366] "The Soviet Union. . . died because it had to, because the grotesque organs of its internal structure were incapable of providing the essentials of life."[367]

The wave of enthusiasm throughout the former European Communist Bloc soon turned to ambivalence. Despite the establishment of new constitutions, the cynicism that had built up over the previous forty years was hard to overcome. Democracy became difficult to achieve by people used to having their major decisions made for them.[368] The lack of a sense of combined purpose in the "new" Russia threatened its economy.[369]

Because of fears of repeating its experience with Cuba, the US supported interventions in governments of a number of Latin American countries rather than considering whether they respected human rights. The US only was concerned with which might become communist and supported a number of repressive regimes. It sent marines to the Dominican Republic in 1965 to suppress a rebellion by officers against corruption; it supported repressive military dictatorships in Nicaragua, El Salvador, and Guatemala in the 1970s; it backed an army to overthrow the Marxist Nicaraguan government in the 1980s. In El Salvador there was ongoing guerilla warfare against the repressive military government that had been denounced by the clergy. The Archbishop of San Salvador, Oscar Romero, was assassinated on the pulpit in March 1980 by the same death squads he denounced. The US did sponsor some organizations supportive of democratic institutions. John Kennedy's Alliance for Progress promoted peaceful reform and Jimmy Carter withheld funds from juntas that engaged in human rights violations.[370]

Mexico defaulted on its debts in 1982, sending the entire economy of Latin America into a tailspin that included severe inflation. The power of drug cartels increased as legitimate means of making a living deteriorated. President Carlos Salinas was able to stabilize the economy to an extent based on the demands of its lenders, mainly in the US. Foreign creditors were allowed to bid for Pemex, the national oil company. Salinas hoped to cement financial reforms by instituting free trade, which led to the North American Free Trade Agreement (NAFTA) in 1994. NAFTA was not popular with many labor groups who saw "free trade" benefiting corporations and making workers more impoverished.[371] In 1995, Mexico once again faced default. US Treasury Secretary Robert Rubin engineered an intervention plan to prevent the collapse of the Mexican currency and economy and to protect the interests of American exporters and banks who had billions of dollars at stake.[372]

Venezuela's economy was helped by the oil boom that lasted from the 1950s to the 1970s, but the non-oil economy did not flourish, creating a dependency on oil for income. Vast differences opened up between the rich and poor. As poverty increased, there was continuing unrest and riots. A coup organized by Hugo Chavez in 1991 resulted in his spending two years in jail, but in the face of ongoing corruption by the government Chavez was elected President in 1998. Chavez put out a referendum for a new constitution that was approved by popular vote, but the constitution concentrated a great deal of power in the hands of its President. Chavez put reforms into place, including social welfare and expansion of education and land reforms. Numerous

attempts to remove Chavez from office by oil and military interests caused him to clamp down more firmly on opposition.[373]

In South Africa, where the black population outnumbered
the white population about five to one, apartheid was strictly
enforced starting in the 1940s. Discrimination in jobs and housing
was openly advocated by the white minority. In 1949, the African
National Congress began a program to protest oppressive conditions. The National (white) Party enacted draconian laws that
could be used to label any dissenters as communists and impose
long jail sentences. Nelson Mandela, one of the protest leaders,
became convinced that a non-violent approach to end apartheid
no longer was working and he was sent to prison for life for his
efforts. Amidst further repression and violence foreign companies
and governments began to refuse to do business with South Africa,
sending its economy into a tailspin.[374] Mandela, who had been writing and communicating with the outside world while in prison,
was released in 1990. The 1994 elections were open to voters of all
races, resulting in the election of Mandela to the presidency.[375]

After the exit of the British in the early 1960s a number of
independent states were established in Africa, including Sierra
Leone, Uganda, Kenya and Zanzibar. Thousands of whites in
the former colonies decided to leave. In French Africa, a similar
state of withdrawal began, with mostly peaceful transitions. But a
violent rebellion in Algeria that began in 1954 caused over a million deaths by the time of the French exit in 1962.[376] A degree of
democracy was established in a number of African states as dictators were forced aside. There were elections in Benin, Congo-
Brazzaville, the Central African Republic, Zambia and Mali. In
Rwanda, war between Hutus and Tutsis resulted in the massacre
of over 800,000. In Liberia, a rebellion in 1980 destroyed any sem-
blance of stability.[377]

When the Communist Revolution assumed authority in China

in 1949 under Mao Zedong, the Party attempted to centralize all authority and undermine the Confucian tradition of family morality. Later, under the decollectivism of Deng Xiaoping in 1978, families were once again inspired to take responsibility for their own farms and the economy sprang back. But the rule of law as developed in the western world never has existed in China, probably due to the traditional monolithic one-state domination of the lives of its people. China never had an Enlightenment tradition like the West to inspire the establishment of individual liberties.[378]

The "Japanese Miracle" after the Second World War prompted management consultants in the West to cite Japanese manufacturing methods as exemplary. In 1985, Tokyo land prices jumped 45%, obviously a setup for a severe downturn to those who view the situation in retrospect. That bubble burst in 1991 due to over-speculation in real estate and the stock market. The Japanese slowdown has continued into the twenty-first century.[379]

The Indian democracy, with a heavy element of patronage running its institutions, continued the traditional division between haves and have-nots. "India. . . has been a remarkably successful democracy since the country's founding in 1947. Yet Indian politicians are still heavily dependent on personal patron-client ties to get elected to parliament."[380]

The post-World War II US presidencies began with the election of Dwight Eisenhower, the war hero, in 1952. Eisenhower transformed the old, slow system of state roads into the modern interstate system still in place today that also stimulated the economy. He regretted his appointment of Earl Warren, a moderate Republican, to the Supreme Court after the court unanimously declared racial discrimination illegal in schools in Brown vs. the Board of Education (1954). In the decision, Warren famously stated "Separate educational facilities are inherently unequal." Eisenhower reluctantly sent federal troops to Little Rock

The World of Wine

In 2002, John and Erica Platter, South African wine writers, took an adventurous, unprecedented tour of nineteen countries on the perimeter of Africa in search of wine. They found, as anywhere else, some fine wines and some not so fine. Vines had to be planted in highland areas to be out of range of the tropical heat.

Morocco, settled by French colonists in 1912, had planted 50,000 hectares, most of them left behind when the country gained independence from France in 1956 and officially became Muslim. But considerable amounts of wine still are made there, which gives a boost to the country's economy. The Platter's tour included Algeria, which once was a source for daily wines in France and still has some production, and Egypt, which was moving into the modern world before the conflict between the army and activists made it a much less safe place to visit.

The Platters book provides an extensive review section of Africa wines. See *Africa Uncorked,* by John and Erica Platter

Arkansas in 1957 to uphold the decision.[381] He warned in his farewell speech about the "military-industrial complex" that seeks to gain power over civilian government, a seer-like prediction of things to come.

Senator John F. Kennedy became President after defeating Richard Nixon in 1960. Although brought up in great wealth he pushed hard for civil rights legislation. He was a vigorous and persuasive speaker, but not persuasive enough to get his most of his legislation through congress. He ordered an ill-fated invasion of

Cuba to overturn the dictatorship of Fidel Castro. When Russian missiles were discovered in Cuba in 1962, Kennedy ordered a blockade at the risk of war, but Nikita Khrushchev commanded his ships to turn back.[382] He negotiated a nuclear test-ban treaty in August of 1963. When Kennedy was assassinated on November 22, 1963, most of the nation was devastated. His brother, Robert Kennedy, who served as his Attorney General, also was assassinated when running for President in 1968.

Under Lyndon Johnson, Kennedy's Vice President, many of the programs pursued by Kennedy were passed. Johnson, the "Master of the Senate" (sub-title of a book by Robert A. Caro), knew how to get legislation passed. He initiated his War on Poverty by doubling anti-poverty funds while cutting taxes and reducing the budget to please conservatives.[383] Medicare, Medicaid, and the Voting Rights Act all were enacted under his watch. Johnson deepened US involvement in the Vietnamese war that was begun by Kennedy. Many Americans feared that was the first of the "dominoes" that might signal a Communist takeover of Southeast Asia. Mounting protests convinced Johnson that his accomplishments were being overshadowed by the war and he did not run for re-election in 1968.

Richard Nixon, who took office in 1969, was so concerned about his public image that he had his conversations in the White House recorded, which proved his undoing. Despite being forced to resign after the "Watergate" scandal, in which he was implicated in covering up a break-in at Democratic Party headquarters, he signed the Clean Air Act and initiated a visit to China in 1972 which broke the ice between the two countries, leading to the beginning of trade agreements.

Jimmy Carter became President in 1977 at a time when oil prices were spiking. The US-backed Shah of Iran was toppled in 1979, installing an ultra-conservative Muslim state that held

52 American hostages for 444 days, being released on the day of the inauguration of Ronald Reagan in 1981. The Department of Energy and Department of Education were established during his four-year term. He put solar panels on the roof of the White House that were removed by his successor. Since his presidency he has established the Carter Center which promotes health advocacy around the globe, and Habitat for Humanity, a volunteer organization to build low-income housing.

Ronald Reagan was elected US President in 1980 and charmed much of the country with an actor's charisma throughout his term. Although the darling of conservatives since his time, he was much more flexible and willing to work with Congress than most subsequent politicians who claim to represent his values. He cut taxes and the budget, and the US went from being a creditor nation to a debtor nation on his watch.[384] Federal indebtedness more than doubled under Reagan.[385] He popularized many myths, including that of "trickle down" economics – cutting taxes to improve the flow of dollars – but the US went into debt instead to make up for lost revenue.[386] Another Reagan myth was that of the "Welfare Queen" – single black women living in luxury on multiple welfare checks – which has been proven unfounded. Despite what many people believe, he raised taxes many times to deal with "loopholes" created by his tax cuts.[387] At the end of Reagan's term his popularity plummeted – there was runaway inflation and a major exit of jobs overseas.

George H. W. Bush took office in 1989 and inherited much of the downdraft from the indebtedness of the Reagan years. He signed the Americans with Disabilities Act (ADA) in 1990, which was intended to extend equal opportunity to those who need accommodation. He sent the US Army into the Middle East after an invasion of Kuwait by Saddam Hussein of Iraq. He was forced to raise taxes despite repeated promises not to do so. He was defeated four year later by Bill Clinton who, in the midst of rampant inflation, emphasized the issue of greatest importance to most Americans: "It's the economy, stupid."

The presidency of Bill Clinton closed the last eight years of the Second Millennium in the US. He was accused of an affair during his campaign but his boyish, magnetic charm allowed him to get away with a denial of many accusations, including the use of marijuana, which he "never inhaled." He raised taxes and reduced the country's deficit, which led to a soaring economy. He cut the military budget substantially, saving billions. He ended "welfare as we know it," depriving millions of mothers of child-care benefits needed to allow them to work. One affair he had in office he couldn't deny, being forced to claim on national television that he "never had sex with that woman." Thus he became the first President to be impeached since Andrew Johnson, although as with Johnson, he later was acquitted by the Senate.

In 1994, Clinton signed a crime bill that made federal penalties for crack-cocaine, used largely by black users, 100 times more onerous than for regular cocaine which is used mainly by whites. Reverend Jesse Jackson stated that Clinton had a chance "with one stroke of your veto pen, to correct the most grievous racial injustice built into our criminal justice system." Clinton signed the bill not long after a speech criticizing the mass incarceration of blacks.[388]

Clinton's financial advisors were men who successfully pushed the revolving door between Wall Street and Government, including Larry Summers, Deputy Secretary of the Treasury, who, when considering how to improve the economy, famously asked his boss Robert Rubin, "What would Goldman think of that?" Thus it was no surprise that Clinton favored bills pushing Wall Street deregulation and overturning the protections the 1933 legislation that had saved the country a reenactment of the Great Depression. Clinton's signature on the 1999 Gramm-Leach-Bliley Act repealed the main

The World of Wine

I live in Northern California, not far from California Wine Country. I arrived in 1970 with $200 in my pocket and no job. Of course I had to sample California Cabernet Sauvignon, which I did. The name of the producer will remain unmentioned.

The oldest commercial winery in California is Buena Vista in the town of Sonoma, founded in 1857, which has beautiful old stone cellars. Napa production began in 1860 by Charles Krug, with Shramsberg, Inglenook, and Beaulieu all founded in the nineteenth century. In 1976, at the "Judgment of Paris," a panel of French judges awarded first place to two California wines over French entries in a "blind" tasting. The judges later said they were tricked.

Robert Louis Stevenson spent his honeymoon in Napa Valley in 1880 on his way to the South Seas. He "squatted" for free at the abandoned Silverado Mine property north of St. Helena and wrote about wine being "bottled poetry." Napa wineries often use that quote, but Stevenson actually wasn't writing about Napa wine. He was waxing so eloquently about the wines of Bordeaux. See *Napa: The Story of an American Eden*, by James Conway

features of Glass-Steagall that had separated commercial and investment banking for 66 years. The results became clear during the financial meltdown nine years later.

As the year 2000 began, a sense of optimism swept the globe. Our TV screens showed New Year ceremonies that began on the South Sea Islands and swept across all time zones for 24 hours, bringing a feeling of unity and appreciation that civilization had progressed so far. After their local celebrations people everywhere went to sleep with a hope for a better world to come.

Summary and Possible Lessons

As far back as we can see, species improved their chances of survival by successful competition with others. Then for some, being able to cooperate speeded the progress of their evolution.

At some point our earliest ancestors developed a sense of self – an idea that they are separate entities from their surroundings and that they have an existence with a beginning and an end. They created stories and myths about themselves and their predecessors, including where they came from and their vision for the future, and imparted this legacy to their children.

Our ability to communicate about new discoveries and cooperate to implement them pushed our advancement far beyond that of any creature that had come before. The skill of making a stone into a hammer or knife could be passed on from one generation to the next. Eventually hunter/gatherer societies succeeded to where they could leave Africa and migrate to other parts of the world.

With the eventual advent of agriculture about 11,000 years ago, we were able to settle in one place and develop elaborate cultures and civilizations. We moved from egalitarian alliances in small groups to larger societies and states that increased our survival chances at the expense of participation in decision-making. Thus we lost much of our freedom as individuals. As societies enlarged, most people no longer had direct contact with their rulers. From that point a conflict between individual recognition and submission to leaders for the good of the group has been a part of the human condition. Religion also introduced the idea of a higher authority to whose representatives we would choose to submit or not.

Rules for behavior were required with the enlargement of societies. The earliest laws and codes – as well as the myths that conveyed the lessons of cultures across generations – were unwritten. The oldest surviving code of laws of which we have a copy is on the stone tablets of Hammurabi, King of Babylon, dating from the eighteenth century BCE. The Iliad and Odyssey of Homer were not written down until about 800 years after the events. Much of what is now the Hebrew Bible was passed on orally for a thousand years before it was recorded.[389]

Top-down organization was considered necessary to address perceived threats from other clans, tribes, or nations. Increasingly larger societies were capable of waging war more successfully and thus war was a key element in organizing the state. But from the earliest societies many rulers were overthrown by those who believed themselves oppressed or who thought they could do a better job.

Since then – at least in the West – we mainly have emphasized individual accomplishment, with the value of cooperation receiving secondary weight. The ability to cooperate and work toward common goals largely is what has made human success possible, but competition – or the achievement of the individual – usually has received more credit.

Competitiveness rose to a high pitch by the time of the ancient Greeks. In the tragedy *Ajax* by Sophocles (alternately translated as *Aias*), the greatest surviving warrior of the Greek force besieging Troy kills himself when he discovers that he will not be awarded the shield of the recently slain Achilles. To the Greeks, reputation was the all-consuming value. This was reflected in their obsession with the competition at their Olympics every four years. With no clear idea of an afterlife, it was how one was regarded in this world that constituted their highest honor, including a proper burial. The Greek populace attended plays by the thousands not just to be entertained, but to learn the values of their society. These values led to continual competition with neighboring states, which sometimes included war.[390]

Yet in some Greek societies an ability to discuss and work together toward common goals was an essential element. The idea began under Solon, the Athenian law giver, at first as an attempt to remove chronic conflicts between classes. It evolved into an attempt at direct democracy that only involved the ten percent of the population who were citizens, but which nevertheless represented a huge step forward. In Athens – if the speech attributed to Pericles is to be believed – the inspiration of a society with "laws. . . that afford equal justice," rather than allegiance to a ruler, inspired men to go to war for their homeland. Democracy did not lead to weakness in war, but strengthened the resolve of those who were inspired to fight for its values.

The Persians, then the Macedonians under Alexander, and still later the Romans, although eventually imploding from over-extension, were able to conquer huge tracts of land that set the stage for rule of law and the eventual establishment of states. In the east of Europe the recognition of human rights took hold more slowly. China continued without rule of law, although exposure to the West – via trade – made the Chinese aware of a world where the rights and needs of people were better addressed.

The churches that developed out of early Christian communities shaped the morality of both the West and East, with the Roman Church exerting political power over its entire domain. Islam, which began in the seventh century, quickly spread to dominate major parts of all continents for 100 years until eventually being checked. The Protestant Reformation that began in the sixteenth century challenged the role of the Church, leading to religious wars. The Jews, who had been expelled from their homeland in Palestine after rebelling against the Romans, constituted a small but influential minority throughout the world, particularly in the area of finance.

Trade and general prosperity expanded as more people moved into towns in the Middle Ages. But disease and plague – the results of many people living at close quarters – decimated the population, especially in Europe, with periodic outbreaks that removed up to one half of the living. Before the establishment of organized states, marauding bands often killed defenseless peasants.

With the European expansion of nationalism and then colonialism in the 1500s, much of the world was dominated by intruders who reduced or destroyed native populations, often under the guise of spreading Christian values. Africa, which had little large-scale political organization, lost part of its population to slavery at the hands of European traders who sold its natives to the plantations of the New World. In South America there were wars among tribes and societies that resulted in the establishment of large nations. Some tribes in the North eventually organized themselves into a peaceful coalition. This mattered little in the long run, as beginning in the 1500s European conquerors and settlers, some seeking wealth and some fleeing persecution, overran Native American societies throughout the hemisphere.

In North America, leaders of Britain's thirteen colonies who had studied the Enlightenment writers who championed human rights went to war to free themselves from colonial domination in 1775. That war, which lasted seven years, eventually established a democratic government. They worked together – despite vast differences – to create a written Constitution devoted to self-governance that guaranteed basic freedoms to "We the People," but the definition of "the people" continues to evolve. This model of democracy has inspired similar attempts in over 100 countries. Following its 1789 revolution, France experienced a series of upheavals and shifting governments for nearly two centuries.

The 1800s saw the advent of manufacturing over agriculture in the West. More people moved to the cities, where they worked long hours under poor conditions in factories. Proponents of capitalism, who had faith in the economic advantages of improved manufacturing methods, and of socialism, who believed that the workers who were the producers of capital should be given a larger share, and of communism, which sought to do away with capitalism altogether, clashed philosophically and, at times, physically.

A result of excluding some groups from a definition of "the people" resulted in the continuation of slavery in the US and a four-year civil war that caused more American deaths than any other fought by that country. Civil wars also raged in Europe and Central and South America in the 1800s, with limited progress in the direction of human rights.

In 1914 much of the world went to war in an expression of hostilities between alliances that already had been built up in Europe. After the defeat of Germany and its allies, the victors imposed harsh reparations and the League of Nations failed to enforce world peace. In the meantime, the 1917 Russian Revolution deposed the Tsar and led to the establishment of the Soviet Union.

The Great Depression plunged much of the world into financial dysfunction, with many losing their saving and becoming homeless. Germany failed to pay its reparations and eventually recovered to again launch war on a world that was unprepared. After its defeat in the Second World War, Germany was divided among the victorious Allies, with the Soviet Union occupying its eastern territory. In 1949 a Communist revolution established a new oppressive regime in China. The Cold War between the two remaining superpowers, the US and the USSR and their respective allies divided the world between democratic and communist ideologies into the 1980s, with each side claiming superiority for its political and economic system. The Soviet Union considered the US not democratic, but capitalistic.

The period following the Second World War was one of economic growth, particularly in the West. Investments in infrastructure – despite high taxes – raised the general level of prosperity to the highest in history. People were provided a living wage and they paid taxes that improved general prosperity, providing governments enough funds to expand infrastructure and recirculate money back into the economy. But a bitter fight over wages took place between companies and labor unions.

The improving prosperity, however, failed to include many members of minorities. In the US, blacks and Hispanics often still were forced to work for subsistence wages. Some blacks moved to northern states to seek a better life. American Indians who had not integrated into society continued to live in desolation. In Europe, many immigrants fleeing poverty and prosecution were isolated and forced to live in poverty.

Toward the end of the twentieth century the Soviet Union collapsed due to an inability to maintain a system that sought to control people's lives. Trade brought a greater variety of products to nations throughout the world. There was general prosperity in the Western world, but there was concern among some that democracy may be weakened by the influence of big money in politics.

As we entered the twenty-first century there was optimism that a new era of prosperity would spread to a greater number of the world's inhabitants.

The Path to Democracy

Somewhere along our journey from the past the idea of freedom became important. Our ancestors decided that they were not simply going to yield to circumstances or overseers. They created a vision of the world in which they wanted to live and they worked together to forge a path in its pursuit.

Human history reflects our efforts to survive and then improve our situation over time, with many steps forward and back. Where we have been most successful as a civilization is in laboring together to identify and move toward common goals. Where we have failed to move forward together is when emphasizing the priorities of some individuals or groups over others.

Our most essential goals as a society only can be pursued successfully with the cooperation of others. An ability to identify common goals and move toward them always has been essential for human progress. This was the basic premise of those who first experimented with democracy in Athens and the American founders who wrote – and rewrote – their Constitution as a team until it best expressed their combined vision.

A desire to recognize human accomplishment always has caused us to honor individual role models – including our great hunters, soldiers, and athletes. But we rarely honor those who have made great strides working together to accomplish far more than any individual could possibly achieve.

1. COMPETITION AND COOPERATION

From the time we are young we model ourselves after our heroes. Our ideas for being the best we can come from watching those who have accomplished much. We want to be like them and experience their victories. They shape our ideas for how to act as productive members of society.

Yet looking at what moves our society forward – from families to schools to teams to businesses to governments – it becomes clear that no one can accomplish much as an individual without the cooperation of others. Those who achieve the most are those who can clearly identify and share goals and then combine their skills and efforts with others to reach them.

In democratic situations the dignity of everyone involved is important. In democratic families children and adults treat each other with respect and listen to each other's views. In schools that prepare students for democracy young minds are trained to develop their own ideas as part of the skills required for success. In democratic organizations a system for integrating the feedback of all members helps to shape policy. And in governments that want to maintain democracy, the dignity of the largest possible number of individuals is addressed.

2. "Us" vs. "Them"

We enter the world without an identity. Eventually we see ourselves as members of groups divided by race, gender, religion, or other shared beliefs or interests.

Those we think of as being like us are most likely to earn our trust and become allies as we confront the world. But as we divide ourselves from others we deny our common humanity. We find ourselves unable to trust those we think of as being part a group different from our own, which reduces the number of allies we might have as we move toward common human goals.

We enter into feuds or go to war based on an assumption that we are different from others. But we actually know very little about those who we force into categories as we ignore the vast potential in each human being. And as we do this to others we also do it to ourselves. The promise of democracy is to recognize the dignity of every human being, and when we deny the value and individuality of others we create a world where the dignity of no one is recognized.

Yet when we admit how little we know about others we find a common humanity. And upon this commonality we can move toward the family, organization, or country we need to ensure human progress.

3. TRUST AND DISTRUST

Humans always have alternated between trust and distrust for others. This affects the mates and friends we choose, the groups we belong to, the associations we form, and the nations of which we consider ourselves members. From the mortal conflict between Cain and Abel to the wars that decimated the human race in the twentieth century, we have decided that those we trust are our friends and those unworthy of our trust are our enemies. In many cases enemies later become friends, and friends become enemies.

Each person who loses a previously held sense of trust believes her or himself to have been betrayed. When this happens we have a choice of working together to reestablish trust or keeping that person (or nation) at a distance. Reestablishing trust requires a serious effort. This only can be done gradually as trust is built back into the relationship. We – and others – must slowly prove ourselves trustworthy to reestablish a viable working relationship.

4. A BELIEF IN JUSTICE

We all believe in justice, at least for ourselves. Most wars and revolutions have been fought by those who think they have been denied justice by others. But humans only have slowly come to the understanding that establishing long-term justice for ourselves must include establishing justice for all. Thus my ultimate best interest is tied to the best interest of you and all of humanity. So to ensure long-term justice for myself I must work toward a world that assures justice – as much as possible – for everyone.

This brings me to the question of whether I am willing to commit myself to doing what I can to bring about a just world. Doing this will change my daily actions. I will treat those around me with greater compassion; I will be more willing to help others;

I will share more of what I have for the good of the whole, knowing that this is the best way to ensure a more just world for myself and mine.

5. EQUALITY VS. INEQUALITY

A key goal of democracy is equality of opportunity. Yet it is impossible to guarantee equality of ability or the outcomes of one's efforts. Opportunity – or lack of it – often is the product of the circumstances of one's upbringing. Those brought up in poverty tend to stay in poverty and those brought up in privilege tend to remain there. Efforts have been made by many governments to level the playing field so that the innate talents of every individual can be recognized and nourished. This promise must be a topic of discussion among those who run governments in countries that consider themselves democratic. Lack of opportunity in youth often leads to adults who are a drain on society. Equal opportunity means that the talents of individuals are encouraged which allows them to become more productive contributors to their world.

6. THE PERSISTENCE OF THE PAST

It has been said that insanity is repeating the same actions over and over, hoping for different results. But often that is what counts for *sanity* in our world. The past can bind us or enlighten our path for a new direction. To avoid repeating ourselves and sending our world into downward spiral of self-destruction we must let go of that part of the past that no longer serves us. We must clarify the direction we want our world to go and identify the steps needed to move in that direction. This is more easily said than done, but creating our visions and working toward them – with others – is our most important task.

The central vision of democracy is the recognition of the validity of every human being. We may be the most advanced of any civilization yet to live on earth but we still are challenged to clarify and move toward that vision. To do this we must be willing to ask: "What type of world do we want to live in?" This leads to having a conversation in which all play a part in moving toward that kind of world. Then can we progress toward identifying and implementing a vision that recognizes human dignity.

7. The Limits of Knowledge

Our knowledge of the world, other people, and ourselves is limited to our concepts, which, if we keep our minds open to new possibilities throughout our lives, are continually changing. Socrates stated that he knows nothing (see above), and Einstein claimed that we choose our concepts (see the quote at the beginning of Chapter III). We need our concepts to function, because if we continually reassess every situation before making a decision we would have a hard time getting through a day. I go into my office with a concept of where it is, where my desk is, where my computer is, and where I left off yesterday, which allows me to sit and write. Now if I could only remember where I put my keys! Without my concepts based on my experience, I would have to continually appraise every situation to continue functioning, much like an infant.

Assuming that our concepts of the world and others always are right has had fatal consequences. We think we know who is good and bad and who our enemies are. We base our conclusions on what we have been told about others and our memories. Both of these sources often are inaccurate. We declare war on each other based on our assumptions, but when we really pay attention we might find that our "enemy" is not the same person that we hold in our minds.

The progress of science has been based on a willingness to acknowledge what we don't know so that we can find new theories to move us forward – from sailing our ships beyond what once was considered the end of the earth to space travel. We have used our knowledge to make great strides, and that will be true when the next generation looks back and wonders why we don't know now what they will know then. Scientific understanding moves along at a galloping pace, rendering much of what we think we know today obsolete tomorrow.[391]

8. Respect vs. Disrespect

I will end this chapter by mentioning one quality that we all are looking for: respect. From our earliest moments we crave being acknowledged and respected by others. We will do whatever we think we must to gain respect and recognition. But ultimately we have much control over the respect we experience. We can hearken back to the old rule that we get what we give.

Much of history can be seen as a contest for recognition as well as survival. We compete endlessly for recognition – sometimes with tragic results. People will risk their lives or those of others; they will go to the ends of the earth to get the attention they think they deserve.

Respect is something we bring to ourselves – or not – based on how we measure up to the standards that we carry within us that were set by our parents, teachers and other models.

Human beings and their civilizations could not have progressed without a shared standard for how we and those around us should act. Yet our standards as often divide as unite us. We can choose to emphasize our shortcomings – and those of others – or the direction we want to go. But progress requires looking beyond rigid ideas of how we or others should be and reestablishing trust as we move toward our goals. Only in acknowledging our common humanity – warts and all – can we supersede the hold of our past and begin to identify and work together toward the world in which we really want to live. That is when the tenets of democracy become a living reality.

And how do we do that?

Stay tuned.

Endnotes

1   This famous quote begins the text of Chapter I, which starts the fourth paragraph of the book.

2   *The Immense Journey*, Pages 130-31

3   "In the primitive past, dramatic and bizarre adolescent rites were performed in an effort to modify and sublimate the adolescents budding manhood." *Childhood and Society*, Page 341

4   *The Origin of Species*, Page 506

5   *The Immense Journey*, Page 127

6   *The Origin of Species*, Page 503

7   *Europe before Rome*, Page 17

8   *1491*, Page 4

9   "The magnificent art of the Upper Paleolithic represents an awakening of the creative spirit, an explosion of our aesthetic senses. Such a transformation may also signify major changes in the minds of the Upper Paleolithic people and/or in the way they viewed the world and organized their lives and society." *Europe before Rome*, Page 62

10   "Band-level societies are highly egalitarian. . . . In this type of society, leaders emerge based on group consensus; they have no right to their office and cannot hand it down to their children." *The Origins of Political Order*, Page 54

11   "Trading in prehistory and protohistory: Perspectives from the eastern Aegean and beyond – Part 1," Incifer Banu Dogan. Istanbul University.

12   "All have developed moral codes and taboos that prohibit anti-social behavior and bring stability to their communities. All human societies show concern for the value of human life; in all, self-preservation is generally accepted as a proper motivation for action, and in none is the killing of other human beings accepted without some fairly definite justification. All human societies regard the procreation of new human life as in itself a good thing unless there are special circumstances. No human society fails to restrict sexual activity; in all societies there is some prohibition of incest, some opposition to boundless promiscuity and rape, some favor for stability and permanence in sexual relationships. All human societies display a concern for truth, through education of young in matters not only practical (e.g. avoidance of dangers) but also speculative or theoretical (e.g. religion). Human beings, who can survive infancy only by nurture, live in or on the margins of some society which invariable extends beyond the nuclear family, and all societies display a favor for the values of cooperation, of common over individual good, of obligation between individuals, and of justice within groups. All know friendship. All have some concept of...title or property, and reciprocity. All value play, serious and formalized, or relaxed and recreational. All treat the bodies of the dead members of the group in some traditional and ritual fashion different from their procedures for rubbish disposal. All display concern for powers or principles which are to be respected...in one form or another, religion is universal." *Natural Law and Natural Rights*, Page 83

13   "Every person and every group has a limited inventory of historically determined spatial-historical concepts, which determine the world image, the evil and ideal prototypes, and the unconscious life plan." *Childhood and Society*, Page 345

14   "...human behavior, and particularly human social behavior, far from being determined by reason and culture alone, is still subject to all the laws prevailing in phylogenetically adapted instinctive behavior. Of these laws we possess a fair

amount of knowledge from studying the instincts of animals." *On Aggression,* Page 237

15   *The Origins of Political Order,* Page 73

16   "...the amount of trust derived from earliest infantile experience does not seem to depend on absolute quantities of food or demonstrations of love, but rather on the quality of the maternal relationship." *Childhood and Society*, Page 249

17   "In projection, we experience an inner harm as an outer one: we endow significant people with the evil that actually is in us." *Childhood and Society,* Page 249

18   *Childhood and Society*, Page 404

19   *Childhood and Society,* Page 235

20   *The Origins of Political Order*, Page 9

21   *A History of Egypt*, Pages 13-26

22   *A History of Egypt,* Pages 27-31

23   *A History of Egypt,* Pages 35-36

24   *Walking the Bible*, Page 174

25   *The Fortunes of Africa*, Page 14

26   "When the people saw that Moses delayed to come down from the mountain, the people gathered themselves to Aaron and said to him: 'Make us gods, who shall go before us; as for this Moses, the man who brought us up out of the land of Egypt, we do not know what has become of him'...So all the people took off the rings of gold that were in their ears, and brought them to Aaron. And he received the gold at their hand, and fashioned it with a graving tool, and made a molten calf, and they said, 'These are your gods, O Israel, who brought you out of the land of Egypt!'" *The New Oxford Annotated Bible*, Exodus 32: 1, 3 and 4

27   "And the Lord's anger was kindled against Israel, and he made them wander in the wilderness forty years, until all the generation that had done evil in the sight of the Lord was consumed." *The New Oxford Annotated Bible*, Numbers 32:13

28   *The New Oxford Annotated Bible*, Deuteronomy 6:4-5

29   *The New Oxford Annotated Bible*, Joshua 6:1-27

30   "They warred against Midian, as the Lord commended Moses, and slew every male...Now therefore, kill every male among the little ones, and kill every woman who has know man by lying with him. But all the young girls who have not known man by lying with him, keep alive for yourselves." *The New Oxford Annotated Bible*, Numbers 31:7, 17 and 18

31   *Europe*, Page 74

32   *The Origins of Political Order*, Page 316

33   *A History of the Middle East*, Pages 2-3

34   *The New Oxford Annotated Bible*, Jeremiah 52:27-30

35   *A History of the Middle East*, Page 9

36   "Minoan ritual...was intense. But it was an important ingredient in the social cement which held a peaceable society together for centuries." *Europe*. Page 89

37   "Thus the hero is the archetypal forerunner of mankind in general. His fate is the pattern in accordance with the masses of humanity must live, and have always lived...the stages of the hero myth have become constituent elements in the personal development of every individual." *The Origins and History of Consciousness.* Page 131

38   *Europe.* Page 111

39   *Europe*, Pages 114-15

40   *The Landmark Thucydides*, Page 549

41   *Democracy*, Page 32

42   *Europe,* Page 98

43   *Democracy*, Page 35
44   *The Landmark Thucydides*, Page 112
45   "The Spartans voted that the treaty had been broken, and that war must be declared, not so much because they were persuaded by the arguments of the allies, but because they feared the growth of the power of the Athenians, seeing must of Hellas already subject to them." *The Landmark Thucydides,* Page 49
46   "The Athenians also took possession of the cities on the continent belonging to the Mytilenians, which thus became...subject to Athens." *The Landmark Thucydides,* Page 184
47   "Hence the result of the discussion, as far as I'm concerned, is that I know nothing, for when I don't know what justice is I'll hardly know whether it is a kind of virtue or not, or whether a person who has it is happy or unhappy." *Plato's Republic*, Section 354, in *Plato, Complete Works*
48   *A History of Egypt*, Pages 96-102
49   *Europe*, Page 102
50   *China, a History*, Pages 28-38
51   *The Origins of Political Order*, Pages 93 and 108
52   *China, A History*, Pages 62-67
53   *China, a History*, Page 70
54   *The Origins of Political Order*, Page 141-48
55   *China, A History*, Pages 53-55, 376
56   *China, A History*, Pages 240 and 382
57   *1491*, Page 211-214
58   *1491*, Pages 21-22, 201
59   *1491*, Pages 281 and 308
60   *1491.* Page 170
61   *SPQR*, Pages 122-25
62   *SPQR*, Pages 147-49
63   *SPQR*, Pages 66-68
64   *A Brief History of France*, Page 14
65   *A History of the Global Financial Market*, Page 10
66   *SPQR*, Pages 531-32
67   "According to Hippocrates, the Europeans were courageous but aggressive and bellicose, while the Asiatics were wise and cultivated but peace-loving to the point of lacking initiative. Europeans were committed to liberty, for which they were prepared to fight and die. Their favorite political regime was democracy. Asiatics, on the other hand, were content to accept servitude in exchange for prosperity and tranquility." *The Birth of Europe,* Page 8
68   *A History of Egypt*, Page 146
69   *The New Oxford Annotated Bible,* Galatians 1:13–16
70   *Europe*, Pages 206-13
71   "First, kings now appeared at the head of the new political formations...Secondly, the laws promulgated by these kings were markedly barbarian in character. The consisted of lists of tariffs, fines, and monetary forms of compensation that applied to offenses and crimes. These varied according to the ethnic status and social ranking of the guilty parties...Rudimentary though it was, the barbarian legislation resting upon the ruins of Roman law did ensure that the Europe of the Early Middle Ages continued to be based on law." *The Birth of Europe*, Page 28
72   *Europe*, Page 292
73   *Europe*, Pages 259-62
74   "Throughout the Middle Ages the encyclopedia was to be a favorite literary genre

for clerical and lay scholars alike, for it provided a distillation of past culture and made it possible to press on further . . . "
The Birth of Europe, Page 17

75   *The Birth of Europe,* Page 24

76   "When he reluctantly became Pope in 590, at a time of serious flooding by the River Tiber a Black Death epidemic in Rome, he organized resistance, both material and spiritual, to these scourges...He defended Rome and the Church's possessions in Italy against the Lombard's. He sent Augustine...to reconvert England. . . . reformed the liturgical chant, thenceforth known as the Gregorian Chant." *The Birth of Europe*, Pages 18-19

77   "It was in the Middle Ages that Europe first appeared and took shape both as a reality and as a representation. This was the decisive time of the birth, infancy, and youth of Europe, even though the people living in those medieval centuries never dreamed of constructing a united Europe nor desired to do so." *The Birth of Europe*, Page 1.

78   *Europe*, Pages 316-17

79   "Roads fell into disrepair, along with workshops, warehouses and irrigation systems, and agriculture declined. It was a technological regression in which the use of stone as a major building material diminished and wood made a comeback. . . . In the place of towns...the large estates now became the basic economic and social entity, with small manors as the units where people lived and farmed...The monetary economy shrank and bartering took its place...Long distance trading almost disappeared." *The Birth or Europe*, Page 27

80   "In a tradition that starts with Karl Marx, "feudalism" is often taken to refer to an exploitative economic relationship between lord and peasant...A more historically accurate definition...was a contractual agreement between lord and vassal by which the latter was given protection and a plot of land in return for serving the lord in a military capacity." *The Origins of Political Order*, Pages 105-106

81   *The Origins of Political Order*, Page 236-40

82   *Europe*, Page 282

83   *Europe*, Pages 251-52

84   "I shall put fear into the hearts of the disbelievers – strike above their necks and strike all their fingers." "People, we created you from a single man and a single woman, and made you into races and tribes, so that you should get to know one another." "You always will find treachery in all but a few of them. Overlook this and pardon them: God loves those who do good." "Live with them (women) according to what is fair and kind."– *The Qur'an*, 8:12; 49:13; 5:13; 4:19

85   *A History of the Middle East*, Page 15

86   *The Birth of Europe*, Page 22

87   *A History of the Middle East*, Page 18

88   *The Birth of Europe,* Page 126

89   *A Brief History of France*, Page 20

90   "In Charlemagne's time...the peasants forced their lords to emancipate them, and thereby formed a free category, exempted from forced labor. The lords were now obliged either to accept a reduction in size of their estates or to reimpose servitude on their peasants. The latter solution was mainly adopted in Eastern Europe and became a further cause of the differences and distancing between western and Eastern Europe." *The Birth of Europe*, Pages 33-35

91   *Christendom*, Volume 1, Page 169

92   *A Brief History of France*, Pages 24-25

93   *Europe*, Pages 321-34

94 *The Fortunes of Africa*, Page 70-71
95 *The Origins of Political Order*, Pages 161-64
96 *The Origins of Political Order*, Pages 171-73
97 The Origins of Political Order, Page 179
98 *The Origins of Political Order,* Pages 185-86
99 *A Concise History of Japan*, Pages 25-27
100 "Arthur, that good King of Britain, whose prowess teaches us that we, too, should be brave and courteous, held a rich and royal court upon that precious feast day which is always known by the name of Pentecost." From "Yvain," in *Arthurian Romances,* Page 180
101 *The Oxford Annotated Bible,* Lupe 23:34
102 *The Oxford Annotated Bible,* Matthew 7:2
103 *The Birth of Europe,* Pages 82-83
104 *The Origins of Political Order,* Page 264-66
105 *The Counsels of the Holy Father St. Francis*, Admonition 27
106 *Europe*, Pages 358-59
107 *A Brief History of France*, Pages 32-33
108 *Europe*, Page 407
109 *The Origins of Political Order*, Page 270-275
110 *The Origins of Political Order*, Pages 257-58
111 *The Origins of Political Order*, Pages 402-06
112 *The Oxford History of Britain*, Pages 141-46
113 *The Origins of Political Order*, Pages 230-34
114 *A Brief History of France*, Page 34
115 *Christendom*, Volume 1, Page 189
116 *Summa Theologiae,* Question 8, Article 3
117 *A Brief History of France*, Page 36
118 *The Birth of Europe,* Page 105
119 *The Birth of Europe*, Page 139-41
120 *The Birth of Europe,* Pages 73-75
121 *The Birth of Europe,* Pages 112-16
122 *The Birth of Europe,* Pages 76-79
123 *The Birth of Europe,* Pages 152-53
124 *The Origins of Political Order*, Page 323
125 *Europe*, Page 357
126 *Europe*, Pages 433-39
127 *Europe*, Pages 470-71
128 *Europe*, Page 349
129 *Enlightening Symbols*, Pages 62-63
130 *The Birth of Europe,* Pages 165-68
131 *The Birth of Europe,* Pages 189-90
132 *The Birth of Europe,* Page 99
133 *Europe,* Page 361
134 *The Birth of Europe*, Page 126-27
135 *The Birth of Europe,* Page 104
136 *The Birth of Europe,* Pages 110-11
137 *The Origins of Political Order*, Page 259-60
138 *Europe,* Page 338
139 *A Brief History of France*, Pages 38-40
140 *Europe,* Page 412
141 "The theme of the *Danses Macabre des Femmes* is the sudden, inevitable event of

death, the great social leveler. By witnessing life's end, readers may be moved to evaluate their prior behavior, to repent, and, by changing their conduct, to attain salvation." *Danse Macabre of Women,* Page 8

142   *Danse Macabre of Women,* Page 72
143   *The Birth of Europe,* Page 155-56
144   *A Brief History of France*, Page 38
145   *Europe*, Page 334
146   *Europe*, Page 386
147   *The Birth of Europe,* Page 186
148   *A Brief History of France*, Page 45
149   *The Birth of Europe,* Pages 177-78
150   *A Brief History of France*, Page 46
151   *The Origins of Political Order*, Pages 328-30
152   *The Birth of Europe,* Page 180
153   *The Birth of Europe,* Page 188
154   *The Origins of Political Order*, Page 236
155   *Europe*, Pages 393 and 453-54
156   *The Fortunes of Africa*, Pages 94-95
157   *The Fortunes of Africa,* Pages 108-110
158   *Europe*, Page 511
159   *The Origins of Political Order*, Pages 310-11
160   *A Concise History of Japan*, Pages 99-101
161   *The Origins of Political Order*, Page 447
162   *Europe*, Page 851
163   *1491.* Pages 11-19, and 189-90
164   *1491.* Pages 50-69
165   *The Birth of Europe,* Page 208
166   *1491.* Pages 20-27
167   *1491.* Pages 74-84
168   *Politics*, Page 24. Section 1260a
169   *A Brief History of France,* Page 51
170   *A Brief History of France*, Pages 66-73
171   *A Brief History of France*, Pages 60-62
172   *Europe,* Page 484
173   *The Oxford History of Britain*, Pages 273-81
174   *The Oxford History of Britain,* Pages 355-58
175   *The Origins of Political Order*, Pages 408-17
176   *The Origins of Political Order*, Pages 419-21
177   *A Brief History of France*, Page 64
178   *Europe*, Page 509
179   *The Prince*, Chapter XXI, Page 79
180   *The Origins of Political Order*, Pages 359-64
181   *Europe*, Pages 531-34
182   *The Origins of Political Order*, Page 359
183   *1491.* Page 148
184   *Europe,* Page 580
185   *Europe*, Pages 649-53
186   *The Origins of Political Order*, Pages 394-98
187   *Russia,* Page 56
188   *Europe,* Page 654
189   *Europe*, Pages 739-744

190 *The Origins of Political Order*, Page 428

191 *Europe*, Page 513

192 *Europe*, Pages 513-17

193 *Europe*, Page 549

194 *1491*. Pages 390-91

195 *Europe*, Page 580

196 *Europe,* Page 637

197 *1491*. Pages 381-87

198 *Europe*, Pages 565-67

199 *A Brief History of France*, Pages 74-77

200 *The Origins of Political Order*, Pages 336-44

201 "Hereby it is manifest, that during the time that men live without a common power to keep them all in awe, they are in the condition that is called war; and such a war, as is of every man, against every man...In such condition there is no place for industry, because the fruit thereof is uncertain, and consequently, no culture of the earth, no navigation, nor the use of commodities that may be imported by sea, no commodious building, no instruments of moving and removing such things as require much force, no knowledge of the face of the earth, no account of time, no arts, no letters, no society, and which is worst of all, continual fear and danger of violent death, and the life of man, solitary, poor, nasty, brutish, and short." *Leviathan*, Chapter 14, Sections 8 and 9.

202 "The State of Nature has a Law of Nature to govern it, which obliges everyone: and Reason, which is that law, teaches all mankind, who will but consult it, that being all equal and independent, no one ought to harm another in his life, health, liberty or possessions." *Second Treatise of Government,* Chapter 2, Section 6, Line 6

203 *The Social Contract* begins with a three paragraph introduction which starts and ends: "My purpose is to consider if, in political society, there can be any legitimate and sure principle of government, taking men as they are and laws as they might be...And whenever I reflect upon governments, I am happy to find that my studies always give me fresh reason for admiring that of my own country."

204 "Every man has the right to believe himself, at the bottom of his heart, entirely equal to all other men." *Philosophical Dictionary*, P. 183

205 "All liberal social contract theories...presupposed a presocial state of nature in which human beings lived as isolated individuals. Such a state of primordial individualism never existed." *The Origins of Political Order*, Page 89

206 *Europe*, Pages 597-98

207 *Europe,* Page 584

208 *Europe*, Page 632

209 *Europe,* Pages 636-37

210 *Europe*, Page 680

211 *The Wealth of Nations*, Book 1, Chapter One, Page 3

212 *The Wealth of Nations*, Book V, Chapter One, Page 406

213 *1776*, Pages 7-9

214 *1776*, Page 54

215 *1776*, Page 37

216 *1776*, Page 99

217 *1776*, Page 118

218 *1776*, Pages 131-36

219 *Common Sense,* Page 5

220 *1776*, Pages 267-83

221 *The Oxford History of the American People*, Page 254

222 *The Oxford History of the American People*, Page 265

223 *Founding Brothers*, Page 5

224 *Founding Brothers*, Pages 7-9

225 *Europe*, Page 637

226 *America's Constitution, a Biography*. Pages 20-21

227 *Founding Brothers*, Page 16

228 *Founding Brothers*, Page 50

229 *Founding Brothers*, Pages 90-92

230 *Founding Brothers*, Pages 90-92

231 *Edmund Burke - the First Conservative*, Page 52

232 *Edmund Burke - the First Conservative*, Page 113

233 *Edmund Burke - the First Conservative*, Page 205

234 *A Brief History of France*, Page 98

235 *Europe,* Pages 693-94

236 *A Brief History of France*, Pages 106-13

237 *A Brief History of France*, Page 116

238 *A Brief History of France*, Pages 118-24

239 *The Fall of the Third Republic,* Page 641

240 *Europe*, Pages 812-28

241 *Founding Brothers*, Page 170

242 *Founding Brothers*, Page 205

243 *An Indigenous People's History of the American People*, Pages 110-113

244 *Europe*, Page 611

245 *Critique of Pure Reason*, Pages 15-16

246 *The Penguin History of Latin America*, Pages 214-16

247 *The Penguin History of Latin America*, Pages 265-67

248 *The Penguin History of Latin America*, Pages 217-21

249 "...persons of rank were driven to America by political and religions quarrels. Laws were made to establish the gradation of ranks; but it was soon found that the soil of America was opposed to a territorial aristocracy ... " *Democracy in America*, Page 29

250 "...in aristocratic states the rulers are rarely accessible to corruption and have little craving for money, while the reverse is true in democratic states. *Democracy in America*, Page 229

251 "I know of no country in which there is so little independence of mind and real freedom of discussion as in America." *Democracy in America*, Page 263

252 "No African has voluntarily emigrated to the shores of the New World...although the law may abolish slavery, God alone can obliterate the traces of its existence." *Democracy in America*, Page 358

253 *Europe*, Page 832

254 *Europe*, Pages 805-811

255 *On Liberty,* Chapter I, Pages 3 and 8

256 *The Oxford History of the American People*, Page 518.

257 *The Civil War*, Pages 39-48

258 *Team of Rivals,* Pages xv-xvi

259 *The Civil War*, Pages 69-80

260 *Team of Rivals,* Pages 549-53

261 *The Civil War*, Pages 358-78

262 *The Civil War*, Page 638

263 *Team of Rivals,* Pages 738-43

264 *An Indigenous People's History of the United States*, Pages 158-59

265 *A Brief History of France*, Pages 150-51

266 *Europe*, Page 775-76

267 *The Fortunes of Africa*, Pages 261-63

268 *A History of Egypt*, Page 236

269 *To End All Wars*, Page 17

270 *To End All Wars*, Pages 23-32

271 *The Penguin History of Latin America*, Page 305

272 Quoted in *An Indigenous People's History of the United States*, Page 162

273 *China*, Page 500

274 *The Communist Manifesto*, Page 76

275 *Creating a Culture of Revolution*, Pages 60 and 79-80

276 *The Penguin History of Latin America*, Page 268

277 *The Penguin History of Latin America*, Pages 459-71

278 *A History of the Middle East*, Page 242

279 *To End All Wars*, Pages 44-50

280 *Europe*, Page 909

281 *To End All Wars*, Pages 81-96

282 *Europe*, Page 1328

283 *A History of Egypt*, Page 271

284 *A History of the Middle East*, Page 181

285 *Europe*, Pages 910-25

286 *To End All Wars*, Pages 347-50

287 *A Brief History of France*, Page 167

288 *Europe*, Page 950

289 *A History of Egypt*, Page 288

290 *Europe*, Pages 937

291 *The Origins of Political Order*, Pages 279-85

292 *Europe*, Pages 960-65

293 *A History of Egypt*, Pages 274-87

294 "The Great Powers at this point failed in their responsibility to 're-educate' Germany in the only way one can re-educate people – namely, by prescribing them with the incorruptible fact of a new identity with a more universal political framework." *Childhood and Society*, Page 351

295 "The Business Cycle Today: An Introduction," in *Economic Research: Retrospect and Prospect, Volume 1.* Page 5

296 *A History of the Global Stock Market*, Pages 10-17

297 *A History of the Global Stock Market*, Page 44

298 *Wall Street, a History*, Pages 5-8

299 *Wall Street, a History*, Pages 178-83

300 *Wall Street, a History*, Pages 197-98

301 *Wall Street, a History*, Pages 191-93

302 *Wall Street, a History*, Pages 224-27

303 *The Oxford History of the American People*, Pages 946-59

304 *A History of the Global Stock Market*, Pages 140-41

305 *The Oxford History of the American People*, Pages 966-67

306 "…The black miracle of Nazism was only the German version…of a universal contemporary potential…For nations, as well as individuals, are not only defined by their highest point of civilized achievement, but also by the weakest one in their collective identity…" *Childhood and Society*, Page 327

307 *Europe*, Pages 973-74

308 *Europe*, Page 978-87

309 *A Brief History of France*, Page 177
310 *A Brief History of France*, Page 178
311 *A Brief History of France*, Page 179
312 *The Warmth of Other Suns*, Pages 8-11
313 *Europe,* Page 987-90
314 *Europe,* Page 979
315 *The Fortunes of Africa*, Pages 501-505
316 *Europe,* Pages 1002-03
317 *Inferno*, Page 11
318 *Inferno: The World at War, 1939-45*, Page 24
319 *A Brief History of France*, Pages 182-89
320 *A Brief History of France*, Pages 192-94
321 *A Brief History of France*, Pages 195-99
322 *Europe,* Pages 1018-22
323 *Inferno*, Pages 74-75
324 *Inferno*, Pages 77-80
325 *Europe,* Page 1008
326 *Franklin and Winston*, Page 105
327 *Inferno,* Pages 107-12
328 *Europe,* Page 1013-15
329 *Europe,* Page 1028
330 *Russia*, Pages 77-80
331 *The Oxford History of the American People*, Page 1002
332 *Europe,* Pages 1031-38
333 *Europe,* Pages 1044-45
334 *A Brief History of France*, Pages 200-202
335 *Inferno*, Pages 611-22
336 *Inferno*, Pages 627-28
337 *Europe,* Page 1073
338 *Europe,* Pages 1052-54
339 *Eichmann in Jerusalem,* Page 22
340 *Eichmann in Jerusalem,* Page 49
341 *Eichmann in Jerusalem,* Page 109
342 *Eichmann in Jerusalem,* Page 277
343 *Europe,* Pages 1063-64
344 *A Concise History of Japan*, Page 274
345 *Europe,* Page 1070
346 "Tribalism in this expanded sense remains a fact of life. India, for example, has been a remarkably successful democracy since the country's founding in 1947. Yet Indian politicians are still heavily dependent on personal patron-client ties to get elected to parliament... "The *Origins of Political Order*, Page 79
347 *A History of the Middle East*, Pages 260-68
348 *A History of Egypt*, Pages 289-306
349 *A History of Egypt,* Pages 312-16
350 *A History of Egypt*, Pages 336-38
351 *A History of Egypt*, Pages 342-46
352 "Of course, in the beginning, this cannot be effected except by means of despotic inroads on the rights of property...In place of the old bourgeois society, with its classes and class antagonisms, we shall have an association in which the free development of each is the condition for the free development of all." *The Communist Manifesto*, Pages 75-76

353 *Europe*, Page 1096
354 *Russia*, Page 30
355 *A Brief History of France*, Pages 226-27
356 *Europe*, Pages 1069-70
357 *A Brief History of France*, Pages 230-31
358 *The Penguin History of Latin America*, Page 338
359 *The Penguin History of Latin America*, Pages 442-47
360 *The Oxford History of the American People*, Page 1087
361 *A Brief History of France*, Pages 246-47
362 *A Brief History of France*, Pages 248-62
363 *The Oxford History of Britain*, Pages 648-56
364 *The Oxford History of Britain*, Page 671
365 *The Origins of Political Order*, Page 325
366 *Europe*, Pages 1122-26
367 *Europe*, Page 1135
368 "The decades 'under water' had conditioned the masses to disbelieve all promises and to expect the worst." *Europe*, Page 1125
369 *Europe*, Page 1134
370 *The Penguin History of Latin America,* Page 326
371 *The Penguin History of Latin America*, Page 585
372 *In an Uncertain World*, Pages 3-4
373 *The Penguin History of Latin America*, Page 593-95
374 *The Fortunes of Africa*, Pages 580-87
375 *The Fortunes of Africa*, Pages 633-35
376 *The Fortunes of Africa*, Pages 556-69
377 *The Fortunes of Africa*, Pages 636-42
378 *The Origins of Political Order*, Pages 120-21
379 *A Concise History of Japan*, Page 282
380 *The Origins of Political Order*, Page 79
381 *Justice for All*, Page 324
382 *The Oxford History of the American People*, Pages 1112-1117
383 *The Years of Lyndon Johnson*, Pages 540-46
384 *Day of Reckoning*, Page *xiv*
385 *Day of Reckoning*, Page 91
386 *Day of Reckoning*, Page 6
387 *Tear Down this Myth*, Page 58
388 "Bill Clinton crime bill destroyed lives, and there's no point in denying it," Thomas Frank in The Guardian, April 15, 2016
389 *Walking the Bible*, Page 21
390 *Aias*, Pages xxiv and xxv
391 "Universe is expanding up to 9% faster than we thought, say scientists," The Guardian, June 3, 2016

"Well, Doctor, what have we got – a Republic or a Monarchy?"
"A Republic, if you can keep it."

BENJAMIN FRANKLIN'S RESPONSE TO A FRIEND AFTER
THE CONSTITUTIONAL CONVENTION OF 1787

CHAPTER II

Democracy's Present

As we have seen, prehistoric humanity, organized as families and small tribes, was essentially egalitarian.[1] Then as larger tribes and states were formed, people compromised their individual freedoms for greater security. Hierarchical and autocratic societies created greater distances between rulers and those who were ruled, periodically leading to rebellions and the removal of oppressive rulers.

Ancient Athens initiated the first known attempts at democratic government starting about 460 BCE. This was direct representation in the daily operations of the state by the ten percent of the population who were citizens. Starting with the Magna Carta of 1215, and then over hundreds of years, England slowly moved toward greater democracy. Parliament gradually gained greater control over the functions of government beginning in 1265. The democratic ideals of government came out of the English model. An insistence on the rights of the individual by the Enlightenment authors beginning around 1700 inspired a revolution by the thirteen British colonies of North America for independence from the British Crown in 1775. Since then, revolutions have overthrown authoritarian governments throughout the world, but often they have been replaced with other authoritarian regimes.

By the late twentieth century the concept of "rule by the people" had gained such credence throughout the world that every major government, no matter how authoritarian, would claim to be ruled by its people. They would write constitutions to demonstrate that they were democratic regardless of the actual level of freedom given their residents.

In this chapter we will trace the waxing and waning of democratic elements in the modern era. Beginning with the major world powers, we will examine the degree to which democracy thrives or is denied in a sample of nations. Constitutions are promises by leaders to their contemporaries and future generations about how their rights will be protected and maintained. We will view a number of constitutions to determine what they state about the level of democracy in each country and compare this with the extent to which that country actually meets its own written standards.

After the third millennium opened, hopes of a kinder and gentler world remained unfulfilled for many. There continued to be trends toward and away from democracy throughout the world. We will review some of those trends starting with the world's six most powerful nations in alphabetical order, including the constitutions they have written to guide their governments. We then will review five other countries on different continents and their constitutions to give us a broader sample. We will see that the degree of real democracy in a country sometimes is based on its constitution – its written promise to its people – and sometimes not. Countries that make great promises to their people often fail to honor human rights in practice, but those with very little in the way of written constitutional guarantees still may practice democracy.

In this section more background information is provided for

countries that were not covered in depth in Chapter I. Our main emphasis is democracy, but governments that are not considered democracies may also – to varying degrees – guarantee the human rights of those they govern. The recognition of human rights and dignity probably is best addressed by democracy in most places, but countries continually evolve, sometimes in the direction of greater recognition of human dignity and sometimes in the other direction. Our real concern is the degree to which the essential validity of every human being is recognized.

BRITAIN

Great Britain currently includes England, Scotland, and Wales; the United Kingdom refers to these three plus Northern Ireland.

Britain, unlike other countries we will consider, has no written constitution. In 1215 the Magna Carta provided protections for nobles from the arbitrary actions of King John. Britain's "unwritten" constitution consisting of laws, precedents, customs and parliamentary decrees has continued to evolve from that time.

The Parliament of England began in 1265 when representatives from counties throughout the kingdom met in London. The original purpose of its representative body was to assist the monarch in making laws and raising taxes. Later parliaments tried to limit the king's power with varying degrees of success. Britain's chief gift to democracy is the concept of common law, meaning in theory at least, that the laws are applied equally and fairly throughout the country. Since the Glorious Revolution of 1688-89 which overthrew King James II, constitutional authority and absolute sovereignty has been vested in the elected Parliament.[2] But Britain has taken a long and winding road toward the realization of its democratic ideals, with a number of rough bumps along the way.

The Britain that entered the third millennium was a greatly

trimmed down version of what it had been 100 years earlier. Deprived of its colonial empire of days past, its gaze was turned mainly inward. At one time, the sun famously "never set" on a British empire that circled much of the globe. But by the early 2000s the entire population of its territories was about 250,000, including such outposts as Bermuda, Gibraltar, and the Virgin, Cayman, and Falkland Islands.

Britain's economy, once based on the benefits of trade within its empire, now mainly revolves around finance and credit. The term "London" refers as much to the financial center of Europe as to a city. A center of manufacturing during the Industrial Revolution of the 1700s and 1800s, Britain now has seventy-five percent of its economy devoted to services.

By the early twenty-first century Britons enjoyed a higher standard of living than ever before. This was negatively affected, however, by the global financial meltdown of 2008. Much of the economic practice that began in the mid-nineteenth century – such as public ownership of industry and redistribution of capital by taxes – had been reduced under Margaret Thatcher in the 1980s.[3] Along with a degree of prosperity came relative internal peace. The large strikes and race riots of the past were mainly gone, although there was concern among many Britons about the neo-fascist British National Party which was, however, not as powerful as similar parties in France and Austria.[4]

Tony Blair, the Labour Party leader who served as Prime Minister from 1997-2007, was immensely popular due to his apparent sincerity and his intentional avoidance of right or left ideologies. He seemed as at home with George W. Bush as with Bill Clinton. In the first few years of his administration, Blair and his Labour party enacted the National Minimum Wage Act and the Human Rights Acts of 1998 (which brought the UK in compliance with the European Convention on Human Rights), and the Freedom of Information Act of 2000, which provided public access to information held by authorities.

The Britain of the early 2000s reflected the general democratic spirit and civilized attitude of its people. Britons were, for the most part, unified in their wish to live in a well-functioning country. In a quaint concession to progress and civility, Parliament outlawed the ancient tradition of fox hunting in 2004 that actually was unlikely to be enforced in practice.[5]

Economic inequalities already in existence became worse under the Conservative policies of Margaret Thatcher, and continued to increase slowly in the Blair years. As in the US, there was movement toward greater economic equality after World War II and up until the 1970s in Britain, but then it began to reverse.[6] Until that time, taxes had been based on income, with a much steeper part of public benefits being paid by the wealthiest. These taxes funded all parts of the cost of government, including roads and bridges, police services, and defense. As taxes were lowered on the wealthy a larger percent of the cost of necessary services of government fell on those with lower incomes.[7]

Blair initiated inner city programs and invested more in public education in an effort to reduce the worst effects of poverty. Yet as late as 2007, before the global financial meltdown, the percent of people living in poverty in Britain remained the same. Meanwhile, the wealth of homeowners and those with market investments continued to rise. Taxes on inherited wealth as well as capital gains also decreased, exacerbating the divisions between those at different ends of the financial spectrum.[8]

The educational level of Britons has increased over the last 50 years, with more than half planning on higher education degrees. More than half of the university enrollment is female. With so many people seeking education, the birth rate dropped at the millennium, with the average age of child-bearing for women increasing to over 30. However, the British population climbed to about 60 million from 56 million in the 10 years leading up to 2010, the bulk of which is believed to have come from immigration.[9]

A new emphasis on individuals' health and freedom took place in early years of the millennium. Smoking, which had been common for centuries in pubs, restaurants, and theaters was forbidden in public places as of 2007. Healthy eating and exercise received more emphasis in an attempt to reduce the love of Britons for sugar and reverse its trend toward diabetes. Homosexuality became more accepted as a lifestyle as civil partnerships and the adoption of children by same-sex partners became more common. Religion, on the other hand, seriously waned, with only about 10% of the population attending Church, although over seventy percent stated they believe in God.

Immigration has been a continual issue in the millennium. After 2000, refugees from war and persecution in Middle East and Balkan countries flooded Britain's shores. Reactions, as elsewhere in the world, have varied from those who welcome asylum seekers, to those who want to keep "Britain for the British." The Commission for Racial Equality has advocated for greater integration and acceptance of immigrants into Britain's culture. As of 2007, Indians were the largest immigrant group living in the country, followed by the Irish and Pakistanis. After joining the European Union in 2007, which made transfers between countries easier, England became a cultural stew of people including many from Poland, Slovakia, Hungary, and Lithuania. The French population of London also increased, while many Britons migrated to France and Spain.

The 2001 attacks on the World Trade Center in New York, which killed nearly 3,000 people, also killed 67 British citizens. Tony Blair declared in Parliament that he would stand "shoulder to shoulder" with the United States in rooting out international terrorism. Britain was the only other country to send a significant number of troops to Afghanistan to remove the Al Qaeda terrorists who instigated the American attacks under Osama bin Laden.[10]

The British tend to hold a degree of skepticism about the transparency of their government, often for a good reason. Many were opposed to the 2003 joint invasion of Iraq, as were many Americans. But as was later revealed, Blair had met with George W. Bush in 2002 and secretly agreed to the Iraq attack. The result of the invasion was massive demonstrations throughout Britain against interference in the affairs of a foreign country. After the "war" was quickly resolved, Iraq descended into near-chaos as there had been no rebuilding plan, although the Americans were quick to exploit the Iraqi oil reserves. The decision to invade Iraq without adequate public consent probably is what cost Tony Blair his job in the next election.[11]

In July 2005 London was rocked by three bombs that killed fifty-two people, detonated by suicide bombers sympathetic to Al-Qaeda in a reaction to the British attack on Afghanistan. The result was a considerable increase in security measures, including extensive searches of airports, trains, and those entering sporting events.[12]

Gordon Brown took over as Prime Minister in 2007. Not long after, the international financial situation began to crumble, due largely to packaged investments in housing securities that were sold to international investors. These collapsed because housing was sold at inflated prices with little or no down payment to many who could not afford the payments. Many brokers were interested only in their immediate commissions and had no long-term concern about whether the buyer could actual meet their commitments. When the banks which had backed the mortgages stopped getting paid, the housing market collapsed and threatened to take the banks along with it. In England there was a run

on Northern Rock and other banks, the first time this had happened in a century. Pictures in the media of customers lined up
outside its doors were reminiscent of the Great Depression.

Brown, who had a Ph.D. in history from Edinburgh
University, introduced an historical perspective during his
administration (2007-2010), with tolerance and love of liberty
as themes. But as a result of the financial downturn, unemployment in industrialized countries rose to over ten percent – and
over twenty percent for some. Banks no longer could loan to
businesses; businesses slowed down and laid off or stopped hir-
ing workers; workers no longer had enough to spend to keep the
economic flow moving. As a result, Brown and his labour party
were blamed for the state of the economy and did poorly in the
election of 2009.

An emphasis on environmental issues began early in the twenty-first century. Climate change had been declared a public threat
by scientists and the British were among the first to propose efforts
to address the problem. Proposals for change in environmental policy included generating more energy from sustainable fuels, and a
plan was put in place to get at least 15 percent of Britain's energy
needs from wind, wave, solar, and biomass sources by 2020.[13]

In 2010, David Cameron became Prime Minister in a coalition between Conservatives and Liberal Democrats, and he
was re-elected in 2015. His government imposed austerity measures as a result of the financial crisis, including government job
cuts. Cameron agreed to a Scottish independence referendum in
September 2014 which resulted in a "No" vote. He is the first
Conservative Party leader to support same-sex marriage. In June
2016 Cameron's promise of a referendum on UK membership in
the European Union took place. Fifty-two percent of those voting
elected to "leave" the EU. Stock markets plunged the next day at
the prospect of reducing free trade with Europe. Some experts

blamed the vote on the anger of voters who have lost financial ground since the 2008 financial crisis and the imposition by the Conservatives of austerity measures.[14] After the vote Cameron announced his resignation.

According to studies, homelessness increased in Britain in the three years leading up to 2014.[15] This may be evidence that contradicts the use of austerity to improve the economy. Even though unemployment is down in all industrialized Western countries as of this writing, a question that must be considered is how to bring the level of wages to the point where at least those who are willing to work can find jobs that provide the basic necessities, including a place to live.

Yet the post-war welfare state — with its guarantees of universal health care and retirement supports — is no longer in dispute among liberals or conservatives in Great Britain. The pivot between political viewpoints is only in the degree that social supports are to be maintained and the extent to which tax policy and economic stimulation affect the public good.

In 2016 London elected Sadiq Khan, the son of a bus driver and member of the Labour party as mayor. He became London's first Muslim mayor after months of acrimonious debate and religious epithets being used against him in the campaign. But with the country's planned exit from the European Union and a reduction in free trade with its European trading partners many economists were predicting a British recession.

Despite having no written constitution, it probably is safe to say that the bulk of British citizens are as committed to their model of democracy as those of any country on earth.

CHINA

The People's Republic of China was established by Mao Zedong in 1949 after pushing out the elected government of Chiang Kai-Shek. According to its written constitution, "The People's Republic of China is a socialist state under the people's democratic dictatorship led by the working class based on the alliance of the workers and peasants." The constitution of China also mentions that "all power belongs to the people." It forbids foreign investment in China by outside powers.[16]

Clearly in China, the words "the people's democratic dictatorship" and "all power belongs to the people" are meaningless phrases. For all practical purposes the Communist Party is "the people."

Although China has many laws, as does every major modern country, the rule of law does not apply there because the Communist Party can change the laws at any time to suit its own purposes. If the Party decides to put everyone in jail who has said anything negative about the government, confiscate a person's property, nationalize foreign investments, or allow environmental degradation in the name of "progress" – and it has done many of these things – there would be no law to stop it from doing so.[17]

Under some of China's emperors there was a sense of responsibility for the good of the people and accountability for actions of government officials, but the accountability always was upward toward the Emperor rather than to a set of laws that affected everyone equally. The current Chinese political system does not greatly differ from the hierarchical systems of the past in this respect, as accountability is not to "the people" in any meaningful sense. Individuals with grievances have no recourse to courts or rule of law. They basically are dependent on the whim of their local officials, who still take bribes, steal peasant lands, and ignore environmental problems that have the potential to disrupt the lives of this population of over one billion. China's authoritarian government is notorious for not overseeing the administrative practices of its provincial rulers, which has resulted in serious workplace abuses and environmental degradation that affects people throughout the country.[18]

Lack of interest in the common good has traditionally led to stagnation of ideas and economic progress, such as when Emperor Zhang (who reigned during the years 75-88) sailed across the Indian Ocean to initiate trade, but subsequent emperors decided to cut back exploration to save funds. A mechanical clock was invented during the Song Dynasty (around the year 1000) and later abandoned.

In the mid-1980s, there was a slight loosening of restrictions on free speech and greater tolerance of protests under the guidance of Party General Secretary Hu Yaobang. Upon his death in 1989, liberals and students mourned him with demonstrations at Tiananmen Square in Beijing. The government labeled the demonstrations as counter-revolutionary. After seven weeks, the conservative regime decided on a crackdown, using tanks to slaughter hundreds of demonstrators. Massive arrests occurred of those considered sympathetic to the democratic movement, and those within the Communist Party who were considered sympathetic were purged. Discussion of the incident was officially prohibited[19] and still is as of this writing.[20]

The backing of new ideas and inventions has greatly improved in China in the twenty-first century with a renewed emphasis on education and personal achievement, resulting in the encouragement of some innovation and development in science as long as it is tied to commercial development. As we can see by the products on the shelves of countries around the world, China now benefits from an ability to learn manufacturing skills and improve them in a way that has given its economy a boost and made it one of the three largest in the world.[417] Yet its industry is largely based on making "improvements" in products originally developed in other countries.

Some historians wonder if a country without "rule of law" like China can continue its exponential growth. There is no accountability to "the people" in any meaningful sense. China is growing rapidly without any of these features seen in Western societies. As the economic life of the Chinese people improves will there be greater demands for democratic accountability? Can China's economy continue to improve without advancing personal freedom?

The economic boom in China has not affected all of its people equally. Many have been forced from their traditional rural homes to industrial sites where they have been treated as serfs. These workers are forced to live under squalid conditions where they are given room and board and very low pay. There has been a spate of suicides among workers forced to work in these situations.

At the Foxconn plant in Wuhan, where electronic equipment for Apple, Sony, Nintendo, HP, and other large companies is made, eighteen workers threw themselves from the roof of the plant in 2010, and 150 also threatened suicide in 2012. According to one worker: "We were put to work without any training and paid piecemeal. The assembly line ran very fast and after just one morning we all had blisters and the skin on our hands were black. The factory was also really choked with dust and no one could bear it." About five percent of the workforce leaves the plant monthly with no clear alternative means of support.[22]

The Communist Party also still frowns on any original thought outside its rigid idea of what contributes to economic growth. Even a depiction of homosexuality is banned in the media.[23]

Despite its poor human rights record, China no longer is at

odds with the rest of world and has become the largest supplier of manufactured goods for its markets. As China sought membership in the World Trade Organization – it was admitted in 2011 – it was forced to make some improvements in the area of human rights.[24] Many have observed that China has in some ways become a capitalist country. Hopefully the economic benefits that have benefited the country as a whole will continue to trickle down to its people at all levels.

FRANCE

France is known for the great beauty of its capitol – Paris – and the varied magnificence of its countryside, from Atlantic seaside resorts to storied Alpine ski country. Its wine is legendary and its food has served as an example for the development of cuisine for many cultures – having great influence on American food and wine appreciation, even having penetrated modern Britain.

There is an ongoing conversation about whether France can be described by the term "exceptionalism" – whether France is different than other nations and has made a unique contribution to the world. Many French people believe that their country, with its history of overthrowing tyranny, its *Declaration of the Rights of Man and Citizen*, and its model of living that many consider exemplary, is an example for the world of the "highest expression of civilization."[25] During its Revolution, France overthrew a Church run by greed and self-serving priests, only to have a majority of its citizens once again become Catholics, until again becoming predominantly secular in modern times. After the French Revolution its goal was to spread its ideas of Liberty, Equality, and Fraternity throughout Europe via Napoleon – whether Europe wanted the favor or not.

France experienced a variety of political regimes after 1789, including a series of revolutions in the nineteenth century, with struggles between conservatives, Catholics, and monarchists of the Right, and republicans and socialists on the Left. With the establishment of the Third Republic in 1870 France finally achieved a fairly stable political system, which endured until World War II. As one author puts it: "France is a country where, since 1789, "every political regime has ended in a coup d'état (a French term), revolution, or war and there have been fifteen different constitutions."[26]

The current French constitution was adopted at the beginning of the Fifth Republic in 1958. After years of chaos and near civil war following World War II, the people backed a new constitution to give the strongest powers to its president – initially Charles de Gaulle – of any major democracy. Article 2 states that: "France is a republic, indivisible, secular, democratic, and social. . . . Its principle is government of the people, for the people, and by the people," which sounds a lot like Lincoln's Gettysburg Address. The President is elected by a majority of the popular vote and all laws are passed by the French Parliament. Article 66 of the Constitution states that "no one is to be arbitrarily retained, and that the judicial authority shall ensure respect for this principle."[27]

Ever since the beginning of the Fifth Republic, the lives of French citizens have been affected by the state to a larger extent than in most countries that could be called democratic. The fact that France is a republic means that it is intended to be a country of equality of opportunity with no hereditary privileges. It has created a social contract where the government reaches into the daily lives of its citizens from cradle to grave. It is routinely involved in their childcare, education, healthcare, work hours, and pensions.

The educational system is standardized in an effort to support equality but leaves little room for creativity, even at the university level. Students are identified early on for their potential and skills that are likely to fit a profile for a profession, and a continuing pursuit of that path is encouraged. Thus, while seen as a democratic society, choice in education – at least in the public schools which the majority attends – is limited. The Grand Écoles (elite schools) are run for those who are identified as having the potential to become the country's leaders. Graduation is based on a make-or-break system of passing strict standardized exams or being left in limbo until they can be retaken, which leads to unemployment and a waste of years by young persons who could be otherwise trained or employed.

As stated in its Constitution, France is a "secular state." All religions are tolerated officially as long as they respect France's traditions.[28] It is considered inappropriate for office holders to espouse religious views, as they are irrelevant to what the French consider qualifications for holding office. The wearing of religious head coverings is banned in state schools, but apparently in practice only for Muslims.

A good deal of major French industry is under government auspices including part of the banking, airline, power and aerospace industries. Yet in the realm of equality of the sexes male chauvinism lives on. Women rarely are promoted to top management jobs and pay is still unequal between men and women for similar positions. However, the disparities are not as great as in Germany and Britain.[29]

Unions represent about eight percent of workers, mainly in the public sector. Yet France's health care system has been highly rated by its citizens for years, and there is generous family leave for maternity and paternity. Taxes remain high to support the welfare system to which the French people have become accustomed – they complain about the taxes but they now are accustomed to their government support system and very few would give it up in exchange for a tax reduction. In 2002, and more recently, the French government attempted some reforms in the welfare system to make it more affordable for the state, but these changes were strongly resisted by the powerful unions.

In relations with the United States, France, under Jacques Chirac, refused to back the attack on Iraq in 2003, disputing the American claim of weapons of mass destruction. It turned out that France was correct.

In 2005, Paris was subjected to riots from North African immigrants living in the *banlieue* (poor suburb) north of the city. They were upset because of continuing high poverty and poor job opportunities, and erupted after two teenagers evading police were electrocuted on the wires of an electricity substation. The riots spread to a number of large French cities which challenged the country's image of a tolerant democracy. Chirac reacted by promising to expand France's employment opportunities.[30]

In the twenty-first century there has been concern among the French left and right that any administration would be unable to control the economy due to the policies of globalization, which allow large corporate players to write their own trade rules with impunity. When Nicolas Sarkozy became President in 2007, he attempted to supersede party politics by claiming a centrist approach and emphasized the importance of religion under a secular government.

Hoping to resurrect the economy in the midst of the world-wide recession that began in 2008, Sarkozy ended the thirty-five-hour work week and provided tax relief that mainly benefited the wealthy. He put limits on immigration and expelled large numbers of illegal immigrants, but amended the constitution to put new limits on presidential terms. Sarkozy emphasized improved relations with Britain and the US as essential to working together to face economic challenges, but publicly stated his displeasure with the American origins of the financial crisis. Budget cuts in

France, Germany, Britain and some other European countries were part of an austerity program that affects the economies of those countries to this day. But these measures have not worked to restore the economy in France or anywhere.[31]

Since 2012, Francois Hollande, a Socialist, has held the office of President. He recently defended labor reforms making it easier for employers to hire and fire employees in an effort to make the economy more healthy and lower government expenses. Strikes in the energy sector challenged his plans, but employer groups do not want Hollande to give in to labor demands for fear of further weakening an already sluggish economy.[32]

France does have an advantage over many other nations in its centrally controlled planning and economy that oversees its infrastructure, industry, and cradle-to-grave welfare system. However, its relative cohesion as a society is expensive – public spending is over one half of the gross domestic product which must be supported by a high level of taxation. This affects annual growth and keeps it below the average of some of its neighboring countries.[33]

One might think, with the historic clash of opinions among the French people between left and right and all gradients in between, that chaos would reign. But as we review the degree of actual democracy in major countries, it seems clear that it is not constitutions alone that make a society democratic. One is tempted to say, with the French, that it is a certain "Je ne sais quoi" (I don't know what) that maintains the country's democratic spirit, but since actually knowing that is the theme of this book, I will give it my best try.

For most French people, a respect for democracy is ingrained in their way of life. Although often engaged in heated arguments on topics ranging from taxes to life's meaning, there is a basic respect for others, including their right to express their views and to disagree. Over time, this view ultimately has resulted in the appreciation of the human creative impulse as well as in stability. There seems to be a general understanding that to disagree can lead to an ultimate agreement or at least an agreement to disagree. This is seen in the lived reality and quality of French life. France's lifestyle – including its food and art – has become a magnet for others and has led to that country being the most visited tourist destination on earth. One might say that the French have a passion for civility.

As of this writing, democracy in France takes another tiny step forward with the closing of the Champs-Elysees, the most famous thoroughfare in Paris with its Arc de Triomphe and array of international flags, to traffic one Sunday per month in deference to pedestrians. For Parisians to give up their beloved cars and traffic jams can be seen as a possible move in the direction of greater human encounter. Its national motto, rooted in its Revolution – "*Liberté, égalité, fraternité*" (Liberty, equality, fraternity) – clearly has become infused into the daily life of its citizens.

GERMANY

Article 20 of the Constitution of the Federal Republic of Germany states: (1) "The Federal Republic of Germany shall be a democratic and social federal state," and (2) "All state authority shall emanate from the people." The Chancellor (Prime Minister) and the cabinet make up the chief executive body. Similar to many democratic governments, the parliament consists of an upper and lower house.[34]

After the Second World War Germany was divided into four occupation zones under each of the victors: The US, Britain, France and the Soviet Union. The first three eventually merged into West Germany (Federal Republic of Germany) and the Eastern zone (the so-called German Democratic Republic) remained under the domination of the Soviets. Germany, like much of Europe, needed many years of extensive rebuilding.

During the trials of Nazi leaders in 1945-46 twenty-two former officers accused of war crimes were tried and ten were sentenced to death. There was a program of "denazification" in West Germany under General Eisenhower, a conscious effort to erase all remnants of Nazi philosophy, laws, symbols, street names, and monuments, and to remove all ex-Nazis from public life. The European Recovery Program, or Marshall Plan, was initiated by the US in 1948 under Truman to provide aid and avoid the radicalization that had led to the rise of the Nazis after the First World War.[35]

The first Chancellor of West Germany was Konrad Adenauer, who served from 1949 to 1963 and organized the Christian Democratic Union, a political party that still is a major player in German politics.

Amidst growing hostilities with the Western powers, the Soviets stopped all access to Berlin, which was surrounded by East Germany, during a one-year blockade beginning in June of 1948. Western Allies began a massive airlift during which over a million tons of food and fuel were delivered. The Soviets were forced to give up after it became clear that the blockade was ineffective.

In the late 1940s the Americanization of West Germany began, with American popular culture being readily adopted, including Coca-Cola, jazz and jeans. East Germany became part of the Eastern European Soviet Bloc under their "centrally planned economy." A number of five year plans only led to chronic economic stagnation.[36]

Once stability was established West Germany experienced rapid economic growth. Over the next forty years – until unification in 1989 – there was considerable jealousy by those in the East, who often risked their lives to escape. The Berlin Wall was erected in 1961 to keep them in, and torn apart in 1989 by those seeking souvenirs when East German authorities no longer blocked migration to the West as the Soviet Bloc of nations began to dissolve.

Helmut Kohl continued as the Chancellor of Germany after unification until 1998. Beginning in the 1950s and continuing to this day West Germany – and then Germany – has experienced an incredible boom and now is the healthiest economic player in Europe. Some of the large international companies headquartered in Germany include Bayer, Mercedes-Benz, BMW, SAP, Volkswagen, Audi, Adidas, Porsche, and DHL. Germany has few natural resources and its economy is based primarily on manufacturing and exports.[37]

In 1992, Germany and its European trade partners formed the European Union to create an economic, monetary, and political alliance and to increase cooperation between nations. The Union has, for the most part, been a success, but Europe has been slow to climb out of the economic slump that began in 2008.[38]

Gerhard Schroeder was Chancellor of Germany from 1998 to 2005. He led a coalition of the Democratic Socialist Party and the Greens to form a majority. Schroeder, a Socialist, initiated considerable reforms, including phasing out of nuclear power in favor of renewable energy and allowing civil unions for same-sex partners. He had exceptional rapport with other leaders, including Putin of Russia and Chirac of France.[39]

All Germans are expected to participate in the national healthcare system that is the oldest in Europe. There are two categories of healthcare membership: a public fund and a private fund for higher income earners. Healthcare premiums are automatically deducted from the paychecks of those who work.

For a long time, Germany has been a magnet for immigration from other parts of Europe, Africa and the Middle East due to its strong economy. In 2001 a new commission set up guidelines for immigration, establishing an asylum process for those who could demonstrate persecution in their native countries.[40] More recently there has been an immigrant crisis in Europe made up of over one million refugees from the civil war in Syria and from poverty and oppression in other countries. Germany has been in the lead in accepting immigrants and working to find a solution to that problem.

Germany refused to become a part of the "Coalition of the willing" of George W. Bush to invade Iraq in 2003, but the war was supported publicly by Angela Merkel, who at that point was Secretary-General of the opposition Christian Democratic Party.

Merkel became Chancellor in 2005 in a close contest and remains in that post as of this writing. She was the first female and youngest person to attain that position at the age of 51. She obtained a PhD in Physics and later switched to Chemistry. Soon after taking office she put forward an Eight Point Program for goals she considered essential to strengthen Germany, including energy, financial policies and health reforms. She was re-elected as Chancellor by her party in 2009 by a large majority.[41]

Merkel has visited Israel on four occasions, and has joined Israel in opposing the Palestinian bid for UN membership. However, she also has criticized Israel for building settlements in Palestinian territory. She has been President of the European Union Council and the chair of the G8 coalition of world leaders, and remains popular as of this writing.

Recently, she has led a coalition of European nations to help bail out the debt-ridden economy of Greece that started during the financial crisis of 2008 when money stopped flowing into that country. Greece could not devalue its currency to increase exports as it now shared the same currency as its partners in the European Union. The low point was in 2015 when banks had to be closed because they did not have enough funds to operate. Greece's debt has been continually renegotiated as its economy slowly improves.

Germany remains economically the strongest member of the European Union. Its unemployment rate has decreased steadily since the 2008 financial meltdown and it retains its place as the leader of interventions when required to ease financial crises in other European countries. With the help of the western powers Germany recovered from the devastating effects of the last World War, which it has admitted – by reparations – that it brought on itself, but it continues to build partnerships with others via the EU and trade organizations that make it a major, and essential, player on the world stage. Despite a recent resurgence of right-wing fanaticism that coincided with difficult economic times, Germany remains a steady partner in fashioning a more democratic Europe.

RUSSIA

In the twentieth century Russia experienced war, revolution and civil war leading to tremendous political and social change and economic transformation. In December 1991 the Soviet Union collapsed. Boris Yeltsin became President of the new Russian Federation and was in office until 1999. He was succeeded by Vladimir Putin, the first elected President of the new Russia.

Russia is considered a presidential-style parliamentary federal republic. Its current constitution was drafted in 1993, two years after the fall of the Soviet Union. It speaks in its Preamble of: "acknowledging the immortality of its democratic functions." Article 1 promises: "The Russian Federation shall be a democratic, federative, law-based state with a republican form of government. Article 2 states: "Human beings and human rights and freedoms shall be of the highest value. Recognition of, and respect for, the protection of human and civil rights and freedoms shall be the duty of the state." Article 120 requires judges to act independently and in a way subject to law.[42]

Russia, the largest country in the world geographically, is stunning in its vastness. The area between Moscow and Saint Petersburg where most of the population lives is covered with what seems like an endless expanse of forests and lakes, and includes the Volga River, which twists and turns majestically for much of the distance between the two cities.

At this writing, Russia is under what some observers call an "electoral authoritarian" regime. Elections take place and other democratic processes and institutions exist, but control is tightly held by the central government headed by Putin, and the rule of law frequently is violated. The school curriculum is standardized throughout the country.

From childhood, Putin wanted to be a KGB agent. Born in 1952, he grew up in Saint Petersburg in one of a series of large apartment complexes built to house an expanding population in the Soviet era. To work toward his goal of becoming a KGB agent he attended Leningrad University while studying martial arts. Fighting and winning were passions. Upon graduation he attained his dream and celebrated with a friend, although he couldn't tell his friend why they were celebrating.[43]

Over the next few years, in the middle to late 1970s, Putin spent much of his time pursuing dissidents under a new law. He also continued his training in a Moscow school for spies in 1984. He then was assigned to Dresden, where he moved with his pregnant wife and child. His assignment was to gather information about westerners, particularly US military operations. He was expected to recruit agents from Latin America to spy on Americans, but wasn't given enough funds to create much interest.[44]

During Putin's time in East Germany the Soviet Union

reached a turning point. Mikhail Gorbachev, seeing the beginnings of the unraveling of the power that held the country
together, initiated a policy of *perestroika* – restructuring of the
State, which then led to *glasnost*, or openness, presumably the
opposite of secrecy. In 1987, Gorbachev commuted the sentences
of 140 dissidents. There were attempts to modernize the state and
install greater flexibility in light of the successes of western economies. But this limited loosening of absolute power only opened
the way for only greater dissention which pried the door open
until the Soviet Union altogether collapsed.[45]

In his next position Putin became an assistant to Anatoly
Sobchak, the first democratically elected major of Saint Petersburg
who he knew through a brief term of employment at Leningrad
State University.[46]

In 1987, as an experiment, more than one name was allowed
on the ballot for the first time in the Soviet Union, thus a degree
of choice and democracy was introduced. In 1988, public speeches
denouncing the Soviet regime and debates discussing democracy
were held in public parks, which were for the most part allowed
by the authorities. Arrests of dissidents were eventually discon-
tinued, and censorship of movies and books gradually ended. A
new election law went into effect in late 1988, allowing voting for
more than one party. In the next year Communist party candidates were soundly defeated, but Gorbachev was re-elected as the
last President of the Soviet Union.[47]

When Gorbachev yielded power to Boris Yeltsin in 1989 it
seemed that the transition to democracy was assured. But in 1990
the Soviet Union could barely produce enough food to fill the
shelves of its shops. Communist hardliners attempted to reverse
democratic reforms in 1991; Yeltsin became a hero as he famously
rode on one of the tanks and the coup eventually failed.[48]

After having survived the oppression of the tsars and purges of the Soviet Union, the Russian people breathed the air of democracy for nearly ten years after the fall of the Soviet State on December 25, 1991. But as so often happens after the fall of oppression – particularly in countries where it is deeply ingrained – there was no clear shared vision of a path to a free society, and the trappings of oppression slowly crept back into place.

As Yeltsin tried to loosen the central control of power, one-time state assets were taken over by private entrepreneurs – often previous government officials – who strangled the economy by monopolizing all major assets and setting themselves up as a new oligarchy. They seized previously government-owned property that had no legal owners. Sobchak, for example, gave away Saint Petersburg apartments to his friends and relatives. Those who obtained timber, oil and other major industries made quick profits.[48]

Yeltsin's popularity plummeted during the latter part of his term. For most Russians the deterioration of the economy under what they considered capitalism and democracy was a great disappointment. The removal of economic controls led to hyperinflation and inequality with pockets of great wealth that had not been seen since the days of the tsars. The general level of income rose slowly during this period but the instability of government created an uncertainty to which Russians were unaccustomed.[50]

As deputy mayor of Saint Petersburg, Putin was largely responsible for security and the flow of information. To implement his duties he used the methods he had learned as a KGB agent, including wiretapping. His next job – which, according to his autobiography, he received through an anonymous "friend" – was as manager of presidential property at the Kremlin.[51]

In 1996 a war for independence in the Republic of Chechnya (in southern Russia) ended in a cease-fire. Hostilities continued, however, and in the late 1990s, there were bombings that killed hundreds of people, mainly in Moscow and the southern part of

Russia in what appeared to be terrorist attacks by Chechen rebels. Vladimir Putin, by then Prime Minister, announced his intent on television to "hunt down" the terrorists, creating an image of himself as the person to be most trusted in times of trouble.

In September 1999, a group of governors of the Duma, Russia's legislative body, wrote a letter to President Yeltsin asking him to yield power to Putin. On New Year's Eve, the largest secular holiday in Russia, Yeltsin resigned, apologizing for the shortcomings of Russian democracy to that point in time: "I am sorry that I did not live up to the hopes of the people who believed that we could, with a single effort, a single strong push, jump out of our gray, stagnant, totalitarian past and into a bright, wealthy, civilized future." This left Putin as acting president.[52]

From that point on, Putin ruled under the constitution left to him by Yeltsin, which allowed him to hold up a façade of democracy while maintaining the same degree of arbitrary power as had existed under the Soviets. All parts of the Russian Federation came under political control of Moscow, including the media.[53] Putin took significant steps to concentrate power in all major areas of government and the economy. Under Putin's "guidance," bills to enact these measures easily were passed in the Russian Duma.

Six days after his inauguration on May 7, 2000, Putin signed a decree and proposed a series of bills to consolidate legislative power. Some of this was based on the need to tighten a loose system of states with individual and contradictory policies, but some of it was simply to concentrate power in his hands. An editorial appeared in a popular daily paper, the *Kommersant*, stating: "The legislation you are proposing will place severe limitations on the independence and civil freedoms of tens of thousands of top-level Russian politicians, forcing them to take their bearings from a single person and follow his will."

In Putin's second day in office, police special forces with black masks and guns entered the office of a magazine editor who had been critical of him, roughed up some of the staff, and made off with boxes of paper files. This would become typical of the types of "warnings" that would be given to individuals and organizations who dared to voice criticism. Eventually the owner of that media group was arrested and charged with corruption in the purchase of another company.[54]

Typical of this tactic of oppression was the takeover of valuable businesses after the arrest of the owner, who would be hit with a series of charges after being exonerated for each charge in succession. Less than a year after Putin's inauguration all three major media organizations in Russia were under control of the state. [55]

Putin soon reversed the country's "no-strike-first" international nuclear weapons policy, which meant that he could use nuclear weapons "if other means of conflict resolution have been exhausted or deemed ineffective." He then established mandatory training requirements for reservists (all able-bodied Russian men).

In the 2003 Parliamentary elections, Putin's United Russia Party took nearly half the seats – a commanding number considering that the remainder was split among a number of other parties. International observers decried the level to which the Russian electoral process had deteriorated to the point where it no longer could be called a representative democracy.[56]

In March 2004 Putin stood for re-election. While he won easily, opposition candidates faced almost insurmountable obstacles, with many threats and irregularities in the conduct of the campaigns and election.

On September 1, 2004, terrorists attacked a school in the city of Beslan. Special forces were sent in and 300 people died. Putin's reaction was to announce that because of the threat to the country, a more central and strong authority was needed. From that time forward he would appoint governors and the mayor of Moscow himself for "security reasons." After that point the only federally elected official was the president himself.[57]

In 1995 the Russian government had asked the country's richest men for loans. When the government later defaulted, Mikhail Khodorskovsky was awarded Yukos, Russia' largest oil company. In the 1990s oil prices were low and things were not looking good for Yukos or its employees. But in the 2000s, when oil prices rose, Khodorskovsky became the richest man in Russia, and embarked on a program of social service organizations, including orphanages, university programs in the humanities, and internet cafés to increase learning and communication between his fellow Russians. Khodorskovsky pushed for his company to meet modern standards and to move in the direction of becoming a multinational corporation.

In 2003 officers of Khodorkovsky's company began to be arrested. Instead of leaving the country, he apparently decided that he was too powerful to be arrested himself and began a national lecture circuit to push his progressive ideas, including the cost to the Russian economy from corruption. In October he was arrested on six charges, including fraud and tax evasion. The next year he was sentenced to nine years in prison.[58] Amnesty International condemned this as one of many prosecutions of Russians at the whim of Putin. By 2011, human rights activists estimated that 15 percent of the Russian prison population was made up of former entrepreneurs.[59]

Alexander Litvinenko, a former FSB (Secret Police) agent, was poisoned in London in 2006. An investigation turned up the agent as polonium, a rare radioactive element that leaves traces everywhere it goes. This allowed British authorities to trace the polonium entering the country to two Russians – a former security agent and his business partner. Neither has faced extradition to stand trial.[60]

In 2007, Putin's two terms were about to expire. He chose Dmitri Medvedev, First Deputy Prime Minister, a lawyer with no leadership experience, to run for President while Putin remained in the office of Prime Minister still basically running the country.[61]

In 2010, Putin declared that human rights activists should expect to be "hit over the head with a stick," a milder punishment than the prison sentences that were given to some who opposed him. Putin became president again after Medvedev's term had run out, and Parliament immediately extended the term of President to two consecutive six year terms.[62]

In June 2012, after his election to his second term as president, Putin had the Duma pass a bill outlawing protests. The law's enforcement began in earnest with jailing three women of a group called Pussy Riot for a raucous political performance.[63]

One only can be astonished at the near-total reversal of what seemed like democratic reform in Russia. Some Russians favor Putin because they are financially better off than under the Soviets, and many also are proud that Russia now appears strong. There is little optimism about the future.[64] But Russians no longer have to fear starvation. Random imprisonment and murder no longer affects millions of people.

Upward mobility in Russia often is based on political affiliation rather than talent. Democratic aspirations routinely are quashed. But most Russians focus on their personal and family lives without encountering the dangers that come with political aspirations. For the time being the Russian government has firm control over political and economic life. Change in the direction of true democracy only can be seen as a glimmer of light in the far distance by those who choose to hold that vision in their minds.

UNITED STATES

In 1940 Vladimir Nabokov, the famous Russian author, took a ship to the United States with his family to flee the Nazi conquest of Europe. He was from an upper-class Saint Petersburg family. What impressed him most upon de-embarkation was the natural and informal way that customs agents treated each other and everyone in line, even telling a few jokes. There was none of the deference to those of wealth and power that was customary in the Europe Nabokov just had left. This was a living example to him of the basic American belief that everyone is as good as everyone else that he encountered in his first few steps on American soil.[65]

The Constitution of the United States was written in 1787 after the Articles of Confederation created by the thirteen colonies that rebelled against England failed to bring about unity of purpose. In their trade and encounters with other nations each colony under the Articles was allowed to pursue its own separate interests, leading to them work at cross purposes and weakening their potential effectiveness as nation.

The Preamble to the US Constitution begins with the words: "We the People" and goes on to state that "all power is originally vested in, and consequently derived from, the people." In 1787 "democratic self-government existed almost nowhere on earth. Kings, emperors, czars, princes, sultans, moguls, feudal lords, and tribal chiefs held sway across the globe."[66] Now let's look at the promises of the American founders to the generations that followed and see how well they were kept.

James Madison had his concerns about the viability of democracy that he expressed in *The Federalist,* Number 55. In "all very numerous assemblies, of whatever character composed, passion never fails to wrest the scepter from reason." Madison knew that the nature of human beings was not always rational, nor even always in tune with their long-term self-interest. And he wondered, as did a long line of thinkers before him, if reason would win out.

The Constitution attempted to undo some of the abuses of privilege of other countries such as England, insisting in Article I that members of the House of Representatives be directly elected, forbidding property rights as a qualification for voting, and eliminating hereditary titles of nobility. Article II provided that the President should be elected by the Electoral College and not attain office by hereditary title. The President would be a public servant who would receive a salary to eliminate the practice of government being run by the elite, and would appoint Federal judges and be the commander-in-chief of the military. Article III provided that Federal Court justices shall serve for life and receive a salary "that shall not be diminished" to avoid manipulation by those opposing them. The trial of all crimes would be by jury. Article IV guaranteed a "Republican" form of government based on the will of all the people, not just for those in positions of power. Article V allowed amendment to the Constitution if legislators did not enact laws that guarantee the rights of all. Article VI stated that all foreign treaties shall be made "under the authority of the United States" and that "No religious test shall ever be required as a qualification to any office." The last Article, number VII, prescribed that nine states would be required for ratification.[67]

The Bill of Rights, composed of the first ten amendments, was adopted in 1791 after some convincing of the others by Anti-Federalists (those opposed to centralized power). James Madison eventually agreed that it was needed to ensure that some of abuses that had been seen under the rule of England would not continue. According to Madison, a Bill of Rights would hopefully "counteract the impulses of interest and passion." It would mitigate the forces of those who would attempt to bend the Constitution to their own interests and whims.

The First Amendment guarantees freedom of speech and of the press, peaceful assembly, and the right to petition the government for the redress of grievances.[68] The Second Amendment states: "A well-regulated Militia, being necessary to the security of a free State, the right of the people to keep and bear Arms, shall not be infringed." The degree to which this amendment affects individual rights to own guns of any type still is being debated. The Third Amendment outlaws quartering soldiers in private homes, with a possible exception of in time of war. The Fourth establishes guarantees against "unreasonable searches and seizures" and states that search warrants only can be issued for "probable cause." The Fifth provides indictment for major crimes by a grand jury, protects individuals from being witnesses against themselves, and forbids the taking of private property "without just compensation."

The Sixth Amendment ensures a speedy trial for criminal prosecution by an impartial jury and the right to confront witnesses; the Seventh ensures trial by jury; the Eighth forbids excessive bail; the Ninth states that rights not enumerated in the Constitution belong to the people; the Tenth, in slightly different language, reserves to the states, or to the people, all powers not mentioned in the Constitution.

For those who wonder if democracy was on the mind of the founders, James Wilson of Pennsylvania, a Constitution signer and one of the original Supreme Court Justices, equated the establishment of the American republic with democracy in a speech supporting the Constitution's ratification: "The Democratic principle is carried into every part of the government."[69]

The American Constitution was a radical document for its time. It enumerated specific rights, and anticipated that new amendments would be needed as the country and world changed.

The founders were among the educated elite of their day and were familiar with the history of the world going back to ancient times. They knew that customs and views of right and wrong continually evolved and created the amendment process so that the new country also could evolve.

Slavery was in great dispute, and the ultimate compromise in the Constitution allowed three-fifths of all slaves to be counted toward government representation. The result, however, was that the Southern states had extra representation in Congress by which they could sway votes. Slavery was not overturned until after the Civil War by the Thirteenth Amendment in 1865, and its ramifications still reverberate in large and small ways in many places in the country, with voting privileges being disputed in our own day, despite the passage of the Fifteenth Amendment in 1870 forbidding the denial of voting rights based on "race, color, or previous condition of servitude."

The Sixteenth Amendment established the Federal Income tax and the Eighteenth prohibited the sale of alcoholic beverages (later repealed).

At the time of founding of the writing of the US Constitution women were not considered likely to even hold jobs or property and it took until the Nineteenth Amendment in 1920 to establish their right to vote, based largely on the urging of President Woodrow Wilson during World War I to consider women as "partners. . . in this war."[70] In light of continued efforts to limit the right of voting based on race, the twenty-fourth amendment outlawed the use of a tax on the right to vote.

As we have discussed, those who were considered to be included in the definition of "The People" at the time of the writing of the US Constitution has continued to evolve. The Founders understood that the Constitution was incomplete and probably always would be, requiring updating as the definition and rights of "We the People" expand.[71]

During the US Presidential election of November 2000, George W. Bush became president with 500,000 fewer popular votes than Al Gore. The last time that the popular vote yielded a different result than the Electoral College was 1888.

Bush campaigned on a platform of "compassionate conservatism" and of being a "uniter" rather than a "divider." After the election, Dick Cheney, Bush's Vice President, was charged with getting the message out regarding the priorities of the new administration. His communication to Republican legislators was clear – they needed to get on board with the new agenda: a trillion-dollar tax cut, a sharp increase in military spending, opposition to the Kyoto environmental agreement to cut greenhouse emissions, and ignoring the dictates of the International Criminal Court. Nothing was open to negotiation or compromise.[72]

While Bush emphasized the need to work with Democrats after such a close election, Cheney pushed the opposite view. His agenda was clear: "We've got a good program, and we're going to pursue it." Education reform was a priority for Bush; it wasn't on the table for Cheney. Getting drugs to seniors was important to Bush; it never was a priority for Cheney.[73]

Beginning in early 2001, Cheney and Bush began to contact Republicans in an effort to create $1.5 trillion dollars in tax cuts. They used ads against Democrats, and Cheney went on air during a talk show to pressure Rhode Island Republican Lincoln Chafee, who had originally opposed the cuts, to support them. They were eventually passed, and would greatly increase the deficit in a country that was about to pay for two expensive wars. Cheney also was able to talk Allen Greenspan, Chairman of the Federal Reserve, into supporting a second round of cuts before the 2004 election.[74]

After the attacks by Al Qaida on the World Trade Center and

the Pentagon on September 11, 2001, most of the US was united behind Bush as he made an eloquent plea for unity:

Terrorist attacks can shake the foundations of our biggest buildings, but they cannot touch the foundation of America. These acts shatter steel, but they cannot dent the steel of American resolve. . . . America was targeted for attack because we're the brightest beacon for freedom and opportunity in the world. And no one will keep that light from shining. . . . America and our friends and allies join with all those who want peace and security in the world and we stand together to win the war against terrorism.

Bush also visited Washington DC area mosques soon after-wards to ensure the American people that the attacks were by extreme terrorists and by no means represented a majority of Muslims.

Soon afterward, combined US and British forces began an effort to remove Osama bin Laden's Al Qaeda organization from Afghanistan, where it had been sheltered by the reaction-ary Taliban Muslim cult. Three years and billions of dollars later a shaky democracy was set up in Afghanistan under Hamid Karzai, who was President from 2004 to 2014.

Soon after the attacks, Dick Cheney saw fit to take the legal leash off of any measures he deemed appropriate to fight the "war on terror." He allowed foreign intelligence agencies to spy on Americans. He supported stripping terror subjects of their traditional rights under international law by claiming a need for confinement and torture as a means to protect Americans and win the "war." Cheney and Bush were supported by the opinion of White House Counsel John Yoo, who held that any measures short of telling a prisoner that you are going to kill him or bury-ing him alive was legal under international law.[75]

In September 2002, Cheney had a meeting with Dick Armey,

Republican Majority Leader of the US House of Representatives. Cheney presented a case to Armey of what he called "weapons of mass destruction" that he claimed were held by Saddam Hussein, the brutal dictator of Iraq, despite the fact that no evidence of such weapons was turned up by US intelligence.[76] This same line of reasoning was used to convince Congress to back an attack on Iraq.

On February 5, 2003, Secretary of State Colin Powell appeared before the UN to argue the case for the dangerous weapons allegedly held by Iraq, but he failed to convince most Security Council members, including France, Russia, China, and Germany. Powell also claimed that there was an association between Iraq and the al Qaeda terrorists for which there was no evidence. Powell later publicly regretted having given that speech.

The US invaded Iraq with its one ally – Britain – in March of 2003.[77] They were able to topple its government in weeks, with Saddam Hussein eventually found hiding. He was hanged in 2006. In May, George Bush stated that major combat operations had ended in Iraq, but that was only the beginning of a quagmire that has lasted until this day. After an interim government Jalal Talibani was elected President in 2005 and served until 2014. The region continues to be rocked by civil war, including suicide bombings and attacks on government personnel. The door also was opened for the Isis cult that threatens to overrun the Middle East.

In the fall of 2008, the US entered into a financial crisis unmatched since the Great Depression of the 1930s. In 1999 the US Congress and President Clinton had repealed the main provisions of the 1933 Glass-Steagall Act, which separated commercial and investment banking. Banks then were free to engage in investment activities with the money of their customers. By 2007, huge profits were being made in commissions by brokers who steered customers to investments in "securities" based on the price of US housing that was bubbling up to unsustainable levels.

People could purchase homes for little or no down payment. That bubble burst due to the inability of many home buyers to make their payments, leading to the most severe economic downturn in seventy years.

The stimulus package that Bush pushed through Congress, the Troubled Asset Relief Program, or TARP, was a $700 billion direct subsidy for banks to keep them in business with the hope that they would loan out the money. For the most part the banks did not loan the money to individuals but held on to the funds or used it for acquisitions.[78]

Elizabeth Warren was asked to come to Washington by Senator Harry Reid to sit on a committee that would oversee the use of the funds. The committee would be called the Congressional Oversight Panel, or COP. The only problem was that COP had no actual legal authority to do its job – it only could "write reports."[79]

One bright spot in Bush's legacy was his funding of relief for Africa. In 2003 he founded the President's Emergency Plan for AIDS Relief (PEPFAR) which has given over $15 million dollars for HIV/AIDS and malaria to people on that continent. Perhaps there is an element of the compassionate conservative in him after all. However, by the time his second term was coming to a close he was extremely unpopular, even among those who had elected him. He was not invited to attend the Republican National Convention of 2008, although he did address the crowd briefly by video.

Barack Obama, an Illinois legislator, came to the attention of the world with his keynote speech at the 2004 Democratic Convention in Kansas City. The most remembered line from that speech was "There's not a Black America and White America and Latino America and Asian America; there's the United States of America." For some this meant that the country should look forward to an era where race does not matter; for others it pointed to an erasure of identity that could omit the elements of cultural difference and history.[80]

In his best-selling book, *The Audacity of Hope*, Obama wrote of the long difficult grind of campaigning for office and having his name confused with the most famous terrorist of the age. He discussed the importance of one of the traits that had helped him succeed since becoming a community activist in Chicago – listening attentively to others. The book offers "Personal reflections on those values and ideals that have led me to public life, some thoughts on the ways that our current political discourse unnecessarily divides us, and my own best assessment. . . of the ways we can ground our politics in the notion of a common good."[81]

He discusses the political process used by the US Senate. Decisions about which bills to support are made off the floor in conference rooms: "In the world's greatest deliberative body, no one is listening." He recalls the national strife when he was sworn in as Senator from Illinois for the first time in 2005: "Across the spectrum of issues, Americans disagreed: on Iraq, taxes, abortion, guns, the Ten Commandments, gay marriage, immigration, trade, education policy, environmental regulation, the size of government, and the role of the courts."[82] He campaigned for President and defeated John McCain in 2008. The economic crisis likely helped him – Republicans were widely blamed for the Great Recession that started that year. After the election, Obama appointed Hillary Clinton as Secretary of State.

Obama's accomplishments as President include a number of areas that have made the country safer and function better. There are other areas in which his policies have been a disappointment to many of his supporters. In fairness, he only had a Democratic legislature during the first two years in office.

The first bill he signed was the Lilly Ledbetter Fair Pay Act of 2009, eliminating the statute of limitations for equal-pay lawsuits. Other laws extended health care coverage for poor children, reestablished funding for embryonic stem cell research, and increased Pell Grants to support College Education for low income students. He has appointed two women to the US Supreme Court – Sonia Sotomayor and Elena Kagan.

In 2009 he signed a Hate Crimes Prevention Act to punish violence against persons based on sexual orientation, and repealed the "Don't Ask, Don't Tell" policy initiated by Bill Clinton which prevented openly gay and lesbian individuals from serving in the military. That same year he proposed new regulations on power plants, factories, and oil refineries for the purpose of limiting greenhouse gas emissions and to slow global warming.

Obama had many of the same economic advisors as did Bill Clinton, including Wall Street insiders such as Timothy Geithner and Larry Summers. Immediately after taking office he signed another stimulus bill, the $747 billion American Recovery and Reinvestment Act. It was expected to provide an additional jolt to the economy and help the auto industry reorganize. But such money was very slow to "trickle down" to the benefit of the average American.

In the Middle East, Obama spoke at Cairo University in 2009 in an effort to improve relations between the US and Arab countries, and then condemned the attack on protestors against the elections in Iran in June. In 2010, he objected to plans by the Israeli government to expand settlements in Arab neighborhoods, but still increased military aid to Israel. He pushed the military to continue the hunt for Osama bin Laden; Navy Seals found and assassinated Bin Laden on May 1, 2011.

A key piece of legislation signed by Obama was the Affordable Care Act (ACA) of 2010, which provided health care for millions, but at considerable expense to employers, many of which were small companies that were severely stressed by the additional expense. Before the 2012 election, Obama announced his support for same-sex marriage, after which public opinion also turned around, as did the US Supreme Court, which overturned the Defense of Marriage Act in 2015.

Obama continued his efforts to build international ties through diplomatic moves. In 2013 the US began negotiations with Iran to eliminate the possibility of developing nuclear weapons, and in 2015 a deal was reached. That same year Obama made a trip to Africa, praising African leaders for progress toward democracy and chastising them for allowing discrimination and perpetuating themselves in office. In 2014, he announced plans to rebuild relationships with Cuba which had been broken since Fidel Castro came to power in 1959.

Obama's campaign promises have not always been realized, sometime due to congressional obstruction. At other times he has not made a clear case for what he wants to happen. After being elected during the economic downturn he promised that he would seek tax increases for families making over $250,000, but abandoned that idea even before being sworn in. He said that he would close the Guantanamo Prison in Cuba that had opened in 2002 where suspected "enemy combatants" have been held since the beginning of the Afghan war, yet it remains open in 2016. In 2011, he promised that the US would be 80% dependent on clean energy by 2015, which was not achieved. In 2014, he promised that the total withdrawal of troops from Afghanistan was to be complete by the end of 2016, but as of this writing, he has decided to leave about 8,000 troops in the country due to continued instability. Obama authorized funds to train rebels in Syria in 2013, and said that he would attack to remove President Assad if he continued to use chemical weapons against his own people, but never followed through.

As the US approaches the 2016 presidential election, Hillary Clinton once again is vying for the job. In her book, *Hard Choices*, she discusses the difficulties of diplomacy: diplomats may do what they think best in any situation but the results always are uncertain.[83] She emphasizes her practice of meeting everyday people, not just leaders, in her diplomatic jaunts around the world, and of her desire to "stand up for dissidents while also seeking cooperation on the economy, climate change, and nuclear proliferation" while in China. She quotes Eleanor Roosevelt: "Where, after all, do universal human rights begin? In small places, closer to home, in the world of the individual person: the neighborhood where he lives; the college or school he attends; the factory or farm or office where he works."[84] This is the populist view that she wants people to have of her as she campaigns to be the first female US President. But she has seriously been challenged by two populists who previously were not considered major contenders.

The promise of the US Constitution is that "We the People" authorize the county's laws and benefit from them. The world before the US founding was one of hierarchies. People were assumed to be unequal in economic and social standing, as well as ability. The radical idea of the US founders is equality of opportunity. But from the beginning what got in our way was how best to live this vision. The concept that all are created equal is meaningless unless all have an equal chance at success.

When de Tocqueville visited in the 1830s he observed a belief in this vision everywhere he went. This was different from what he saw in his native France despite its revolution. But he also expressed concern about the treatment of blacks and indigenous peoples whom many Americans, including President Andrew Jackson, did not consider to be a part of "The People" for whom the country was founded.

What is meant by "The People" continues to evolve. In our

minds, which have been shaped by evolution, we easily can think of "The People" as being those who look and act like us – with the others being not quite as human. But we have gotten to this point due to the ability of our cooperative selves to supersede the competititive tendencies within us.

The aspiration of all people is to be recognized as valid human beings. If Americans are to live up to the promise of their Constitution they must continue to expand their definition of "The People" to those who once were denied that validity, including those of all backgrounds – all nationalities, genders, religious or non-religious beliefs, ethnicities, sexual identities, and those with various types of disabilities. This is – and always will be – an ongoing process. But those committed to the vision of the US Constitution will work to embrace the diversity that is America. When we celebrate the diversity of others, we acknowledge the diverse nature and potential of our own human makeup and become more free. At the point where progress toward our understanding of who constitutes "The People" stops, then democracy in America – whose vision lives in the minds and hearts of its people – no longer really will exist.

In his 1996 seminal book, *American Exceptionalism*, sociologist Seymour Martin Lipset criticizes American over-emphasis on competition: "In a country that stresses success above all, people are led to feel that the most important thing is to win the game, regardless of the methods employed in doing so." He criticized the idea that "the end justifies the means."[85] Winning the game is a satisfying emotion that only lasts until the next competition. The game becomes more in tune with real American values when we expand the playing field so that all of "The People" are seen as worthy of being included.

In the current election cycle in the US there is competition among candidates to prove who among them is the most in touch with real American values. This is as it always has been and should be. But this election has taken an unusual twist. Candidates who represent alternatives to the established system are doing extremely well. Perhaps this means that many people believe they have been forgotten in what America has become.

The only way to a stable society is a return to those values with which our founders once shook the world. It is tempting for "us" to blame "them" when we feel that the promise of the Constitution is not being kept. But if "The People" are to remain sovereign there can be no "us" or "them." There only can be a continually expanding understanding of who we are.

Next we will review the constitutions of five other major nations. We will consider what their constitutions promise, and the success, or lack of success, of their governments in creating democratic societies. These five nations were chosen to serve as examples of what can happen when societies see a clear path to democracy, and also what can happen when democratic impulses are set back.

BRAZIL

Brazil is the largest country in Latin America. It was discovered in 1500. The development of sugar cane failed at first because the natives were not amenable to the long work schedules required for plantation life. The Portuguese began enslaving natives, who then began to attack the Europeans. As the native population thinned from subjugation and disease, imports began of thousands of African slaves to work the sugar plantations. Eventually the descendants of all three groups created a mixed race.[86]

The discovery of gold in 1695 spurred the next stage of development, followed by diversification into cacao, rice, cotton and coffee. A hierarchical society emerged, with plantation owners at the top. The merchant class also became prominent. A degree of equality among classes resulted from involvement of the Church where all were considered equal in the eyes of God.[87]

Brazil became independent in 1822. Throughout Latin America movements to become independent from Spain and Portugal resulted in new rule by the elite rather than representation being more democratically spread among the population. The structure of the society and economy favored the white landowners, with non-whites still working the mines or plantations. Once the elite were in a position to rule and make their own trade deals with other countries they saw the need for a state to represent their interests. A conflict between the expressed democratic values of the elite and their actual lack of support for real democratic reform that affects all levels of society has shaped Latin America to this day.

Increased trade with the rest of the world did bring greater prosperity that improved stability throughout the 1800s.[88] The armed forces in Latin America, including Brazil, became gradually more powerful. The military, which had become a force for independence, declared Brazil a Republic on November 16, 1889 in a bid to make that country a world power. A new constitution was drawn up, modeled after that of the US, giving Brazil twenty self-governing states with a national government and an elected president answerable to the senate and chamber of deputies.

The idea of the new constitution was to spread power, but governance remained in the hands of the wealthy. Coffee, the biggest source of income, was centered on the town of Sao Paulo. Since only literate males could vote, the voting population was limited to about three percent of the population. The governing power in each province was determined by the most powerful local clan. Rebellions were organized by the rural poor throughout the country, but were violently put down.[89]

Throughout the twentieth century the military played a major role in politics. Attempts to combat nationalism, communism, and fascist movements often led to a disregard for human rights. The US was closely involved in Brazil's affairs as a source of loans and investment.[90]

The revolution in Cuba inspired insurgencies that were stopped by another military coup in 1964, after which Brazil was ruled by the military for twenty years.[91] The country stabilized while cutting back on imports and increasing exports. Neither industrialists nor labor were satisfied with the poor showing of the economy, which led to demonstrations and strikes. Urban guerilla warfare erupted as it did in other Latin American countries such as Argentina and Uruguay. The guerilla groups were defeated by the military over the next few years as the bulk of Brazilians continued to live in poverty.

By the 1970s, largely due to oil exports and inflation, Brazil was the world's fastest growing country. The biggest corporations were state owned, including oil and telecommunications. Private banks were allowed to compete with state banks. Exports and the general standard of living reflected improved annual growth rates.

In the 1980s an oil crisis put a crimp on the economy. Yet pay and retirement benefits for civil servants still increased considerably. Recession again raised its head as the military sought a social consensus for ruling the country, but since the military could not be removed by popular vote the result was political stability but greater repression.[92]

In 1985 there was an inflation rate of 230 percent, which was devastating to the poor and those on fixed income. Inflation continued and repaying debts in foreign currencies proved nearly impossible. Land redistribution to peasants was met with great resistance from large landowners. Wage and price freezes could not be retained because of the strength of labor unions. Food riots in the late 1980s showed that many segments of the population were not helped by the latest round of reforms. The extremes between inflation in a loose economy and recession in a tight economy continued.[93]

In 2002 Luis "Lula" de Silva, a candidate of the Workers' Party (PT), was elected President. He promised to eliminate hunger and inequality. He managed to slow inflation and make the next large loan payment to the International Monetary Fund. The improved world economy helped conditions. Silva raised the minimum wage and increased welfare payments which boosted his popularity. Members of his party were accused of offering bribes to win votes in Congress, but he still prevailed in the 2006 election. He had to deal with a police abuse scandal, violence in poor areas, and serious environmental threats to the Amazon. But in 2008 Brazil was ready to lobby for a permanent seat on the UN Security Council.[94]

As in most of Latin America, there was great optimism in Brazil at the beginning of the twenty-first century that democracy would succeed at last. However, the level of corruption and an inability to collect taxes due to underreporting by the wealthy has left Brazil's government chronically underfunded. This means that taxes to support government must come primarily from sales, which puts the tax burden primarily on the poor.[95] Despite increased economic stability overall, inequality still is rampant. Although there are regularly held elections, most of Latin America is plagued by high levels of corruption and crime.

As of this writing, Brazil is scheduled to host the 2016 Olympic Games for which it has been making expensive preparations since being awarded that honor in 2009. However, the country continues to be rocked by economic downturn and scandal. The worst recession in 25 years continues, and the Zika virus, which causes severe birth defects, seems to be peaking. There has been a two-year investigation into bribes involving Petrobras, the state-run oil company. And with all these problems, Olympic ticket sales have been extremely slow.

Brazil's President since 2011, Dilma Rousseff, was chair of Petrobras from 2003 to 2010, when much of the corruption is alleged to have taken place. Many Petrobras executives already have been arrested or imprisoned. Rousseff was accused of hiding a budget shortfall to make the budgetary picture look better before her 2014 re-election. In May 2016 she was impeached by Congress, removing her from office for 180 days until the fate of her legal battle is determined.

There have been seven constitutions in Brazil, with the latest version put in place in 1988, but this has been revised many times since. Each new government tries to get its own party's ideas put into in the Constitution. The Preamble states that Brazil is "a democratic state for the purpose of ensuring the exercise of social and individual rights, liberty, security, well being, development, equality, and justice."

Article I states:

The Federative Republic of Brazil, formed by the indissoluble union of the states and municipalities, and of the federal district, is a legal democratic state found on 1. sovereignty; 2. citizenship; 3. the dignity of the human person; 4. the social values of labor and of free enterprise; 5. political pluralism. All power emanates from the people, who exercise it by means of elected representative or directly, as provided by this constitution.

Article 2 states that the powers of the union shall be the legislative, executive, and judicial which shall be "independent and harmonious." Article 3 states the country's objectives of eradication of poverty and substandard living conditions.[96] Article 5 is dedicated to "Individual and Collective Rights and Duties." But the Constitution is not always followed, for example, regarding minimum wage, which according to Article 7, clause IV, should be enough to pay for the basic needs of a family.

Brazil, like much of Latin America, has democratic aspirations but a tradition of authoritarian and military rule that goes back to its founding. Popular and idealistic politicians have risen many times, only to be implicated in scandals, which lessened their popularity and effectiveness. Democracy is difficult to accomplish when there are vast differences between those at the economic top and bottom and when powerful interests offer temptations that provide comforts that otherwise may not be available to those in politics. Only by a revamped commitment among those who run the country to meeting the needs of the entire population will the country be able to overcome chronic divisions and scandals. Such a commitment by those at all levels of Brazilian – and Latin American – society would stabilize their governments in a way that would benefit all.

GREECE

Greece is universally recognized as the fount of western democracy. It originated the concept that – however imperfectly – people can govern themselves.

One still can visit the sites in Greece that gave birth to Western Civilization: the Acropolis where representatives of the people of Athens met; Epidaurus and its theater with perfect acoustics that still causes our voices to cascade back to our ears after more than two millennia; Delphi, home to the Oracle, high in the hills, where people of all walks of life had to wait their turn to learn of their fate; Olympia, origin of the greatest of all games; and Mycenae, once thought lost but rediscovered, home of King Agamemnon who spent ten years retrieving the stolen Helen while destroying Troy in the process.

After Athens's defeat by Sparta in 404 BCE, Socrates taught his students about the "examined life," and Aristotle speculated about the ideal state ruled by a wise king. Alexander, a student of Aristotle, conquered the known world, after which Rome governed. Upon Rome's decline, Greece became part of the Christian Byzantine Empire for a thousand years until 1453 when the Ottomans conquered Constantinople and dominated the area. The Greeks rebelled and obtained independence in the early 1800s. After equivocation, Greece eventually fought on the side of the Allies in World War I. A coup and counter-coup led to a republic being declared in 1924.

At the beginning of the Second World War a mobilization of Greeks formed an army that put off the Italians until the country at last succumbed to the Nazis.[97] After World War II Greece's economy developed quickly with help of the Marshall Plan. The military seized power in 1967 and established a junta that lasted until 1974. After a rebellion against the Junta, Greece elected a new Prime Minister. In 1981, the Socialist Party candidate Andreas Papandreou became Prime Minister and was in power for most of the years until his death in 1996.

Greece has undergone nine constitutions under governments dominated at times by a monarch imposed by European powers, more than one episode of military dictatorship, and now, under a democratically elected government.[98] It has modeled much of its democracy on the European parliamentary model, particularly that of West Germany, limiting the powers of the president.

Greece adopted its current constitution in 1975, making it a parliamentary democracy with a president, prime minister and cabinet, one house of parliament, and a judiciary with a constitutional court. Its constitution affirms the role of the Greek Church as a guide to the principles of government. It starts: "The Constitution of Greece, In the Name of the Holy and

Consubstantial and Indivisible Trinity, The Fifth Reversionary Parliament of the Hellenes Resolves. . . "

Article 1 established the type of government:

1. The form of government of Greece is that of a parliamentary republic.

2. Popular sovereignty is the foundation of the government.

3. All powers derive from the people and the nation; they shall be exercised as specified by the constitution.

Article 2 states that the role of the government is to respect and protect the value of people and that Greece follows the principles of international law.

Article 3 outlines the relations of the Church to the State, to which it is firmly linked, unlike other Western countries. It requires that the president be a Christian.

The rest of the Greek Constitution deals with individual and social rights, including "equality; personal freedom; protection of life, honor and liberty regardless of nationality, race, language, and religious or personal beliefs; freedom of movement; protection in the home; the right of petition, assembly, and association; freedom of religion, opinion, the press, art, science, research, and teaching; protection of property and compensation for public taking; secrecy (privacy) of communications; the right to judicial protection; protection for the family, marriage and motherhood; the right to work, join trade unions, and to strike. The right to establish and belong to political parties is also guaranteed." The Greek constitution only can be amended by a majority of two successive legislatures.[99]

Greece joined NATO in 1980, the European Union in 1981, and adopted the Euro in 2001. The Greeks still consider themselves a proud and independent people with a zest for life. The plaza beneath the Acropolis is a bustling scene where one can hear Zorba's dance incessantly, acting as a siren for shoppers to linger and consider the many well-made – and some not so well-made – articles for sale.

Modern Greece has a population of about ten million. Its economy is based mainly on agriculture and some small industries, plus international shipping companies.

The country enjoyed considerable prosperity after becoming democratic in 1975. Until recently the Greek economy was stable and the country was a model of a progressive European country. However, in 2009 the Greek economy became a victim of the international financial crisis as its exports and tourism declined. When the economy started to fail it required massive loans from its European trading partners to keep the country afloat.

Greece had debts to European banks that it could not repay on time. As a result the country's debts were rated as junk bonds which caused a crisis in the financial markets, resulting in the need for loans of over 200 billion Euros by European countries and the International Monetary Fund. The loans were backed by demands for extreme austerity measures, greatly reducing government expenses including healthcare and pensions, with some people reportedly unable to afford rent or food. This resulted in years of civil unrest. For one period in the summer of 2015 tourists and locals alike were unable to withdraw money from banks due to a limit of cash liquidity. Eventually that crisis was relieved with another infusion of European cash.

There remains much concern in the European Community about the stability of the Greek economy.[100] A document prepared by the European Stability Mechanism (ESM) predicts a decline in the country's economic growth, and therefore in its ability to pay its debts. The EU continues to consider ways to extend the Greek debt to European bankers (which already has been done many times), redefine the terms of the loans, or cap interest. This is in light of the need for further infusions of cash to keep the economy afloat. New measures would be contingent on Greece living up to its short-term obligations.

The situation with Greece and other countries that accumulate large, unsustainable debt has been – and still is – a cause for ongoing international concern. Some of the countries whose economies that have been threatened and needed support by larger, more prosperous nations over the last twenty years include Mexico, Japan, Portugal, Spain, and Italy.

At the most basic level, trade between people and/or countries should, by definition, be equal. Money is a relatively recent measure of value. Historians tell us that in the most ancient times, before the advent of money, items were bartered. The earliest known European coins go back to about 600 BCE in Ephesus (not far from Greece, now a part of Turkey and the source of the Ephesians Epistle from Paul in the New Testament)[101]

A barter system is based on equality: "I will exchange this shirt that I made for your equally fine handmade necklaces." Then money was introduced to represent value, as it easily could be transported and stored (many items have been used as money such as beads or tulip bulbs). From ancient times there was a prohibition on loaning money for interest in some cultures. Jesus criticized the money lenders who were doing business at the Temple. Loaning for interest also is forbidden in the Qur'an. But for those who have saved money, they expect to deposit it in an investment or a bank and receive a return, either as a way make a living or to support their retirement.

We all hope to continue the lifestyles to which we have become accustomed, as most of us, not unreasonably, expect a return on our investment of work or money. We put our money in a bank which loans it to others, or we are the recipient of loans based on an assumption that we will be able to pay them back. When our lender/borrower agreement appears to be coming apart – such as during a financial meltdown or bank failure – our world appears threatened. The only sustainable solution is a compromise that restores our trust and working relationship; then we cooperate to re-negotiate a mutually beneficial contract. There are people whose lives can be affected – positively or negatively – at both ends of every financial arrangement. A financial crisis is not just something that happens to us, but something that we create and therefore can resolve[102]

Before the financial meltdown of 2008, Greeks were selling produce abroad, engaging in small industry and manufacturing, and managing shipping businesses that resulted in a more or less equal situation with their trading partners. The country supported a healthy – but not wealthy – economy that provided a decent lifestyle for its citizens, including healthcare and retirement benefits. One ongoing challenge has been that Greece traditionally has found it difficult to collect taxes from its most wealthy citizens due to poorly enforced record-keeping and reporting laws.

When the 2008 financial crisis hit, Greece needed to borrow money from its European trading partners to keep its lifestyle in place. One trick to improve exports that many countries use is to allow its currency to devalue, which buys less abroad but makes its imports more attractive. This option was unavailable to Greece because by the time of the crisis it had adopted the Euro, the European common currency.

At this writing the Greek financial crisis continues despite a general improvement in the world's financial situation, and also continues to be tenuous in some of the other countries mentioned. Greece has taken on a huge amount of debt that is expected to be paid back with interest but has no real prospect for repaying those funds under the current terms, which is why the loans need to be continually renegotiated. Germany, which is prosperous and a large exporter of cars to Greece, is backing many of these loans and expects the loans to be repaid. World financial markets often go up or down depending on the latest status of the Greek financial crisis, so this ongoing issue threatens to undermine not only the economy of Greece but the underpinnings of democracy everywhere.

As of May 2016 a renegotiation of the Greek debt was undertaken under the new Prime Minister, Alexis Tsipras, leader of the leftist party Syriza. Tsipras once promised confrontation with Greece's lenders, but has focused on working with them toward an agreement to end the crisis since his election in September 2015. The lenders, who hope to avoid default, as does the new Prime Minister, are considering loosening the terms of the deal and providing more payments as conditions slowly improve. According to Tsipras: "This will create the financial room not just to relaunch the economy but also widen social protection."[103]

If creditors are serious about helping Greece get out of debt and on its own feet they will need to work with that country to establish more financial independence. An old proverb, attributed to Confucius among others, states: "Give a man a fish and you feed him for a day; teach a man to fish and you feed him for a lifetime." Greece has many marketable strengths. The country needs assistance to develop new industries, or perhaps improve the export of its marvelous produce or stylish clothing that will allow it to become more independent. Greece needs an open hand – rather than a closed fist – from its European partners to again become an equal player in the world economy.

EGYPT

Except for the roads, a visit to Egypt puts one squarely in touch with a different time. The Pyramids, of course, are timeless. Colorful tombs of nobles, though of great antiquity, still tell the stories of those who built them. There are tombs of Pharaohs in museums containing layers of sarcophagi for protection against vandals, and three-story statues of ancient kings have been unearthed. Perhaps the clearest sign that the country still has a foot in the past is seeing merchants bringing their produce to market on the backs of donkeys.

Egypt today is the product of revolution and counterrevolution that has spun it around, but at this point, unfortunately, it has landed in a place close to where it always has been. Having overcome generations of kings and dictators to at last throw off an oppressive regime, the country once again is under the thumb of its military. This is despite the efforts of many intelligent and determined revolutionaries who have staked everything on a vision for a more democratic country.

Egypt was the main stage of the "Arab Spring" that began in early 2011. After years of underground organization and public protest, Hosni Mubarak was forced to resign as President. Mubarak had been in power since 1981 and was the subject of growing dissidence throughout the country due to suppression of the democratic impulses of his people. At 6PM on February 11, 2011, the Vice President of Egypt announced:

In the name of God the merciful, the compassionate, citizens, during these very difficult circumstances Egypt is going through, President Hosni Mubarak has decided to step down from the Office of President of the Republic and has charged the High Council of the Armed Forces to administer the affairs of the country. May God help everybody.[104]

When protesters who had been occupying Tahrir Square, the central gathering place in Cairo, for weeks, heard this announcement their reaction was electric, as it was throughout the country and beyond.

According to those who had opposed Mubarak, he was a

tyrant who "rewarded greed and punished integrity and hard work." His corruption and control reached to every level of government and of the everyday functioning of the country: to government employees, police, judges, lawyers, journalists, and media executives.[105]

Upon his resignation Mubarak ceded his authority to the Supreme Council of the Armed Forces, a group of about twenty generals who convened to deal with emergencies. The SCAF dissolved the constitution and promised to move out of power as soon as new laws, an elected president and parliament could be put in place.[106]

But the military maintained control, while arresting and torturing protestors who kept pressing for real democratic reform. Protestors called for a trial of Mubarak for corruption and the deaths of dissidents. He eventually was tried, which the military perhaps thought would put an end to protests. But confrontations and arrests continued as the same officials that served under Mubarak remained in place.

The US was heavily involved in the situation as it had supplied money and arms to the military. When Hillary Clinton visited Egypt as Secretary of State in March of 2011, she met with representatives of citizen groups and visited Tahrir Square. When asked if she would continue to support democratic changes in Egypt she replied: "I have no opinion."[107]

By January of 2012 the military continued to confront protestors, killing many. The Muslim Brotherhood made a deal that they wouldn't hold protests during the upcoming election. They and other conservative Muslim groups dominated the results. A member of the Brotherhood, Mohamed Morsi, became president in June and tried to impose his extreme views on the country. One year later, 10 million protestors contested the presidency of Morsi, and the military deposed him, putting Adly Mansour in his place as interim president, but the military still dominated the government. Then over 1000 Muslim Brotherhood protestors were killed in protests against the deposition of Morsi. Defense Minister Abdel el-Sisi won the presidency in 2014, again supported by the military. Most Egyptians were glad at that point to vote for any candidate who did not represent the Brotherhood.[108]

As of 2016, "Almost every revolutionary and member of Egypt's opposition is either in prison or has left Egypt."[109] Revolutions throughout the Mideast have degraded into civil wars or been turned back in Morocco, Jordan, Syria, Yemen and Libya. Only in Tunisia is there a tentative collaboration of Islamic and non-Islamic peoples, which many Tunisians hope will be a model for the Middle East.[110]

Since 1923, Egypt has had five constitutions that have, at least on paper, slowly created greater power-sharing by their leaders. This started with King Farouk, who established a Parliament. Farouk was overthrown in a coup by Abdel Nasser in 1952 whose constitutional revisions included quotes from *The Communist Manifesto*, but who, despite his popularity and egalitarian speeches, created a police state.[111] It was revised again by Anwar Sadat who was President from 1970 until his assassination in 1981, but real democracy still eluded the country due to the near-dictatorial status of its presidents.[112]

After a temporary constitution was established under the military in 2012, the new administration was charged with putting an updated version in place in 2014. The Constitution claims to protect basic human rights, but as in all authoritarian regimes, the rights guaranteed under this document don't correspond to the reality experienced by the people.

The 2014 Egyptian Constitution has six Parts and 247 Articles. It starts: "In the name of Allah, Most Gracious, Most Merciful, This is Our Constitution. Egypt is the gift of the Nile for Egyptians and the gift of the Egyptians to humanity."

Part I, Article 4 states: "Sovereignty belongs only to the people, who shall exercise and protect it. The people are the source of powers, and safeguard their national unity that is based on the principles of equality, justice and equal opportunities among all citizens."

According to Article 8, "Society is based on solidarity. The State shall achieve social justice and provide the means to achieve social independence, in order to ensure a decent life for all citizens." Article 9: "The State shall ensure equal opportunity for all citizens without discrimination." Article 11: "The State shall ensure the achievement of equality between women and men in all civil political, economic, social and cultural rights." Article 17 establishes social insurance for incapacity to work, old age, and unemployment, Article 18 provides for health insurance for all and Article 19 promises education for everyone.

The Arab world seemed ready to embrace democracy in 2011. But the Arab spring has become a winter of discontent. The extreme difficulty of working together to reach consensus about how to run a government points to the distance between the idea of democracy and its practice. The victory in an election by an extreme group that doesn't support democratic principles in Egypt points to a contradiction: a democratic election can result in non-democratic government. Democracy must be discussed, practiced, and understood by the bulk of individuals before it can become present on a larger national stage.[113]

Like many revolutions that don't result in democracy, a spark of self-governance and human dignity is now ignited in the Middle East that will undoubtedly once again be kindled because its people – like all people – will not rest until they see themselves as free.

INDIA

I will never forget seeing the movie *Phantom India* by Louis Malle (1969). India comes to life in that film. The people, the sights, and the sounds so immerse the viewer that one even can taste and smell what is on the screen. It celebrates the great passions of the Indian people in their spirituality, their interpersonal lives, and even their poverty.

In Chapter I, I dwelled extensively on the history of this, the world's largest democracy, so here we will mainly discuss India in modern times.

But first, its Constitution.

India's Constitution of 1950 has eleven parts and 395 articles. It is the longest in the world and the only constitution that India has ever had. It has been amended exactly 100 times as of 2015. India's Supreme Court has ruled that amendments cannot overturn "the basic structure" of the Constitution. Due to the great inequalities in that country, the constituent assembly that gathered to write the constitution in 1947 attempted to give special preference to its poor. Its drafters sent representatives to the US, Canada, and Ireland to seek models for what they were about to create.[114]

The Preamble states that the country is "a sovereign socialist democratic republic" that intends to secure for all its citizens justice, liberty, equality, and fraternity (clearly inspired by the French constitution).

Part 3, Fundamental Rights, guarantees equality before the law, prohibits discrimination on grounds or religion, race, caste, sex, or place of birth, establishes equality of opportunity in public employment, abolishes the caste of the untouchables, outlaws traditional titles, guarantees freedom of speech, provides protections for those accused of criminal offenses, guarantees protection of life and person liberty, promises freedom of religion, prohibits child labor in factories, and protects other rights.

Article 53 gives the President, elected to a five-year term, "executive power of the union." The President is elected by an indirect system through members of both houses of Parliament and legislative assemblies. The Prime Minister reports to the President the decisions of the cabinet. The members of the Supreme Court are appointed by the President in consultation with the other Supreme Court justices.

The Brahmins of ancient India established a social system that limited the political power of its people and taught that individuals were in the place determined by their karma. Literacy was seen as unnecessary for those of the lower classes. Thus a tradition was begun that still affects the poor, and many remain in poverty due to the limited mobility built into that system. Despite the constitution, tradition reigns supreme in much of Indian society. For example, the courts still administer family law based on religious principles.[115]

But there are many who have risen to a high level in India's international economy due to education and an ability to innovate. Some of the fields in which Indians have become successful include information technology, medicine, entertainment, and economics.[116]

During World War II, the Japanese occupied parts of India, and members of the Nationalist Party showed a willingness to cooperate. To prevent India from becoming a part of the Axis powers, Britain promised to grant independence after the war, which it still was reluctant to do until confronted with the mass insurrection led by Mohandas Gandhi.[117]

Gandhi, who was influenced by Thoreau's essay *"Civil Disobedience"*[118] in addition to the *Bhagavad-Gita* while leading the movement for Indian independence, was to further influence two of the great peace movements of the century – those of Martin Luther King, Jr. in the US and of Nelson Mandela in South Africa.

Partition came as India was moving toward becoming an independent state in 1947. The northeast and northwest were predominantly Muslim, and there had been ongoing enmity between the Muslims and Hindus in that area. Perhaps a million died in the wars between them that affected many communities, and up to ten million were uprooted as they were forced to move from their homes to one of the new countries that were carved out on religious lines – from India to Pakistan or in the opposite direction.[119]

In 1975, the Indian High Court invalidated the election of Prime Minister Indira Gandhi for election irregularities and banned her from office for six years. She was the daughter of Jawaharlal Nehru, who served as India's first prime minister from its independence in 1947 until his death in 1964. She chose not to step aside and challenged the ruling. She evoked emergency powers and told the country that the court order was part of a conspiracy against her. She therefore needed to temporarily rule by decree.

There were massive arrests, censorship of the press, and general suppression of civil rights. Mrs. Gandhi used the press to tell the country her views and then promoted those she thought should be in power, including her son, Sanjay, and their other nominees to run the government. Many in the country and abroad feared that India's experiment in democracy was over. Her two-thirds parliamentary majority followed her directions to amend the constitution and strip the judiciary of essential powers.

It was a surprise to some observers that a country so diverse in religions and with such inequality had been able to maintain its democracy for thirty years. Democracy was an enigma in Asia. India was the only country that held up at least the idea of human dignity in that region. Mrs. Gandhi appeared to some to be another Asian autocrat who was determined to overturn the rule of law. Under her decree many went to jail and were tortured. The government controlled the press, and there was a persistent underground movement by activists to restore the country's civil rights. In 1977, thinking herself secure and favored by the people who would then exonerate her at the polls, she called special elections, but was soundly defeated.[120]

Despite the subservience of generations that had been subject to the ancient caste system, Indians boldly reasserted their rights when once again given the vote. Some have speculated as to what has allowed India to continue its democratic traditions when so many other countries have faltered. Perhaps the key factor was the culture of democracy to which its people had become accustomed, but the country only had emerged from colonialism thirty years before.

So why does democracy succeed in India when it has failed to thrive in other one-time British colonies, particularly some in Africa? Perhaps one answer lies in the ancient culture of India itself. Hinduism – in all its many facets – is the dominant religion. Despite the caste system from which some began to emerge at the time of the writing of the Indian constitution, inequalities are ingrained in the culture. But, in contrast to a country like China, where absolute rule has existed for thousands of years, the religious tradition of India emphasizes one's relationship to the divine One, not to others.[121] This has some parallels to the One God orientation of the ancient Israelites. A person's Karma – or place in the universe – is not something that another human being can determine. Hinduism teaches that human souls are inherently perfectible and ultimately perfect, although realizing this may take many incarnations. Thus in a way, the basis of Hinduism is respect for everyone and everything, and patience that all will eventually find their place in the universe.

When Indira Gandhi established what amounted to martial law, Indians waited. And when given a chance to reassert their self-determination, they did not hesitate. There was not only a resurgence of the press, but of civic activism.

India is a study of diversity within unity. Federalism, the ability to combine efforts by diverse states within a country, has allowed for the recognition of local differences in language and tradition to merge into one large unit, erasing the need for the traditional wars that are a part of the country's tradition, although skirmishes still break out.

India also has numerous civic organizations that bring people from differing backgrounds together to advocate for democratic principles. The People's Union for Civil Liberties targets injustice and the remnants of the caste system. There are groups that challenge destruction of the environment, gender discrimination, and corruption in government through marches, fasting, and frequent use of civil disobedience in the style of Mahatma Gandhi.

Voter turnout in India hovers around 60 percent of eligible voters, more than the average in many countries. One reason may be that Indians have seen their democracy work. Elections are competitive with many parties vying for votes. Even so, organizing a national election is a gargantuan task. About 900,000 polling stations must be established all across the huge expanse of the country, some of which only can be reached by elephant. Yet those who believe in democracy in India are determined to do whatever it takes to keep it. To ensure that the reach of democracy extends to the people, the Supreme Court has established circuit courts throughout the county to intervene in personal disputes, such as debts, when needed. However, there remains a huge backup in the local court system.

Quality of life gradually has improved under democracy in India. Life expectancy rose from fifty to sixty-six between 1970 and 2015. The fertility rate has come down from an average of six children for every woman to less than half that. India currently has a population of over one billion and is expected to overtake

China in a few years. Yet poverty remains a serious issue that is not likely to be eliminated any time soon.[122] The gap between rich and poor actually has grown larger since 1991.[123]

But the overall Indian economy has picked up pace since 1991. This has resulted in accelerated job growth in the agricultural and industrial realms. Still, the manufacturing jobs of the past are quickly disappearing and must yield to the automated workplace of the future. The median age of the population is 26, with 300 million Indians under the age of 15. India's young now are seen as the future of which its elders are proud: "it's crowning asset." To keep all these young people employed the country must create at least 10 million jobs for them each year. There also is a gender imbalance – only 919 girls are born for every 1000 boys.[124]

India's booming economy slowed in 2011 and foreign investors, no longer receiving the expected profits, began to pull out. Some claim that the glaring inequalities of the country are to blame for the slowdown. Although it has the second fastest growing economy (next to China), a vast number of children still are unprepared for the type of work that will be required to sustain the younger generation. Schools that the poor attend still are inadequate; opportunities for young women are limited due to ingrained traditions. Malnourishment still affects about 30 percent of young children, immunizations are not on track, and one in four Indians still live in poverty on less than the equivalent of $1.25 per day.[125] Those in possession of the "new wealth" are segregating themselves in gated communities. They use private hospitals and their children attend private schools.[126]

Women, though still underrepresented in India's Parliament, are making some headway. Between 2000 and 2010 more women than men became literate. Rape victims are less likely to fear coming forward, and are publicly accusing their molesters[127]

The old animus between Muslims and Hindus is still very

much alive. On November 28, 2008, ten gunmen began well-planned attacks on various targets in the city of Mumbai. The attackers shot indiscriminately into crowds at a railway station, killing fifty-eight, then moved on to other sites in the city, where they fired into crowds, took hostages, and set off bombs in hotels, killing another sixty-three people. The attackers were found to be Pakistani citizens; of those left alive some were hanged and others imprisoned.

But Indians are becoming more focused on their future and less on past animosities. Now that their economic situation – at least for some – is looking more secure they seem to have less need for negativity and revenge. Although the short legacy of their democracy is filled with pitfalls, they seem to be squarely on the road to creating solutions to their problems and moving steadily forward as a democracy.

SOUTH AFRICA

South Africa was forged in intolerance.

Up until the year 1900 there was a series of wars for independence by the Boers from the British colonialists. The Boers were Dutch speaking descendants of settlers from the Netherlands. They eventually lost. English became the required language and children were sent to schools to learn their duties as British subjects. Leaders of white Afrikaners, who spoke Afrikaans, opened their own Christian schools.[128]

There were skirmishes between Afrikaner rebels and British troops at the beginning of World War I. Afrikaners, who often were farmers, became victims of industrialization, forced to leave their farms and seek employment in the cities. Lacking in education and English language skills, they did menial tasks to survive, while most lived in poverty. Many children did not complete their education for lack of clothing and shelter.

Most of the majority black community was even worse off. Segregation was severe and kept blacks in a subordinate role. A commission in 1905 recommended that blacks and whites should be kept separate in their political organizations as well as living and land ownership in clearly marked areas. This led to a legally sanctioned segregated society. Black land owners were forced to sell their land and work for whites as urban laborers and farm hands. This destroyed a generation of previously prosperous farmers and forced many black families into the status of migrants looking for shelter.

In 1910, The Union of South Africa, with its vast diamond and gold reserves, gained independence from Britain under white minority rule.[129] The government gave white mineworkers a monopoly on skilled occupations. In 1912, a meeting of prominent black leaders organized what later became known as the African National Congress, or ANC, but their means of protesting segregation, which were mainly legal, had little effect. The 1913 Native Lands Act prohibited Africans from purchasing or leasing land in white areas and limited blacks to preserves that only took up about 7% of the available land. A result was overuse of the land which led to soil erosion and degradation. Many headed to the towns to find work, but a 1924 law gave preference to white workers. Black voters were excluded from the voting lists in 1936, restricting a right they had held for eighty years.[130]

Afrikaners had, by the 1930s, created their own nationalist organization, the Broederbond, that promoted the view that they eventually would "rule South Africa," claiming persecution by the British and blacks, as well as their own superiority. At the same time, there were movements to unite all whites into one party. By a narrow vote, the South African Parliament voted to bring the country into World War II in 1939 on the side of the British.[131]

In the 1940s, the white rulers of South Africa watched in dismay as the countries around them gained independence from their colonial rulers with blacks in roles as leaders. Some of these included Southwest Africa, (Southern) Rhodesia, Angola, and Mozambique. During that period, unemployment of blacks in South Africa was high, with many moving into squatter camps on the outskirts of Johannesburg, the country's largest city. Trade unions formed which led to strikes, including one in 1946 by black mineworkers. In the meantime the black population was increasing at about twice the rate of whites.

To keep the black population under control, the government created the policy of apartheid in 1948 to totally segregate them, using the Bible as justification. The nationalist Afrikaners – 60% of the population – won the election that year, purging the English speaking minority from well-paying government positions. People were forced to move into separate segregated areas based on race and sit separately in restaurants, on transportation, and at all public places. [132]

In 1949, the ANC began a program to combat these draconian measures, including disobedience, boycotts, and strikes. Nelson Mandela rose to the top of the organization. He was inspired by Gandhi, but advocated using means other than nonviolence if needed. The government passed the *Suppression of Communism Act* to use as a weapon toward any organization by which it felt threatened, including the ANC, which answered by civil disobedience. Many were imprisoned, and some accused of high treason.

In 1959, the new president declared that South Africa would become a "multinational state" with totally separate living areas for each of its populations. Amidst pressure to end discriminatory practices, the government cancelled membership in the British Commonwealth in 1961. The ANC was deemed illegal. Mandela organized a strike which had little effect, and he decided to engage in an armed resurrection which landed him and his co-conspirators in jail for life in 1964.[133]

Mandela spent twenty-seven years in prison, during which he earned a law degree and wrote his autobiography, *Long Walk to Freedom*. Mandela's views evolved in prison, where he swore off violence. A memorable line from his book summarizes his views: "To be free is not merely to cast off one's chains, but to live in a way that respects and enhances the freedom of others."[134]

In 1991, President de Klerk released Mandela after years of international political pressure and boycotts. Mandela met with black and white leaders to negotiate the details of how the country would operate after the end of apartheid. This set the stage for a new constitution after a peace memorandum was signed. De Klerk and Mandela earned the Nobel Peace Prize in 1993, and Mandela became President the next year in the country's first multiracial election. He then launched investigations to combat interracial violence and created new anti-poverty programs.

South Africa guarantees rights in its Constitution that are not seen in many nations inside or outside of Africa. These include the right to join a union plus guarantees of housing and healthcare. Its human rights provisions have been used to permit same-sex unions, a rarity in Africa.[135]

The 1996 South African Constitution is divided into 14 Chapters and 243 Sections.

The Preamble reads:

We, the people of South Africa,

Recognize the injustices of our past;

Honor those who suffered for justice and freedom in our land;

Respect those who have worked to build and develop our country; and

Believe that South Africa belongs to all who live in it, united in our diversity.

We therefore, through our freely elected representatives, adopt this Constitution as the Supreme law of the Republic so as to

- Heal the divisions of the past and establish a society based on democratic values, social justice and fundamental human rights;
- Lay the foundations for a democratic and open society in which government is based on the will of the people and every citizen is equally protected by law;
- Improve the quality of life of all citizens and free the potential of each person; and
- Build a united and democratic South Africa able to take its rightful place as a sovereign state in the family of nations.

May God protect our people.

Chapter I, the Founding Provisions, state that "South Africa is one, sovereign, democratic state founded on the following values, which include human dignity, non-racialism and non-sexism, and universal adult suffrage." It assures equal rights to all citizens and describes the official languages (there are twelve).

Chapter 2 is the Bill of Rights, which includes equality before the law, human dignity, a right not to be deprived of freedom without just cause, a right to privacy, religious freedom, freedom of expression and the press, freedom of assembly and association, freedom of movement, and a right to join a union. It also includes a right to "an environment that is not harmful," keeping one's own property except if needed for the public interest, housing, health care, and education.

I believe that it is safe to say that South Africa, despite old attitudes that still persist among some, has recast itself in a new spirit of tolerance. It has become a testament to what can be achieved when people work together to create and forge a new vision.

SUMMARY AND POSSIBLE LESSONS

We have compared the promises of the constitutions of eleven nations with the level of democracy experienced by their people. All constitutions promise the rule of law, but this does not guarantee an actual respect for human rights. Thus constitutions are not the only way to determine the extent to which countries are just and democratic.

Our historians and social scientists tell us that primitive societies generally were egalitarian. As they enlarged, hierarchies developed that created more distance between those with greater and lesser authority. But those at the top of a society always were – and are – in danger of having their power usurped.

Democracy requires power sharing and a commitment to human dignity, but its ultimate purpose is for people at all levels of a society to identify and work together toward common goals, directly or through representatives. There is considerable distance between the top and bottom in nearly all countries. Those who see themselves as oppressed always will try to equalize their situation. But if real power sharing and financial opportunity is extended to all members of a society, stabilization is much more likely that benefits those at all levels.

Stability and Instability

There are some essential differences between governments that are run democratically and those that are not, regardless of their written constitutions.

True democracy that honors those at all levels of society still is an unrealized ideal in our world. Some western democracies come closest, but there are many individuals who experience discrimination and lack of opportunity in every country. This leads to a degree of instability everywhere. Even in countries with constitutions that claim to honor the democratic aspirations of their people, equal opportunity often still is lacking.

In autocratic and dictatorial countries we find discontentment among those who believe themselves left behind, and continuing threats to those in power from those who want their share of it. As those in lower positions do move up there still will be others demanding a voice. This pattern will repeat until when – and if – real democratic reforms are put into place.

It is only by ongoing democratic dialogue that begins at the level of basic education and moves up through all levels of society that people begin to believe themselves included and appreciated as individuals. Inclusion is the key to stability rather than rigid rules that undermine the contributions and recognition that people seek. Yet people rarely are trained to engage in ongoing conversations that allow them to work with others respectfully toward common goals.

The Role of Government in Encouraging or Discouraging Human Potential

In real democracy each of us is encouraged to do and be the best we can. When those at all levels of a society are allowed – and trained – to live up to their potential, there is a much greater degree of contentedness. People become more fulfilled while making the maximum contribution of their skills and talents. Countries then become more economically and socially stable. This is much easier than suppressing those who channel their energy into rage and resentment.

Failing to allow people to maximize their potential only makes the democratic impulse stronger. Wise leaders move to create situations that recognize and reward human potential, rather than suppressing it. But doing this requires a clear idea for how it can be accomplished. It requires leaders committed to creating and working toward a shared and inclusive vision. But moving toward greater democracy in the real world requires continual effort to maintain it as our vision of equality evolves.

The actual form of a government is less important than that it recognizes the humanity and diversity of its people. Socrates and Aristotle were suspicious of democracy because they thought it invited mob rule. A government can increase its chances of staying in power if it engages in honest and ongoing dialogue with the bulk of its people. No one country can assume that its methods are superior or the best for others, especially because every nation is far from living up to its own ideals. The best that the leaders of a nation can do is to engage in honest conversation about what actions they can take to realize the ideals expressed in its constitution, and then really *listen* to the views of others.

Questions to Consider

Here are a few questions we can ask to clarify our values and how to work toward them:

(1) What are the most essential human values?

(2) How do we determine "the will of the people?"

(3) How do we forge a vision and communicate it so that it affects real people in the real world?

(4) How do we recognize the diverse views and needs of people while moving toward a unified vision and plan of action (*E Pluribus Unum*)?

Economic imbalance incites resentment and resurrection. So do leaders who fail to give people a voice. Those who do well financially should work toward greater economic balance to

ensure their own futures and to stabilize the economy for everyone, including themselves. If people really believe they are being
heard they will see themselves as participants in incremental
change. This will make them less likely to seek radical change.

A Delicate Balance

Democracy is a delicate balance. In Athens democracy already
had become difficult to manage with too many people sharing in
the decision process. 500 jurors voted at the trial of Socrates. A
streamlined method of decision making is needed. Yet the voice
of the people cannot be lost.

One question to always ask is "Who are the people whose
voices are being heard?" If the answer is not "All," we still have
much work ahead of us. If some voices drown out others there is
a tyranny that some will resent. That is why an ongoing conversation is needed about what course of action best serves the greatest
number of people. That conversation can take place at all levels of
society, starting with the family and working its way up through
every organization to the level of the nation. Complaining about
the state of affairs is easy, but creating a clear vision and moving
toward it requires determination and foresight.

People often are persuaded to vote for a politician based on
promises. We should demand that those who would lead us reveal
how they intend to fulfill their promises, and if fulfilled, how they
will serve the vast majority of people. To make democracy work,
leaders and those they lead must combine efforts in an atmosphere
of trust that affects every conceivable level of a society.

For more on that, turn the page.

Endnotes

1 "Band level societies are egalitarian and engage in considerable food sharing, something that becomes impossible once agriculture and private property are adopted." *The Origins of Political Order*, Page 455
2 *Constitutions of the World*, Pages 294-96
3 *The Oxford History of Britain*, Page 677-78
4 *The Oxford History of Britain*, Page 681
5 *The Oxford History of Britain*, Page 682
6 *Capital in the Twenty-first Century*, Page 42
7 *Capital in the Twenty-first Century*, Page 499
8 *The Oxford History of Britain*, Pages 683-84
9 *The Oxford History of Britain*, Page 708
10 *The Oxford History of Britain*, Pages 696-97
11 "Chilcot delivers crushing verdict on Blair and the Iraq war," The Guardian, July 6, 2016.
12 *The Oxford History of Britain,* Page 702
13 *The Oxford History of Britain*, Page 707
14 "David Cameron's Austerity Bomb Finally Went Off," Foreign Policy Magazine, June 24, 1016
15 "Number of homeless in England has risen for 3 years in a row, report says." The Guardian, December 13, 2013.
16 *Constitutions of the World*, Pages 48-49
17 *The Origins of Political Order*, Page 248
18 *The Origins of Political Order*, Page 384
19 *China*, Pages 533-34
20 "Families of Tiananmen Square victims accuse Beijing of three decades of "white terror." The Guardian, May 31, 2016.
21 *The Origins of Political Order*, Pages 314-17
22 "Mass suicide protest at Apple manufacturer Foxconn," The Telegraph, January 11, 2012
23 "China bans depiction of gay people on television." The Guardian, March 4, 2016
24 *The Origins of Political Order*, Page 475
25 *A Brief History of France*, Page 266
26 *A Brief History of France*, Page 268
27 *Constitutions of the World*, Pages 83-86
28 *A Brief History of France*, Page 297
29 *A Brief History of France*, Page 273
30 *A Brief History of France*, Pages 289-90
31 *A Brief History of France*, Pages 295-301
32 "Francois Hollande resists union pressure to abandon labour reforms," The Guardian, May 27, 2016.
33 *A Brief History of France*, Page 306
34 *Constitutions of the World*, Pages 89-91
35 *Three Germanies,* Pages 29 and 38
36 *Three Germanies,* Pages 52-58
37 *Three Germanies,* Page 267
38 *Three Germanies,* Page 247
39 *Three Germanies,* Page 269
40 *Three Germanies,* Pages 275-76
41 *Three Germanies*, Page 290

42 *Constitutions of the World*, Pages 238-40
43 *The Man without a Face*, Pages 50-56
44 *The Man without a Face*, Pages 60-62
45 *Russia, A History*, Page 462
46 *The Man without a Face*, Page 98
47 *Russia, A History*, Page 452
48 *Russia, A History*, Pages 464
49 *The Man without a Face*, Pages 124-25
50 *Russia, A History*, Pages 479-83
51 *The Man without a Face*, Pages 137-40
52 *The Man without a Face*, Pages 26-31
53 *Russia*, Pages 254-55
54 *The Man without a Face*, Pages 153-55
55 *The Man without a Face*, Page 174
56 *The Man without a Face*, Pages 227-28
57 *The Man without a Face*, Page 190
58 *Russia, a History*, Page 504
59 *The Man without a Face*, Page 266
60 *The Man without a Face*, Pages 202-03
61 *Russia, a History*, Page 522
62 *The Man without a Face*, Page 265
63 *The Man without a Face*, Page 294
64 *Russia*, Page 141
65 *1491*, Page 379
66 *America's Constitution, a Biography, Page 8*
67 *America's Constitution, Pages 14-16*
68 *The Second Bill of Rights*, Pages 110-111
69 *America's Constitution*, Page 17
70 *America's Constitution,* Page 425
71 *America's Constitution*, Page 425
72 *Angler: The Cheney Vice Presidency*, Pages 61-64
73 *Angler*, Pages 67-69
74 *Angler*, Pages 74-77 and 256
75 *Angler*, Pages 132-33 and 177
76 *Angler*, Pages 215-17
77 *A Brief History of France*, Page 287
78 *A Fighting Chance*, Page 112
79 *A Fighting Chance*, Pages 84-85
80 "Seven days, three speeches, one week in the life of having a black president,"
    Stephen W. Thrasher, The Guardian, May 9, 2016,
81 *The Audacity of Hope*, Pages 4-9
82 *The Audacity of Hope*, Pages 15-16
83 *Hard Choices*, Page 19
84 *Hard Choices*, Page 111
85 *American Exceptionalism*, Page 47
86 *The Penguin History of Latin America*, Pages 167-72
87 *The Penguin History of Latin America*, Pages 188-90
88 *The Penguin History of Latin America*, Pages 233-34
89 *The Penguin History of Latin America*, Pages 410-12
90 *The Penguin History of Latin America*, Pages 418-19
91 *The Penguin History of Latin America*, Pages 426-27

92   *The Penguin History of Latin America*, Pages 431-32
93   *The Penguin History of Latin America*, Pages 433-35
94   *The Penguin History of Latin America*, Pages 580-82
95   *The Origins of Political Order*, Pages 355-56
96   *Constitutions of the World*, Page 26
97   *Europe*, Page 1010
98   *Constitutions of the World*, Pages 97-98
99   *Constitutions of the World*, Pages 98-101
100 "Euro zone Greek debt analysis shows serious concerns over its sustainability," The Guardian, May 9, 2016.
101 *The Ascent of Money*, Pages 24-25
102 "Once the principle of equal respect or dignity is articulated, it is hard to prevent human beings from demanding it for themselves...successful liberal democracy requires both a state that is strong, unified, and able to enforce laws on it own territory, and a society that is strong and cohesive and able to impose accountability on the state." *The Origins of Political Order*, Page 479
103 "Greek Deal ends 'six years of darkness.' " AFP, May 10, 2016
104 *You are under Arrest for Masterminding the Egyptian Revolution*, Page 243
105 *You are under Arrest*, Page 245
106 *You are under Arrest*, Pages 246-47
107 *You are under Arrest*, Pages 257-68
108 *You are under Arrest*, Pages 257-68
109 *You are under Arrest*, Page 288
110 *A Rage for Order*, Page 221
111 *A History of Egypt*, Page 291
112 *Constitutions of the World*, Page 72
113 *A Rage for Order*, Page 4
114 *Constitutions of the World*, Page 117
115 *The Origins of Political Order*, Page 273
116 *The Origins of Political Order*, Page 171
117 *Western Civilization*, Page 824
118 *The Oxford History of the American People*, Page 527
119 *The End of Karma*, Page 14
120 *The Spirit of Democracy*, Pages 153-54
121 *Philosophies of India*, Page 242
122 *The Spirit of Democracy*, Pages 158-68
123 *The End of Karma*, Page 19
124 *The End of Karma*, Pages 7-11
125 *The End of Karma*, Page 12
126 *The End of Karma*, Page 19
127 *The End of Karma*, Pages 177-79
128 *The Fortunes of Africa*, Pages 507-08
129 *The Fortunes of Africa*, Page 527
130 *The Fortunes of Africa*, Pages 509-13
131 *The Fortunes of Africa*, Pages 514-17
132 *The Fortunes of Africa*, Pages 580-82
133 *The Fortunes of Africa*, Pages 585-86
134 *Long Walk to Freedom*, Pages 624-25
135 "Senegal's Sall Says West Should Accept Africa Gay Rights Stance," Bloomberg, May 12, 2016

"All concepts, even those that are closest to experience, are from the point of view of logic freely chosen conventions, just as is the case with causality."

AUTOBIOGRAPHICAL NOTES in
Albert Einstein, Philosopher-Scientist [1]

CHAPTER III

Democracy's Future

Our most ancient ancestors saw their world as a whole. Their quest for knowledge was focused on the skills they needed to survive.

To the Greeks, all knowledge was a branch of philosophy. They and other ancient civilizations developed calculations to help them predict the movements of the planets. We eventually called this skill mathematics.[2]

Gradually we created more and more categories of knowledge to enable us understand our universe. We invented geography, biology, chemistry, history, and an expanding number of disciplines to help us more effectively interact with our world. The results have been extremely beneficial. We were able to calculate that our planet is round (or at least pear shaped), which allowed us to circumnavigate it; we have used our knowledge of biology to wipe out many diseases that once were rampant; we have discovered how to use the chemical elements that make up the universe for our benefit; we have studied the rise and fall of civilizations, which we hope will guide us in preventing the demise of our own.

From the beginning of our formal education we are taught subjects such as math, geography, history and science. But the world itself knows no such divisions – we have devised them to guide us in our pursuit of knowledge. We segment our world to help us better understand it. As time goes on we create new fields – and then sometimes combine them – to facilitate yet better understanding. Biochemistry, for example, a union of biology and chemistry, was conceived to help us better decipher the chemical processes of the body.

Eventually we relegated most knowledge to the realm of specialists and began to rely on experts in every field. We depend on professionals because of our own limited knowledge, whether it be in law, medicine, or auto mechanics. We rely on scientists to explain the rules that govern our natural world; we depend on doctors to do our healing; we count on professional teachers to teach our children, usually with good results.

In our world of specialization we defer to the experts and put aside our own ability to come to independent conclusions. Education has become more about repeating truths that others have discovered rather than making our own discoveries. The process of what we call learning rarely involves developing our own thoughts and conclusions.

But there is another way to view human knowledge, which is that it is a process that continually evolves. At all times in history – including our own – people have assumed that their knowledge was complete. At any point in time we think that our model of the universe represents the truth. Greek concepts of the physical universe stood for two thousand years. But Isaac Newton, known in his day as a "natural philosopher," overthrew all previous understanding of how the universe works. He created new laws to explain what could be observed by everyone – he just thought about things differently.[3] During the eighteenth and nineteenth centuries Newton's view of the world was considered incapable of improvement. When Einstein began graduate school he was told by his professors that he should not go into physics because there was nothing new to be discovered. He then brought our understanding of the universe far beyond the Newtonian model that had been in place for over 200 years. Our knowledge of human origins also is continually changing based on discoveries of bones and relics in remote places, as well as newer methods of unraveling the secrets of those findings.[4]

What we consider "knowledge" is tentative; our concepts change based on an expanding vision of reality. Our model of the universe continues to evolve. Yet it is difficult to see this from where we stand. Evolution and continental drift, for example, took years of observation to confirm, and then each of those theories shifted our entire view of how the world works.

So what does all this have to do with democracy?

Much of our history is about gaining new insights that have improved the lives of the average person in ways that could have only been imagined as recently as, perhaps, two hundred years ago. But two hundred years ago – a span that barely can be measured on the scale of time humans have been on earth – most women and minorities were not included in the concept of what is a valid human being. Much of Africa was under colonial rule and Africans were considered by many Europeans and Americans as only fit to be slaves. The caste system – including the avoidance of contact with subhuman "untouchables" – was firmly in place in India. The people of China were subservient and inferior to their emperor. Those included in "We the People" in the US did not include women, blacks, or indigenous peoples. Members of these groups could be enslaved or discriminated against – and were

– with impunity. "He" was the standard pronoun to refer to any person. Justice was not an option for those who were considered to be not quite human.

The innovations of the Greeks in the realm of democracy, as well as democracy's resurrection in the North American British colonies, were revolutionary for their times. But the real meaning of the democratic revolution still is unfolding. The US founders, even with their far-reaching vision, could not have imagined those for whom the rights of their constitution would be extended to cover – voting rights for blacks and women; programs to support the poor; government sponsored retirement insurance; equal access for persons with disabilities; marriage rights for mixed race and same-sex couples.[5]

Human beings use their concepts about others to assess their compatibility with them and their worth. But what do we really know about other people? What we think we know often is limited to the categories into which we place them. People can be white, black, Hispanic, Asian, or of another race; female or male; an office worker or mechanic; good looking or not so much so.

You may be of another political party or income category from me. You may like a different sport or type of music. I am limited to my concept of you by the categories I impose upon you. But the reality of who you are is different than any category into which I might place you. My concepts always fall short. I only can begin to know you by putting aside everything I think I know. The way to come closer to knowing you is to watch and interact; even then my understanding will be limited.

And what do we know about the world around us? Our advancement of knowledge has brought us from the use of sharpened stones as knives to the nuclear age and beyond. Yet we basically are the same human beings we ever were. Our knowledge is limited by the apparatus of our minds and the concepts that our brains can generate. In other words we can't know anything or anyone beyond the range of where our limited abilities and understanding will take us.

Over the millennia we have developed gradually improving concepts, yet every concept falls short of totally capturing the nature of the people and universe around us. Knowledge evolves when we gradually pay better attention – often aided by science – and are willing to let go of concepts that no longer fit. Over time our means of experimentation and observation improve – recently for example, by the use of the electron microscope and nuclear telescope.

Our understanding of the world has evolved, but our way of seeing others hardly has budged. We still divide people into those we like and those we don't; into our friends and enemies; into those who really are human like us and those who are not. We team up with those we find to be our natural companions and go to battle with those who we determine are not like us at all.

Those who wrote the Declaration of Independence and Constitution in the US were able to work past their differences to create documents that expressed the essence of the nation they wanted to create. This is because they were determined to agree on a clear vision for how to move that nation forward, despite weeks of wrangling and disagreement.

Democracy, at its best, allows us to move past our pre-established concepts and categories to identify what we have in common – to work with others to move toward shared goals. It encourages us to expand our idea of those who are worthwhile human beings. It pushes us to enlarge our possibilities so that we can work together with an expanding group of individuals in our personal and work lives, as well as our private and government organizations.

Not long ago in the US there were no women or minorities in the legislatures, but now such a thing is commonplace. In the past, it was pointless for those of minority religions, including Muslims, Jews and Catholics, to apply for work in many places. People who considered themselves homosexual had no chance of attaining political office. But that all has changed as we have been willing to expand our definition of "We the People" to include many for whom we now fail even to understand why they ever were excluded. The definition is expanding – at least in the Western world – to those with mental handicaps and intellectual disabilities. If given a chance, everyone has something to contribute. It's impossible to know where ongoing revisions of those we consider valid individuals will lead, but it is likely that people we have not previously even considered will be included in the future.

Going back to the beginnings of democracy as we know it, Socrates, in Plato's *Republic*, states that he knows nothing.[6] When I become aware of the limits of what I know about others I find it difficult to judge them. When aware that my knowledge of the world around me is tentative I see that I must continually be open to new discoveries.

Awareness of the limits to our understanding provides us a chance to acknowledge that we have much to learn, which then allows us to move on to new insights. We become more willing to give up old ideas as they become obsolete. We realize that what we think we know must continually yield to what other people and the world have to teach us. We return to that humble place where we once were beginners in exploring our universe and we are relieved of the burden of holding on to a past that no longer serves us.

One promise of democracy is that it will bring us to a continual new awareness of the meaning of equality. We are all different in beliefs and abilities, yet in the view expressed by many of the world's constitutions we all are equally valuable citizens of this world (see Chapter II). This means that in situations that we might call democratic, from the family to the nation and beyond, we seek solutions that reflect the value of every human being. We include those who express themselves well and those who do not, and those who are wealthy or not, in decisions that affect us all. As we do this we honor the integrity of every human being, including ourselves.

At the core of every major religion and philosophical tradition is an admonition to treat others as we would like to be treated. This principle also is the central vision of democracy. It includes relationships and governments in which we protect the potential of all to thrive to the maximum extent possible.

In every time and place there have been those who have imposed – or tried to impose – their will on others. This has happened in tribes, city states, monarchies, autocracies, communist or socialist states, and even democracies. Within all countries there are those who attempt to use their influence to gain a disproportionate share of power for their own short-term gain.

Democracy is threatened everywhere, and in whatever form it exists. Those countries we consider "democratic" are not exceptions. When those who rise to the top within any nation use their influence to bend the functioning of government to their own purposes, the laws of that nation usually provide inadequate protections for the average person. Those who have the most power often seek to increase it at the expense of the bulk of the population until the effects of inequality – and short-sighted behavior – cause a disruption in the lives and economies of those at all levels of society. This has happened during numerous worldwide depressions, including that of the 1930s, and the Great Recession that began in 2008.[7]

In the pages that follow we will consider how democratic ideals apply to a number of areas in which human beings function and interact. We will describe how the influence of real democracy – interactions and government that respects the needs and wishes of the vast majority of people – can affect the workings of our world.

CHILDHOOD

Democracy – for those who believe in it – starts in the home.

We each enter the world with no clear identity. Then we gradually learn who we are – female or male, members of a race or nationality, and many other factors that make up our eventual idea of ourselves. Yet these concepts of who we are – and those concepts we impose on others – are not even close to being the totality of what it means to be human.[8] There are many other aspects of the personality that we develop that effect our future lives. Among these are our interpersonal skills, our mechanical or artistic ability, our preferences in food, music, or art, and our basic enthusiasm or pessimism about life.

Creative play helps children begin shaping their ideas about right and wrong, heroes and villains, males and females, and a host of other factors that eventually become a part of how they see themselves. Our parents, friends, and others in our early lives influence our tastes and preferences. For most of us, our creative potential slowly wanes as we learn to live within the narrow confines of the person we eventually believe ourselves to be.

We slowly become comfortable or uncomfortable with the identity we have created for ourselves. If we are brought up so that our self-esteem is not threatened for acting outside a narrow range of behaviors we will be more comfortable with who we are, including being a person who makes mistakes. We also will be more comfortable living in an uncertain world. Those brought up with inflexible standards often are less comfortable with who they are, including their faults. They find it more difficult to act outside the straitjacket of a rigid idea of themselves.Our self-concept revolves around our ability to meet standards that others have set for us or we have set for ourselves. Once identified as good at academics or athletics, for example, we pin much of our self-esteem on how we succeed in those areas. What we consider success sometimes emphasizes individual accomplishment and at other times emphasizes what we can accomplish together.

The suppression of our spontaneity and creative potential in childhood results in anger or sadness that can last a lifetime. Often we later blame this on those around us. Resentment that builds up can result in harm to others or ourselves – emotionally or physically.[9] The stress of being brought up in poverty also often limits our options.

Our creative potential always exists beneath the surface, yet to be rediscovered.[10] More flexible and less rigid ideas about who we and how we must act lead to greater confidence in ourselves and to more creative interactions with our world. With children, simple questions such as "How was your day?" or "What do you think?" or "Where shall we go on our family outing?" teach confidence in an ability to work with others to make decisions.

The crux of democracy is acknowledging the rights of each of us to recognize and express our individuality. Once our basic needs are met we want to be free to make the major decisions that affect our lives. We will rebel against repressive forces in our home or government. Children need to learn to channel their creative forces and clarify their values as they grow older. This requires practice in self-expression and interpersonal skills. An upbringing that doesn't prepare us for a responsible adulthood by practicing self-expression makes it less likely that we will be able to function successfully in a democratic environment.

Parents are likely to bring up their children much as they were brought up. Those who were raised strictly amidst rigid rules are most likely to pass that way of thinking on to the next generation, and those who are raised more flexibly are likely to continue that practice. But trends also can change with the times. In the most recent generation of parents we see a bending of the old models. More fathers, for example take roles in child care, perhaps because more mothers work or perhaps because of the newly popular philosophy of shared child-raising.

We can move past some of our traditional patterns as we become more attuned to a changing world. Parents who were brought up to follow rigid rules in their own childhoods and who were not allowed to develop their own ideas of right and wrong still can begin to provide more respect for individual expression in their home environment. Morality can be taught by example and promoting choice, rather than imposing inflexible rules that inspire rebellion and don't prepare children for democracy.

If we hit or berate a child we are teaching that violence and bullying are solutions to problems, which a quick review of history will dispel.[11] Those brought up with a view that physical punishment improves behaviors can look at the literature on the subject or at their own family lives to see that violence begets itself. *The Bullying Antidote* (2013) by Louise Hart and Kristen Caven discusses different types of parenting styles, including the "autocratic," that gives children little say in family decisions and the "permissive," that provides little of the guidance that children want and need. Their recommendation is to "balance strictness with nurture" – to provide the structure needed while still practicing empathetic and democratic interactions.[12]

The best way to teach democracy in a family is by daily conversations. Of course when children engage in dangerous behaviors, such as hitting or running out in the street, they must be told to stop. But if we ask our children, for example, what could happen if they run in the street, they will begin to internalize the behavior patterns that we want them to learn. If we ask them what they could have done instead of hitting when they are angry, they will learn to create non-violent solutions to their problems. Then asking children to practice the behaviors that have been established via our discussions makes them more likely to become ingrained.

When we have these conversations with our children we are teaching them to become the problem solvers that are needed to sustain democracy. In many cases, what we call democracy is about competition rather than cooperation – about a confrontation between "us" and "them." The most important question you can ask your children is: "What kind of world do you want to live in?" They will surprise you with the wisdom of their answers, and perhaps become our own best teachers in the process.

History is punctuated with individuals who are remembered as the most hateful of all time. Some people choose a violent path. But we never know if history would have been different if each of them had been treated more kindly in childhood or beyond. This is why each of us must do all we can to demonstrate kindness and trust to the children in our lives.

EDUCATION

For many people, learning begins and ends in their school years. They have little interest in expanding their education beyond that period. For others, learning is a lifelong process that involves them not only in academics, but in the ongoing lessons that life provides.

If we believe that students are capable of making the major decisions that affect their lives – or can be trained to do so – then our educational system must prepare them to do this for their own good and that of their community and world. Teaching can demonstrate a faith and trust in students that they internalize and take with them into their lives. But if we believe that students are to be distrusted and are incapable of real independence, our instruction will be in the form of rigid rules that will discourage them from believing in themselves or their abilities to come to their own conclusions. The best teachers find a way to use examples to make their lessons relevant, which encourages student interest and participation. Making it relevant is what makes it come alive.

Some educational systems reflect a belief that people can be trusted to make the best decisions for themselves and their society; they can learn to come to appropriate conclusions and work together toward common goals. Other educational systems express the view that people are not to be trusted; they should doubt their ability to make the right judgments and will forever need to be guided like children who never will develop an ability to come the right conclusions. One system inspires self-confidence; the other sows self-doubt. The first expresses a faith in democracy; the second reflects a belief that people never will be ready for self-rule.

Those who teach in democracies can bring democratic methods into their classrooms. Teachers can express faith in students to come to useful conclusions that relate to the real challenges of the world. Students then learn thinking habits that allow them to become innovative and creative in their lives and careers. Democratic educational systems focus on preparing students for thinking by the use of creative projects and learning to trust their ability to take on challenges and find solutions. This makes them more likely to have successful careers and be capable of becoming genuine participants in democracy.

In his *Politics*, Aristotle stated the view that education should be public rather than private because all students must be trained in how to be good citizens as well as to advance themselves. Thus education should be the responsibility of the state:

Since the whole state has a single end, it is clear that education must be one and the same for all, and that it must be in public, rather than private, hands. . . . It is indeed quite false to imagine that any citizen belongs to himself. . . . The correct view is that all belong to the state because each is a part thereof.[13]

Education in the earliest societies was simply passing on survival skills from adults to children who participated in the same activities as their parents as soon as they were able. As societies became more complex and skills became more specialized, the training of young people took longer. In Greece, where students were seen as needing a long period of education to be productive members of society, academies focused on understanding the world as well as obtaining skills. In the ancient world practical arts and philosophy were separated into what we would call science and humanities. Cicero, in the year 55 CE, advocated combining the practical with the theoretical when he wrote in Latin of the *artes liberales*, what we have come to call the liberal arts.[14]

In Europe of the Middle Ages, most children entered apprenticeships, which could take years, depending on the vocation. Education essentially was training for a trade or profession, and most children learned skills needed to continue the family trade from their parents.[15]

Education underwent a resurgence when Charlemagne created schools that prepared the sons of aristocrats to take their roles as part of the educated elite that ruled the empire (see Chapter I). Under the advisors to Charlemagne, the writing style was reformed to make it easier to read.[16]

Early universities were established to teach religion in the 1100s, but with the advancement of knowledge they began to teach practical skills like mathematics and astronomy. Then the thirteenth century saw a number of universities open throughout Europe that emphasized philosophic and scientific enquiry.

In Egypt, secular education was introduced as an alternative to the Koranic schools by Muhammad Ali in the 1830s. In Central Africa, many of the first schools that taught subjects outside tribal rituals were founded by missionaries. In the 1930s colonial governments started educational programs to prepare locals to take their place in the administrative bureaucracy in a number of African countries. Eventually the graduates of these schools became national leaders as colonialism ended. But after the days of colonialism it was difficult for the new leaders to maintain an educational system amidst disorganization in countries where the bulk of the population was subsistence farmers.[17]

As mentioned in Chapter I, education was frowned upon by the early Chinese emperors who feared promoting too much independence among the masses. With its vast population, today's China has huge numbers of every extreme of income. There is a large group that lives in dire poverty and are essentially homeless, never getting to participate in the education system. The school and university system, though not as prestigious as those abroad, has an excellent record of admitting those from all classes, except for the poorest, who are unprepared. Amidst higher income groups, many children are sent abroad to prestigious schools in England, such as Eton or Harrow, and the brightest among the elite attend the great universities of Europe and America.[18]

In Brazil, as in much of Latin America, the education of children lags far behind much of the civilized world. In 2000, only about half of Brazilian children finished school. Three out of four adults were functionally illiterate, and the country was last in a study of basic educational standards. The elite, of course, send their children to private schools. But in Latin America there is a growing awareness that a poor education holds people back.

Starting in the 1990s the Brazilian President, Fernando Henrique Cardoso, put through funding to increase the number and quality of public schools, which has continued despite Brazil's economic problems. The country is trying new incentives to get schools to improve, but Brazil is a long way from reaching the goal of providing an education for all of its children to lessen the level of the county's deep poverty.[19]

In northern New England, education was provided by public funds during the 1600s. Compact villages throughout the area made it easy to set up a school in or near the town square. The Bay Colony of Massachusetts required settlements with fifty or more families to hire a schoolmaster. The emphasis was on the three "R's, which was progressive for its time. Schools were exclusively for boys above the age of six.

A small college opened in a cow yard donated by the town of Cambridge, named after its first benefactor, the Reverend John Harvard. The school attracted students from all over the Eastern seaboard, and allowed them to pay tuition with farm produce and cattle during the depression of the 1640s.[20]

In 1830, Ohio passed a free education law for elementary students. Pennsylvania followed in 1834, Indiana in 1848, and Illinois in 1850. Even then, only about half the children attended. Blacks in New England were included in the system. Most colleges of the period were founded by Christian denominations, and free public libraries also were beginning to be established.[21]

The modern idea of a college – buildings designed for study around a quadrangle with residences nearby – developed first in England. Oxford, and then Cambridge, developed the earliest models in the 1200s.

In the US, Harvard and Yale eventually copied that model. Those schools combined an emphasis on the sciences with the humanities in an attempt to develop a fully rounded person.

Amidst the debate about practical versus theoretical skills, the Yale faculty issued a report defending its practice of combining the two in 1828. It claimed that the basis of a liberal education is "not to teach that which is peculiar to any one of the professions; but to lay the foundation which is common to them all." Real success is an ability to understand the principles behind education and to bring these principles into our vocations and lives.[22]

The debate still rages, especially in the US, about the purpose of education. Is it to provide practical and job skills, or is it to develop a well-rounded person who is comfortable with whatever challenges one may meet? Both clearly are essential. Perhaps a more relevant question might be: "In what order?"

In 1952, Robert Maynard Hutchins, who at that time was the Associate Director of the Ford Foundation that made educational and humanitarian grants, testified before the *House Select Committee to Investigate Tax-exempt Foundations*. Hutchins had been Dean of Yale Law School and President of the University of Chicago, where he and his colleague Mortimer Adler introduced what they called the "Great Books" program in the 1930s. That program eventually led to the establishment of the Encyclopedia Britannica. Hutchins was a strong believer that a truly educated person must be versed in the classics going back to the ancient Greeks.

The Great Books curriculum, which had originated at Columbia University in the 1920s, centered around small seminar classes where the goal was to develop critical skills that reflected the great thinking of all time. Hutchins believed that developing these skills would impart an ability to make one successful in one's chosen career.

Hutchins was testifying because of his concern that the US defense budget – which provided large research grants to universities – was steering professors to be lackeys of the Pentagon rather than researchers in pursuit of knowledge.

Here is his testimony:

Now, a university is a place that is established and will function for the benefit of society, provided it is a center of independent thought. It is a center of independent thought and criticism that is created in the interest of the progress of society, and the one reason that we know that every totalitarian government must fail is that no totalitarian government is prepared to face the consequences of creating free universities.

It is important for this purpose to attract into the institution men of the greatest capacity, and to encourage them to exercise their independent judgment. Education is a kind of continuing dialogue, and a dialogue assumes. . . different points of view.

The civilization that I work toward. . . could be called a civilization of the dialogue, where, instead of shooting one another when you differ, you reason things out together.

In this dialogue, then, you cannot assume that you are going to have everyone thinking the same way or feeling the same way. It would be unprogressive if that happened. The hope of eventual development would be gone. More than that, of course it would be very boring.

A university then, is a kind of continuing Socratic conversation on the highest level for the very best people you can think of, you can bring them together about the most important questions, and the thing that you must do, to the uttermost possible limit, is to guarantee those men the freedom to think and to express themselves.[23]

Hutchins told the committee that he thought there was a great danger in training people to think all in the same way. It could lead to totalitarianism. Rather, education that truly supports democracy demands the encouragement of independent thinking. Perhaps his most important point is that discussing issues in a rational and respectful way is a viable alternative to "shooting one another," a point probably not lost on the committee members whose nation had recently emerged from a war that killed more than any in history.

The point that a major goal of education is to train students in independent thinking has been echoed in many recent books.

In *Excellent Sheep*, by William Deresiewicz, a former Yale professor, the theme is similar. He claims that even the brightest students are trained throughout their educational careers to do what they are told and to think what they are told to think. The author claims that schools like modern Yale and Harvard are no different – the emphasis is on students avoiding original ideas and spitting back what they are given, all in the interest of procuring a career where they also will do what they are told:

> *The problem is that students have been taught that this is what education is: doing your homework, getting the answers, acing the test. Nothing in their training has endowed them with the sense that something larger is at stake. They've learned to "be a student," not to use their minds. . . . Very few were passionate about ideas. Very few saw college as part of a larger project of intellectual discovery and development, one that they directed by themselves and for themselves.*[24]

He further complains that:

> *What is not reasonable is that we have constructed an educational system that produces highly intelligent, accomplished twenty-two year olds who have no idea what they want to do with their lives: no sense of purpose and, what is worse, no understanding of how to go about finding one.*[25]

He goes on to state that, in most of higher education, "There is no vision. . . of what an educated human being is."[26]

In a similar vein, in *The Test*, Anya Kamenetz, an education writer for Public Affairs, states her concern that the measure of an education in the US has become how one does on tests:

> *I have seen how high-stakes tests are stunting children's*

spirits, adding stress to family life, demoralizing teachers, undermining schools, paralyzing the education debate, and gutting our country's future competitiveness. . . . The way much of school is organized around these tests makes little sense for what young humans need developmentally. Nor does it square with what the world needs.[27]

She claims, similarly to Deresiewicz:

A flood of recent research has shown that creative problem solving, oral and written communication skills, and critical thinking, plus social and emotional factors, including grit, motivation, and the ability to collaborate, are just as important in determining success as traditional academics. Scores on state tests do not correlate with students' ability to think.[28]

She goes on to discuss what she considers the real work of educators, which is to teach – to interact with students and give them feedback in a way that doesn't judge them or threaten their self-esteem. This provides an atmosphere where learning can take place in a nurturing classroom that emphasizes real learning – one that prepares students to function in the world.[29]

We have discussed democratic educational methods: now let's take up how such methods actually can become implemented in the classroom. Students come to class with views and backgrounds as diverse as they are. Each is an individual, and each deserves to know that her or his views are respected, no matter how ill-formed. But it is the responsibility of teachers to educate – to find a way to allow the subject material to integrate into the world view of their students. Parallels to students' lives always can be found.

If our purpose is to have students mimic our lessons back to us, then teachers barely are needed in the classroom – computers can do just as well. If, however, we intend for our students to understand the material in a meaningful way, we must build on their current level of understanding. The best way to do this is to bring students into a conversation – allow them to develop and express their own views; encourage them to create internal concepts that really reflect an understanding of the material in terms that they can integrate into their own world scheme. This only can be done by providing an opportunity for discussion.

And, you ask, how can we bring topics into a discussion format without inviting chaos? The well-managed classroom – no matter how large or small – borders on the edge of chaos because it generates excitement, the same type of excitement that every scientist has experienced while about to make a discovery. A few well-placed questions that allow students to relate the material to their experience leads to much more enthusiastic participation in the classroom. Opening up to student questions can be limited to the time allotted, and teachers must frame their own questions in a concise manner so that the essence of the material can be communicated and conveyed. This is the type of classroom that imparts the skills students need for success in any career or situation that involves working with others toward common goals and solutions.

When I taught in a small elementary school in the 1970s we had many students with learning problems. To engage their interests we individualized the curriculum and made it relevant to their lives. Students could advance through each subject area at an individual pace, and there was no stigma to being at the level they were. They could move through the math, science, and reading curriculums with a minimum of guidance when they were ready. We also showed them the relevance of these skill areas to their interests: horses, tornadoes, dinosaurs, earthquakes, etc. which made them willing participants in their lessons.

Later, when doing motivational workshops for non-profits, I

asked participants to identify their own ideas about the purpose of their organization. Then we created a group composite of that purpose and emphasized the best way to bring it into the workings of the organization.

In my current work I train people of all backgrounds in health care and management skills. The most important skill for the health care worker is to have a clear vision of how to meet the needs of those they serve. Rather than telling staff what they should think, which makes a limited impression, I ask them to share their own vision of how best to meet residents' needs and then concentrate on more and more specific examples of how to make this work. This engages participants much more fully in the training than telling them what to think and how to act. It brings them to an awareness of how best to serve people rather than any lesson that could come from me.

Humor also is important in effective teaching. If lessons always are serious it creates a separation between teacher and student. Admitting to the perpetual imperfection of our state of knowledge – and of ourselves – adds a realistic human element.

A situation that occurs in many classrooms and schools is the domination of one student over another, sometimes resulting in bullying. Whether physical or verbal, bullying can lead to a lifetime pattern of aggressive behavior on one hand, or a lack of self-confidence on the other. Children who are bullied can, in extreme cases, develop such a lack of self-esteem that they try – or in some cases succeed – to kill themselves.[30] A primary role of teachers – at all levels – is to teach social skills. When there is a disagreement between students, or one tries to dominate others, they should be required to sit down and work out their differences. If they can't, a teacher or counselor should help them to communicate toward a solution that works for all. This simple practice leads to a lifelong skill of being able to work with others toward common understanding, which may be the most important lesson that teachers can convey.

To sum up, teaching that prepares students to live in a democratic society must be democratic. It must respect the uniqueness and individuality of each student. It must provide a broad enough understanding of the principles that underlie all knowledge to prepare them for the uncertainty that life provides. It must impart the essential skill of collaborating with others toward common understanding and goals. Only then will students be prepared to continue their education and lives as citizens in a democracy.

JUSTICE

Of course we all want justice for ourselves. But what is justice, exactly?

Is it an eye for an eye? If I accidentally cause someone to lose an eye, should I therefore lose mine? And what if I cause someone to lose an eye intentionally? Should my family also suffer as a result of my actions, as was done in some ancient societies? What if I think that for others justice is punishment for the harm they do, but for me it is forgiveness?

And for those of us who care, how do we act justly toward others? Do we treat those close to us the same way as strangers, or treat everyone equally? And since every situation is different, how do we even know when we're being just?

In all societies there is an ideal of justice so that people can live together and learn to control their impulses for the greater good (see Chapter I). But it is not always easy to determine the nature of justice. In the real world every situation is different and each interpersonal dispute requires a different solution. Most disputes can be worked out among those involved. When that is impossible society needs to step in. In democracies we administer an imperfect justice as best we can according to the concept of fairness.

Let's look at what some well-know writers on justice have to say.

John Rawls, who taught at Harvard, has written what probably are the most widely respected works on justice. In *A Theory of Justice* (1971), Rawls discusses his essential concept of "justice as fairness."

1. The Role of Justice: Justice is the first virtue of social institutions, as truth is of systems of thought. A theory however elegant and economical must be rejected if it is untrue; likewise laws and institutions no matter how efficient and well-arranged must be reformed or abolished if they are unjust. Each person possesses an inviolability founded on justice that even the welfare of society as a whole cannot override. For this reason justice denies that the loss of freedom for some is made right by a greater good shared by others. . . . An injustice is tolerable only when it is necessary to avoid an even greater injustice.[31]

Here, Rawls tries to set up the idea of justice as an absolute. Justice and freedom are rights except where exercising them would lead to injustice.

2. The Subject of Justice

For us the primary subject of justice is the basic structure of society, or more exactly, the way in which the major social institutions distribute fundamental rights and duties and determine the division of advantages from social cooperation. . . . The institutions of society favor certain starting places over others. These are especially deep inequalities. Not only are they pervasive, but they affect men's initial chances in life; yet they cannot possibly be justified by an appeal to the notions of merit or desert. It is these inequalities, presumably inevitable in the basic structure of any society to which the principles of social justice must in the first instance apply.[32]

In a just society inequalities will be addressed.

3. The Main Idea of the Theory of Justice

The guiding idea is that the principles of justice for the basic structure of society are the objects of the original agreement. They are the principles that free and rational persons concerned to further their own interests would accept in an initial position of equality as defining the fundamental terms of their association. . . . The principles of justice are chosen behind a veil of ignorance. This ensures that no one is advantaged or disadvantaged in the choice of principles by the outcome of natural chance or the contingency of social circumstances. . . . Justice as fairness begins. . . with one of the most general of all choices which persons might make together. . . . Then, having chosen a conception of justice, we can suppose that they are to choose a constitution and a legislature to enact laws. . . all in accordance with the principles initially agreed upon.[33]

There is an agreement for justice implicit in the formation of a society. "Justice as fairness" means that we reach an understanding of justice that is separate from any of our own subjective circumstances, and then create laws that follow from that principle.

Amartya Sen, currently also at Harvard, is considered by many to be the top writer on justice and ethics of our era. He won the Nobel Prize in Economics in 1988, but in my view, his key contribution is in the area of ethics. His field is Welfare Economics, meaning an emphasis on what, beyond wealth, leads to improving the lives of individuals. His books include *Ethics and Economics* (1988) and *The Idea of Justice* (2009), which we will consider below.

To understand the world is never a matter of simply recording our perceptions. Understanding inescapably involves reasoning.[34]

What we think we know is challenged when we engage in reasoning, which by its nature brings us into communication with others.

Democracy has to be judged not just by the institutions that formally exist but by the extent to which different voices from diverse sections of the people can actually be heard.[35]

Justice must consider the diverse ways that people really are and act rather than the way we think they should be.

He refers to justice in the world of fish, where a big fish can freely devour a small fish.[36]

Similar to the concept of democracy held by some people?

We may do the right thing and yet we may not succeed. Or, a good result may come about not because we aimed for it, but for some other reason.

We can do our best, but must resign ourselves to the possibility that things may not work out as planned.

One of the issues to consider is the possibility that the critics of relying on reason are influenced by the fact that some people are easily over-convinced by their own reasoning.[35]

There is a difference between reasoning on our own, that can be self-serving, and discussing issues with others, that can open our minds to new possibilities.

The assumption of the completely egoistic human being has come to dominate much of mainstream economic theory.[36]

Most economists take the view that self-advancement always is a person's main priority.

Happiness and frustration relate, respectively, to our successes and failures to achieve the fulfillment of our objectives.[39]

Sen emphasizes the importance of our identifying and pursuing objectives as individuals, not just the objectives of society, which may be violent or materialistic and not well thought out.

Benjamin Friedman completes our Harvard trio. Friedman's work also is about the interplay between ethics and economics.

In *The Moral Consequences of Economic Growth* (2005), he considers the following:

One important question. . . is whether progress – again both material and moral – is inevitable. As we shall see, there are plausible reasons why a rising standard of living, broadly distributed across a society, fosters positive developments in spheres of life beyond economics. . . . Within the lifetime of any person, or any generation, whether progress occurs depends in large part on the choices and actions people take, both individually and collectively.[40]

There are actions that we take as a society that move us forward and those that do not.

After World War I the US economy stagnated according to Friedman, and the Klan flourished.[41] To combat poverty and intolerance during the lows of the Great Depression, FDR, who understood the importance of human dignity, began programs to establish not only "social justice," but "an economic bill of rights."[42] Social Security then was expanded by Eisenhower,[43] and Medicare and Medicaid were started under Johnson.[44] These programs were expanded by Nixon, who also recognized the need to respect our environment by signing bills to create the Environmental Protection Agency and OSHA.[45]

In Europe, Friedman points out that tolerance for people of different races and religions was stronger during periods of economic strength from the late nineteenth century until Word War I. We all know of the intolerance upon which the German nation was built after that war.[46] In Asia, greater prosperity lowered the gap in incomes during the 1970s and led to greater equality.[47] As more money has been entering China over the last twenty years (much of it from the US), more economic freedom and decision making has been allowed as authorities see that entrepreneurship leads to greater prosperity.

As Friedman sees it, spreading economic opportunities through all levels of society is most likely to lead to respect for democratic ideals. "What matters for this purpose is not just the size and vitality of the growing middle class but that its members be distributed widely throughout society; not only business people but doctors, lawyers, teachers...and others...with democratic values and whose economic success gives them a sense that they have a stake in helping to promote a stable, modern society."[48] Perhaps most important is a vision among people that they can work together cooperatively to overcome their societal woes. "The willingness to think and act in new ways – to adapt, to innovate, to create – also matters for economic growth."[49] A vision that includes the importance of making available publicly supported education that prepares students for the world of the future is essential. "Providing scholarships and loans for children of lower-income parents has...raised America's overall level of education."[50]

And how is an equitable society financed? By expecting those who can afford it to invest in a world that will benefit them as well as society as a whole. "Critics of the 1993 budget package warned that. . . higher taxes would squelch the still fragile recovery. . . . The critics were wrong. After 1993 the business expansion gained momentum, incomes and profits surged ahead, and the resulting increase in tax revenues contributed enormously to decreasing the deficit."[51] We also need to invest in keeping up the supply of skilled workers to keep the economy functioning at a high level, which increases tax revenues and leads to an increased ability of our government to meet its obligations. "It also is an investment, and the evidence makes clear that the return, in terms of added productivity for the economy as a whole, can be large." [52]

More recently, Elizabeth Warren, Senator from Massachusetts, has written *A Fighting Chance*. Warren was involved in the establishment of the Consumer Financial Protection Bureau, but when denied the opportunity to chair that agency, she ran for Senate. She is known as a crusader for updating banking regulations to protect consumers, but her main emphasis is on what she sees as the lack of justice that has resulted from the US banking and investment system.

Ever since the days of the Founding Fathers, the United States has had laws in place that made it illegal to lend money at extraordinarily high interest rates. . . . With usury laws and the 1930s banking regulations as a backdrop, banks played a really important role in helping America's economy grow. They lent money to people to buy homes. . . financed cars and college educations . . . helped small businesses get a start. . . . It all worked pretty well. Until the 1980's that is . . . thanks to a Supreme Court ruling. . . and an amendment quietly passed in Congress, the cap on interest rates was effectively eliminated. [53]

Usury laws were eliminated due to pressure on Congress from the banking industry.

Other things being equal, the middle class might have made it through – no richer than their parents, but no poorer either. But other thing weren't equal, because costs went up for stuff that was a lot harder to live without, like health care and education. . . . Single income families found themselves falling further and further behind. . . . On average, once the basic bills were covered. . . the modern two-income family had less money left over than the one-income family of a gen-eration earlier.[54]

The buying power of the average family has shrunk over the last 50 years.

News broke that Treasury had made a huge new commitment to Citibank, a giant bank that had already received $25 billion in TARP money. . . . I kept coming back to one number: $700 billion. We could have fixed our roads and bridges and public transportation. We could have launched universal preschool and made state universities afford-able again. We could have doubled our federal investments in medical research and scientific research for the next twenty years.[55]

During the 2008 financial crisis bailout money went to banks rather than to investments in people.

In fact, there was a long tradition of executives and regulators moving back and forth between government and private sector jobs, which meant that the key players in the financial industry almost never received serious input from anyone with a different world view.[56]

The main advisors to our presidents during the crisis had worked in big banks and investment firms, so of course their advice was to save the banks first.

Money – it whispers everywhere in politics. It twists a little here, bends a little there. And far too often it tilts in the same direction: in favor of those who have buckets of cash to spend. . . . To level the playing field so that everyone gets a chance, the money part of politics has got to change.[57]

Politicians must rely on contributions to campaign for office. Large contributors expect favors in return and usually get them.

The US Supreme Court has the responsibility of determining

which laws are in line with the US Constitution (known as "Judicial Review"). This began with the famous case of Marbury vs. Madison (1803), when Chief Justice John Marshall wrote: "The essence of civil liberty consists in the right of every individual to claim the protection of the laws, whenever he receives an injury." Marshall also believed that the courts should follow the intent, not the letter, of the Constitution: "Laws and institutions must go hand in hand with the progress of the human mind."[58]

William O. Douglas, who served on the US Supreme Court from 1939 to 1975, affirmed the evolving nature of the idea of justice in the US as reflected on the Court. "The Constitution," he wrote, "is written in general terms and uses terms like 'due process' without definition."[59] Regarding changing ideas about segregation: "Plessy vs. Ferguson, decided on May 18, 1896, was an eight-to-one decision holding that segregation of blacks on railroad coaches was constitutional, and that state laws requiring such segregation did not violate the Equal Protection Clause of the Fourteenth Amendment."[60] Regarding how actually to apply groundbreaking decisions: "The storm broke on May 17, 1954, the day the decision in Brown vs. Board of Education was initially announced. The opinion, though unanimous, did not represent that solidarity which unanimity implies. . . . We emphasized that the federal courts should require the local boards to 'make a prompt and reasonable start toward full compliance.' "[61] And on the injustice that can be promulgated in the name of democracy: "Holmes did our society a grave injustice when, in 1903, writing for a majority of six, he held that Negroes could not bring an action in the federal courts to protect their constitutional right to vote. . . . Why? Because, he said, the issue was "political" and not "justiciable."[62]

In his book *A Matter of Interpretation* (1997), Supreme Court Justice Antonin Scalia took a different stance. He stated that he does not believe that judges should make law: "If the courts are free to write the Constitution anew, they will, by God, write it the way the majority wants. . . . This, of course, is the end of the Bill of Rights, whose meaning will be committed to the very body it was meant to protect against: the majority. By trying to make the Constitution do everything. . . we shall have caused it to do nothing at all."[63]

Scalia's Supreme Court colleague, Stephen Breyer, in *Active Liberty* (2005) stated almost the opposite: "It is clear that themes, approaches, and matters of emphasis can make a difference. This book will describe one such theme, that of active liberty."[64]

Even though the US justice system serves as a model for many in the world, US Supreme Court members often disagree. One recent case in which some justices stated they were upholding the constitution and others said it was being violated was Citizens United v. the Federal Election Commission of 2010, which was decided by a 5-4 decision. This decision overturned laws that had previously limited large donations to politicians. It was based on the Free Speech provision of the US Constitution (under the First Amendment) and interpreted the contribution of money to politicians as "free speech." Because the US Constitution is one of the shortest among major nations, much of it is open to court interpretation. Whether or not we agree with a decision, it shows that in many ways our courts do create law, although most justices would claim the opposite. Nominations to Federal courts by the President that must be confirmed by the Senate have been accompanied by more and more contentious debate in recent years.

Our ideas about justice also are reflected in how we treat those who have broken laws. Much evidence points to a problem with the justice system in the US and in some countries: many people emerging from these systems have not reformed but continue to commit crimes. They often don't have opportunities to learn new skills and behaviors that would allow them to reenter the economic stream.

In the US over 2 million people are in prison at a rate much higher than any other major country. The so called "war on drugs" has swelled the ranks of the prison population since the 1980s. Minor drug offenses put blacks behind bars at a much higher rate than whites[65] The criminal justice system in the US costs an annual average of about $1 billion dollars per state,[66] and the cost per inmate in prisons far exceeds the average cost spent on students in schools.[67]

The vast majority of prisoners are admitted for either nonviolent crimes, such as burglary, drug offenses, robbery, or parole issues. A disproportionate number are young African American males who lack a high school education. Many are married with children, which leaves families with one parent trying to hold a job and raise a child.

One solution: abandon a failing system that America can ill afford. Instead provide programs that include training in job skills and social interactions that can be done at a much lower cost financially and to society. Perhaps most importantly, provide programs that let people know that society cares about what happens to them.[68]

Democracy makes many promises. The US Constitution, upon which many are modeled, states in its Preamble that its intent is to "establish justice." It is doubtful that the US Founders agreed on the practical nature of justice – its meaning in everyday life – when they wrote it and that certainly continues to be debated in our own day. But I think that the concepts of "justice" and "democracy" are intricately tied.

If the laws of a country tip toward a majority that imposes its will on the minority, such as with slavery, clearly that is not justice. If the scales become unbalanced toward the priorities of a wealthy minority, that also is not just. If any part of the population prevails over any other part we actually are moving away from democracy toward autocracy. But if our guiding principle for justice becomes that which serves the vast majority of people, and we bring a discussion of how best to do that into our interactions as a society, we then are engaging as many people as possible in moving toward clarity about how best to make democracy work for all.

We also experience justice for ourselves as we become more committed to acting justly and fairly toward those around us. Thus we create a more just world in the immediacy of our own lives.

So how do we combine the desire to blame and that to forgive? True justice always includes respect for the integrity of the individual. Corrective action only can be about improving future behavior since the past – by definition – is over. Except for those few who are incarcerated for life, all must be prepared to re-enter the world. This only can be done by training programs that prepare those who make mistakes to take their roles as productive members of society.

THE ECONOMY

Economics, once called "the dismal science," affects each of our lives every day. Everything we purchase to put on our bodies and in our homes, what we drive and where we live, and our optimism or pessimism for our future all are affected by the economic policies of our own countries and their interactions with other nations.

We usually think of economics as being about money. But as has been pointed out in the first two chapters, there was trade long before there was money. Trading events also were social events.

People met with their neighbors regularly to exchange goods or services, and then this was expanded over gradually greater distances. Markets originally were democratic; the value of items was determined by bartering. Money eventually was used to facilitate trade and store value for the next time. Thus economics ultimately is not about money, but about the circulation of goods and services.

Even now, money only has the value that we agree that it has. Its only real use is what it will buy for us and its ability to store value. But if everyone were to agree that the money we have worked so hard for (or gotten by other means) is useless, it would be reduced to scraps of paper with pictures of some of our favorite historic figures.[69] This is what happened, for example, to the Deutschmark after World War I, and has occurred numerous times in history, such as in Brazil which experienced over 6000 percent inflation in 1990.[70]

In the late 1920s, and leading up to the Depression of the 1930s, a singer named Al Jolson popularized the song: "I'm Sitting on Top of the World." Songs like these, along with films of the time, provided a glimpse of optimism in contrast with the grim reality that most people experienced during that downturn. The opening lines in the song went: "Don't want any millions, I'm getting my share, I've only got one suit, that's all I can wear." There were many who, although experiencing severe losses due to the drop in the stock market, remained wealthy during the depression. But the reality was, and still is, that no matter how wealthy you may be you still only can wear one suit. You only can eat a limited amount, ride in one car at a time, and be in one room at one time, no matter how opulent the room. The rest of one's wealth only can be experienced by viewing a spreadsheet or holding an image of all of that accumulation in one's mind.

There are very few people who wouldn't welcome a chance

to be rich. Some are excellent at saving and investing, some have inheritances, and then there are lotteries. Some have sources of income that could be considered illegal. But no matter how much money we accumulate, its real value is in what it can purchase.

When I buy a shirt, I'm giving up money that I worked for in exchange for something that I agree to be of equal, or near equal, value. If I don't agree with its purchase price I am less likely to buy it. Then the person to whom I transferred my money uses it in exchange for items that he or she, or a corporate entity, considers of value. Thus money only serves us as it becomes a part of the economic flow that moves in an ongoing manner from one person to another, and then to still another continuously.

Going back to the origin of markets, some people became good at accumulating money. They may have been good at saving, made a commission on items they bought or sold, or were in a high paying profession. Looking to increase their funds, they lent to those were short of money and seemed likely to pay them back.[71] Or they may have invested in trade organizations, such as happened in ancient Rome (Chapter I), or in companies investing in new lands, such as the Massachusetts Bay Company. Another option was loaning money to the government (actually our fellow citizens) by buying government bonds that, although usually providing a low yield, usually were reliable.

Inequalities often occurred as money was handed down from one generation to another. Those with an inheritance could invest it to have enough to meet their needs. Eventually those at the top of the economic pyramid were able to establish large households or fiefdoms. Some eventually became royalty. As history shows, royalty often clashed until only a few governed increasingly larger territories. Those who dominated were those who could inspire – and pay – their armies.

Some in positions of power treated those under them with

respect, while others took advantage of their positions to make those with little or no funds serfs, or even slaves (Chapter II). Leaders often were threatened by those who coveted their position and wealth. Often having no reliable sources of information due to their isolation from the commoner, kings and queens took the word of their advisors about whom to trust.

Leaders needed to collect taxes to support the country's expenses. Wars were particularly costly. European sovereigns depended on their colonies for revenue after the year 1500. Many plundered their colonies to bring in gold and other items that would increase economic flow.

At the time of the American Revolutionary War, the legendary economist Adam Smith was concerned about the inequalities he saw around him: "Wherever there is great property there is great inequality. For one very rich man there must be at least five hundred poor, and the affluence of the few supposes the indigence of the many. The affluence of the rich excites the indignation of the poor, who are often both driven by want, and prompted by envy, to invade his possessions."[72]

In the eighteenth century the King of England needed funds to support his armies as he engaged in long-term conflicts with France and Spain. He decided to tax his New World colonies to bring in those funds, but many in his colonies were educated individuals who had read the Enlightenment authors and considered themselves equal to the citizens of Britain. Thus started the American Revolution that was the beginning of the end of colonialization throughout the world.

Turning to the present day, it is no secret that there is great economic inequality in much of our world. Some may think it is because some people are smarter than others, or because some are luckier than others, or because some have stolen from others. But inequality – not in the value of human beings but in the accumulation of wealth – is a fact of our world.

Thus we might say, with Jesus: "You always will have the poor with you."[73] There have been poor people as far back as history goes. But even in biblical times, the accumulation of too great an amount of funds by a few individuals impeded economic flow. Rulers collected taxes to sustain the supervision of their dominions, as was the case with Rome which ruled the world in the time of Jesus. Armies had to be paid and so did those who built the magnificent structures left to us by antiquity.

But those who accumulate excessive wealth and block its circulation ultimately harm themselves. Global economic crises – and there have been many historically, on the average of one every ten years during the twentieth century – rarely have been about shortages of goods, but usually have been about funds failing to circulate.[74] Leading up to the worldwide Depression of the 1930s, people focused on accumulation of funds. Eventually there were not enough funds to go around. Goods and services failed to circulate in response. A lack of food, housing, clothing and other items did not cause the slowdown. It was caused, rather, by a sudden shortage of funds based on overspeculation. Everyone was hoping to accumulate money and get rich at one time, and there just wasn't enough money circulating to keep the economy moving.[75] The trust needed to sustain the economy was shattered.

Now let's look at what some economists – denizens of the dismal science – have to tell us about the nature of an economic crisis.

Thomas Piketty, a French economist, surprised the world of publishing when his *Capital in the Twenty-First Century*, a six-hundred-page study of the history of economic inequalities, appeared in 2013. The first printing of the English translation, which appeared in 2014, sold out quickly. Those wanting to wade through his long arguments supported by a plethora of charts had to wait a few weeks.

Piketty's book was especially popular because of the 2008 Great Recession that was still on everyone's minds. His essential argument is not complex. He states his premise right from the beginning:

When the rate of return on capital exceeds the rate of growth of output and income, as it did in the nineteenth century and seems quite likely to do again in the twenty-first, capitalism automatically generates arbitrary and unsustainable inequalities that radically undermine the meritocratic values on which democratic societies are based. There are nevertheless ways that democracy can regain control over capitalism and ensure that the general interest takes precedence over private interests.[76]

It doesn't exactly read like your average best seller. But the basic premise is important and worth understanding. There are those who make enough returns off their investments that they don't have to work. In many cases they have inherited their funds. I want to be clear I am not blaming them for that. Most of us wouldn't mind being in their position. Their accumulated funds, as a group, continue to increase and, unless regulated some way, slowly outstrip the funds of those who work for a living, creating income gaps. There is no way that those who work, no matter how hard, can catch up. This means that income inequality, if left alone, will continue to grow indefinitely.

Why is this a problem? As those of us who have been around for a while know, prices rise over time. In the US $100 per week was enough for the average middle class worker to buy a home and support a family in the 1950s. And that was with only one person working in the home. That's $400 per month, or about $5000 per year. But inflation has multiplied the amount required to support a family about ten times since 1950.[77] That's about $4000 per month or $50,000 per year. Those making less than that amount have lost ground, and in many areas of the US, that is still not enough to provide basic necessities and still make house payments.

Imagine having to still live on that $100 per week today. Those whose income has gone up with the rate of inflation in the last sixty years would be able to live at the same level as always. Those with investments that kept up with inflation would be fine. But there is a growing income inequality in the US and many western countries that causes resentment among the large numbers of workers whose wages have not kept up with inflation. According to a recent study by the Economic Policy Institute: "The rise of top incomes relative to the bottom 99 percent represents a sharp reversal of the trend that prevailed in the mid-20th century."[78]

Later in his book, Piketty points to the results of long-term gaps between interest earners and wage earners: "In my view, there is absolutely no doubt that the increase of inequality in the United States contributed to the nation's instability. . . . It is important to note the considerable transfer (15 %) from the poorest 90 percent to the richest 10 percent since 1980. The richest 1% absorbed nearly 60% of the total increase."[79]

He takes a final swipe at the concept of Americans that they are a just society: "Modern meritocratic society, especially in the United States, is much harder on the losers, because it seeks to justify domination on the grounds of justice, virtue, and merit."[80]

Piketty does not spend as much time on his solutions to inequality as on the problems it causes. He recommends raising taxes on the income from investments (capital gains) to plow those funds back into the system.

Robert Reich was Labor Secretary during the presidency of Bill Clinton, although his real strength is economics. He now writes books and creates videos about how to make our economy strong again in addition to holding a professorship at UC Berkeley in California. In his latest book, *Aftershock*, Reich discusses how inequality hurts the economy – a theme he has been emphasizing for years. He also created a film, *Inequality for All*, based on his book.

He admits that some inequality is inevitable. Some people are more talented than others and some just more fortunate. But he has become alarmed at the negative effects of growing inequality on the world economy, particularly in the US: "at some point inequality becomes so wide that it undermines democracy."[81]

Reich states that, although workers have continued to work hard, improvements in productivity did not help to prevent the financial meltdown of 2008. This is because the gains of their efforts went primarily to those at the top of the economic scale, creating more imbalance. To keep pace, people went into debt early in this century, borrowing on housing that seemed like it would go up forever. But many found that they couldn't pay their increased mortgages which contributed to the meltdown.

He points to studies showing that the inequalities before the 2008 crash were the largest since 1928, right before the Great Depression. The reason that inequality leads to economic downturns is that economies are dependent on spending. Most businesses, and the banks that loan to them, need spending from the bulk of people to stay afloat.[82] When economic flow slows down, it leaves many businesses unable to repay their bank loans.

Reich also discusses the inadequate response of governments to the 2008 economic downturn. Most governments of Europe resorted to austerity, which means they cut spending.[83] While austerity might temporarily look good on the balance sheets of nations, it cuts into the economic flow needed to keep businesses afloat. This in turn reduces the tax flow to governments, making it difficult for them to provide the services that they have promised.

During the Great Depression of the 1930s the US government as well as governments around the world at first cut back on expenditures to save money. But this made the situation worse, and before long the new President, Franklin Roosevelt, began spending money to stimulate the economy. But the economic slowdown was stubborn and stimulation didn't work for a long time, largely because people had become afraid to spend. At last World War II forced a government spending binge that stimulated the economy.

John Maynard Keynes, a British economist, published his *General Theory of Employment, Interest, and Money* in 1936. For a long time there was general resistance to his theories in England and the United States, and with good reason. His ideas seemed to contradict common sense. The essence of his main idea was that, during economic slowdowns, one should "prime the pump." This meant that instead of cutting funding, the government should borrow money and invest heavily in creating employment to increase the amount that consumers contribute to the economy. This would, in turn, generate more taxes so that the government could continue its stimulus and increase the general economic flow. He challenged the previous thinking that free markets would eventually adjust themselves – this clearly hadn't worked out during the Depression that was in its sixth year when his book was published.

This book is couched in difficult economic terms and rarely quoted. Nonetheless I will cast a buoy in the murky waters of his seminal work and see if it floats. In the chapter entitled "The General Theory Re-Stated," Keynes writes:

> *An increase (or decrease) in the rate of investment will have to carry with it an increase (or decrease) in the rate of consumption; because the behavior of the public is, in general, of such a character that they are only willing to widen (or narrow) the gap between their income and their consumption if their income is being increased (or diminished).*[84]

Now if your eyes still are focused on the page I'll try to inter-pret what that means. If we want to improve the economy we (that is the government) must increase investment, which then will create more jobs, and that then will stimulate the economic flow as people have more to spend. This was done in the United States during the Depression to a limited extent, but it did ease the lives of many who might otherwise have starved or lived in the street. Much later, when the US was in its 2008 economic downturn, Keynesian methods were used with generally good results rather than hoping that the economy would right itself, which once was the theory of mainstream economists.[85]

Opposing the Keynesian theory were the "free market" economists led by Milton Friedman and the Chicago School of Economics. Essentially, they believed in minimal governmen-tal interference in the economy. Friedman was an advisor to both Ronald Reagan and Margaret Thatcher. Allen Greenspan, Federal Reserve Chairman in the US beginning in the 1980s, also espoused theories called monetarism, which held that the money supply should be regulated to improve the economy. More money would go in – via lowering interest rates by the Federal Reserve – when the economy needed stimulation, and interest rates would be raised when the economy overheated. The problem was that Greenspan kept rates low despite an expanding economy. He became a cheerleader for an economic bubble that could not sus-tain itself. He warned of "irrational exuberance," but never raised interest rates when the economy overinflated in the years leading up to the Great Recession of 2008.[86] He then expressed his surprise and regret at not having seen what was coming.[87]

Societies have economic systems as a part of their basic struc-tures which, when working well, allow us to enjoy an expanding range of goods and services. Money is a tool to help facilitate our access to the things we need and want. But when money remains accumulated in too few hands for too long, it impedes our ability to get our needs met. It also causes economic slowdowns that negatively affect those at all levels of income.

Taxes can be a tool to increase economic flow while investing in the services we need, such as roads and police services that benefit everyone. Government agencies also can be wasteful and need continual monitoring by citizens or legislators. But even those individuals who are financially well-off and have no concern about the effects of stagnation from slowdowns will benefit from economic flow. When consumers at all economic levels have funds to make purchases, this stimulates the economy which benefits everyone.[88]

Economic policies have consequences. They never are neutral. Markets may have begun with a neutral playing field long ago, but as some gained the upper hand they eventually had advantages over others. Equality is about adjusting the playing field so that all once again have a chance. Playing a rigged game benefits no one.

And so the question we might ask ourselves is "Do we really believe in democracy?" If so, what does it look like in the real economic world, between individuals, in government, and particularly in the marketplace? We need an ongoing conversation about this issue. As in all areas, we need to agree on specific ways to move toward a vision of how a healthy economy facilitates democracy. And then we need to invest to maintain economic flow at a sustainable level. As history has repeatedly shown, lessening the flow of funds within economies via tax cuts for those at the top is harmful to those at all levels of income.[89]

As the world entered the 1990s, the consequences of globalization became more obvious.[90] The interdependence of nations became pronounced as trade barriers were reduced and goods, capital, technology, and workers were more easily able to move across international borders, accompanied by the creation of firms that were more international than aligned with any one nation. To agreements such as the European Union were added the likes of the Association of Southeast Asian Nations (ASEAN) and the North American Free Trade Agreement (NAFTA) designed to "eliminate barriers to trade."[91]

The stated purpose of these agreements was to bring economic benefits to the people of participating countries, but from the viewpoint of many economists most of the benefits went to corporations able to move their businesses or take advantage of cheaper labor and taxes. Jobs were lost in the US as factories closed, particularly in the auto and steel industries. The impact on many workers was that their jobs disappeared or their wages were reduced. Large sections of cities like Detroit became ghost towns. Oppressive labor conditions were introduced in countries that produced consumer goods (see China in Chapter II). Public perception of the benefits of trade agreements that had been touted by politicians dropped significantly.[92]

The leaders of all large world powers claim to be pursuing economic policies that support the principles of democracy, but the actual affects of these policies – as seen and experienced by many – are to create inequality and negatively affect the financial situation of people worldwide A large number of economists and politicians believe that our policies and trade agreements must be reevaluated and redesigned to benefit those at every level of the economic spectrum.

The needs of people at all economic levels must be brought into the conversation about what works best for economic growth. To quote John F. Kennedy: "A rising tide lifts all boats." People eventually will rebel or, in democracies, vote out politicians who they see as not addressing economic inequality.

THE ENVIRONMENT

If, in a democracy, the will and needs of the people are to be respected, then the environment upon which we depend also requires respect. This means that our air, water, food, mineral, and fuel sources are maintained in a way that does the least damage while still meeting the needs of people. Our ideas about how to do that continue to evolve.

When automobiles were introduced, no one thought that the fumes would eventually clog the planet. Coal once was a life-saver supplying fuel for furnaces that radiated heat in buildings that previously were cold in winter. At first people were not concerned that coal would be a dirty and damaging fuel. As the redwood forests in California were cut down to build homes it was not apparent that those vast groves could be decimated. And when gold was discovered no one anticipated the destruction to lives and the environment that would result. Eventually environmental destruction became – for many – just the cost of doing business.

As mentioned, views of what is important change within a society over time. There is no evidence in the art or writings of the ancients that they paid much attention to their natural environments, despite the beauty that we now see upon visiting natural places. The possible exceptions were Chinese scenes that depicted natural motifs in a stylized way. Landscape art, which reflected – and then affected – attitudes of western society toward nature only became popular in the mid-1600s.

When the first trains and steamboats were developed to haul passengers, no one anticipated the soot that would ruin their clothes and sting their lungs. Since then competing camps gradually developed, with some favoring more use of environmental resources in the name of "progress" and some wanting to slow down the pollution that comes with more people and the abstraction of fossil fuels.

Fortunately, in the last half of the twentieth century, more alternative fuels were developed that were less destructive of the environment. Scientists also charted a rise in air and ocean temperatures that correlated with the rise in fossil fuel use. The lobbying of the fossil fuel industry – and their influence on legislators, particularly in the US – has given rise to climate change "deniers," even in the state of Florida that is seeing the clear consequences of rising oceans due to melting ice caps. Yet the use of fossil-fuel energy continues to rise, particularly that derived from oil.[93]

As of this writing, some scientists say that we are on the verge of getting the bulk of the energy we need from renewable and non-polluting sources, including hydroelectric systems such as dams, wind turbines, solar power, hydrogen fuel cells, and non-fossil fuels, such as those based on algae.[94] Distributing energy via grids is a challenge because it also uses energy, particularly over long distances.[95] Considerable progress is being made in saving energy by innovative technologies such as electric cars, LED lights, and solar water heating.

Unfortunately bio-fuels based on plants such as corn have not lived up to expectations because of the cost of producing the crops from which the fuel is made and the limits to the amount of farmland that can be converted to that purpose. This also limits the production of food from the same land.[96]

Recently, there has been a movement to obtain previously unavailable fuels from underground sources by the use of a technology known as fracking (hydraulic fracturing). This process drills in places to extract fuels from underground shale deposits and has increased the supply of natural gas and oil. But fracking destroys the environment in the area above ground and has been correlated with an increase of earthquakes below ground. It uses a tremendous amount of water as it pumps chemicals into underground water reservoirs. The fuel derived from this process still is a pollutant when burned.[97] There is a limit to the amount of biofuel in the ground, so viable alternatives must be found sooner or later.[98] At this writing there is an encouraging trend: clean energy jobs are surpassing oil drilling jobs.[99]

As the world population passes seven billion, there is growing competition for the land needed to feed everyone. Fertilizers, increased water supply, and crop efficiency contribute to greater yields from the same land area. But with the population increase the past problem of food overproduction now is being replaced with a need to boost production.[100]

In areas of the earth torn by war and environmental degradation a meal has become a luxury for many. The war in Sudan, for example, killed at least 1.5 million and left eighty-five percent of the population as refugees. Starvation has killed thousands as the land is devastated and unable to support life.[101]

Water also recently has been recognized as a limited resource. Dumping raw sewage in European rivers such as the Thames and Seine once led to death from typhoid. Eventually modern water and sewage systems developed, but as seen even in rich countries such as the US, water supplies, if not maintained can deteriorate and cause illness.[102] Many cities are considering reuse systems, especially for irrigation, to alleviate anticipated water shortages that come from expanding populations and drought.[103] Desalination plants are used by necessity in dry places like Israel and are being considered for drought-prone areas like California.[104] But these plants also use much energy. Lawns are being replaced in many areas with plants that use less water, such as Texas, Colorado, New Mexico and California.[105] Much water from rains goes to waste in these areas that could be captured by underground reservoirs.

An encouraging sign is the new environmental education emphasis in many schools, making the adults of the future more aware and respectful of their environment. In Santa Rosa, California, the Center for Climate Protection conducts programs for high school students to teach active ways to lessen their environmental impact. Its mission, according to its website: "Is to inspire, align, and mobilize action in response to the climate crisis. We work with business, government, youth, and the broader community to advance practical, science-based solutions for significant greenhouse gas emission reductions."

Only a hundred years ago, when automobiles were attempting to replace horses and buggies, the disparaging expression used to harass those trying to make their gasping new cars gallop down the road was "get a horse." For the earth – and democracy as we know it – to continue, environmental awareness will be a prerequisite. Discussing the issues and presenting facts to those who have, for some reason, not gotten the message hopefully will go a long way to convincing them to eventually give up their horses for the energy solutions of the future.

HEALTH CARE

In most industrialized countries that are considered democracies health care is a basic human right.

Germany has the oldest universal health care system in the world. It was started in 1883 as the Sickness Insurance Law under Otto von Bismarck, otherwise known as the tough and aggressive Iron Chancellor. This plan created the model for many similar plans with shared employee-employer contributions. Currently, the German plan provides insurance for over 80 million residents regardless of legal status. The plan covers doctors, dentists, chiropractors, physical therapists, psychiatrists, and hospital stays. The

World Health Organization puts the German system near the top for services provided. There is an adequate supply of providers because they are well paid, thus there are no long waits for services. Patients can choose any doctor or hospital and bills are paid by a private health care plan which only can charge fixed prices. The plan is expensive by European standards – at eleven percent of the country's gross domestic product it is second only to the cost of health care in the US that costs about seventeen percent of the GDP.[106]

In France, patients present the *Carte Vital* upon entering a doctor's office, showing registration with the national plan. The healthcare system reimburses doctors for about seventy percent of the cost of visits, the rest is charged to the patient upon arrival. Despite costing a fraction of US healthcare, the French system is rated #1 by the WHO and the French life expectancy is higher than in the US. As in Germany, the cost of the plan is shared between the employee and employer. However, insurance plans are non-profit which means that they save much of the approximately 25% of the administrative overhead of US insurance companies. If a French employee suffers a job loss, the government picks up that share of the tab. All practitioners in the country are covered by the *Carte Vital* so there are numerous choices.[107]

The British National Health Service has no insurance premiums or co-payments – all is covered by the government. Health insurance is covered by taxes that are high even by European standards. Although Brits sometimes find their system slow, it costs about one third of health care in the US. Yet the British system seems to ensure a longer lifespan than most countries. When concerns were expressed about overuse of a system that is totally free, a few charges were introduced, such as a small fee for prescriptions, glasses and false teeth, but they are waived for children and the elderly. There is some rationing of expensive drugs. The National

Health Service is huge – it is the largest employer in Europe. No one – Conservative or Labour – would dare threaten to end it.[108]

In Japan, a wide range of treatment options are covered, from acupuncture to radical surgery. The mandated coverage – which uses private insurance plans – pays about seventy percent of the bill. The Japanese system gets more usage per patient than any European or American system, and doctors make house calls. Japanese people are either naturally healthy or their healthcare system works because they have the highest life expectancy on earth. The costs run about eight percent of GDP, half of the US. Most insurance is obtained through work plans, but retirees and the self-employed have a separate plan. Medical costs are capped and the insurers must pay every bill.[109]

The benefits of the booming Chinese economy do not trickle down to all citizens. During the first thirty years after the Communist takeover, there were impressive benefits to the health of its citizens. Infant mortality dropped and life expectancy doubled to sixty-eight years. But in the early 1980s the health care system was dismantled due to an attempt to "decentralize" government. Central health care funding dropped in half, while responsibility was transferred to local governments. Wealthy areas did well, while poor areas lost services, and much of the treatment was privatized. The central government did maintain price controls on treatments, but only those who could afford health care received it.[110] Just two percent of the national budget goes toward health care, and only one third are insured. Most doctors and hospitals are privately paid. Because there is no single payer buying system, medications can be high. People pay about ten percent of their individual incomes on medical care.[111]

In Russia, the entrenchment of oligarchy has especially devastated the health care system. The death rate from heart attacks is rising.[112] Medical care has become inaccessible for a growing portion of the population; mortality in hospitals – and the death rate in general – are increasing as doctors no longer can keep up with workloads. Health clinics have been slashed due to lack of funding. Cuts in staff have resulted in an inability to provide a cohesive system of care.[113] In the small town of Chapaevsk, south of Moscow, there is a wasteland created by the remnants of chemical plants. In 1985 and on other occasions there were blasts in the factories that killed thousands of people; the land and water still are toxic. But no officials ever acknowledged the problem. Discussing it with the press or outsiders can lead to the loss of one's job or worse.[114] Russian authorities continue to pretend that the health of its citizens is improving, and almost no one dares to contradict the official line.

In the US, the Affordable Care Act was signed into law by President Obama in 2010 with its provisions to gradually be put in place. The ACA mandates healthcare for most people who lack it, prevents insurance companies from denying coverage for a pre-existing condition, establishes healthcare exchanges to find the best-suited program for enrollees not covered under their employer, subsidizes low income earners, reforms Medicare, and provides a penalty for employers who do not provide insurance. A survey by the Gallup Poll reported that the percent of uninsured in the US went from eighteen percent in 2003 to eleven percent in 2016 under the ACA. The law has been challenged in court numerous times, but its basic provisions were upheld in 2013 by the US Supreme Court. As in any large system change there have been some losers and winners – some whose premiums have gone up and some whose premiums have gone down. Other complaints come from employers who are likely to have their insurance rates go up. Some have suggested that simply expanding Medicare to more of those who cannot afford health insurance would have been a simpler and cleaner path, but the process of developing this bill was closely watched by the health care industry which would not have benefited as much by a simple expansion of Medicare.

In 2000, a book came out that considered the correlation between health and inequality. *Is Inequality Bad for Our Health?* by Norman Daniels, Bruce Kennedy, and Ichiro Kawachi describes the costs of poverty to society.

We have long known that the more affluent and better-educated members of a society tend to live longer and healthier lives. . . . Our health is affected not simply by the ease with which we see a doctor . . . but also by our social position and the underlying inequality of our society.[115]

The health of individuals and families is affected by their position in society.

If social factors play a large role in determining our health, then efforts to ensure greater justice in health care should not focus simply on the traditional health care sector. . . . We should be looking as well to improve our social conditions – such as access to basic education, levels of material privation, a healthy workplace environment, and equality of political participation – that help to determine the health of societies.[116]

All aspects of poverty must be considered if we are to improve the health of those who are impoverished.

Numerous studies have provided support for this relative income hypothesis, which states, more precisely, that inequality is strongly associated with population mortality and life expectancy across nations.[117]

The death and life expectation rates in all nations are affected by the level of inequality.

The poor in many countries lack access to clean water, sanitation, adequate shelter, basic education, vaccinations, and prenatal and maternal care. As a result of some, or all, of these factors, infant mortality rates for the poor exceed those for the rich.[118]

Many factors affect the health of those at the bottom of the income scale.

What sorts of social policies should governments pursue to reduce health inequalities? The menu of options ought to include policies aimed at equalizing individual life opportunities, such as investment in basic education, affordable housing, income security, and other forms of antipoverty policy.[119]

To improve the general health, all aspects of poverty must be addressed.

Growing evidence points to the importance of the early childhood environment in influencing the behavior, learning, and health of individuals later in the life course.[120]

Children can be disadvantaged by factors in their environment right from the beginning.

In a just society, health inequalities will be minimized and population health status will be improved – in short, social justice is good for our health.[121]

Justice demands addressing inequalities and creating programs to alleviate them (see above discussion of John Rawls).

As we review health care in a number of countries, it becomes clear that those which are most democratic are those that address the needs of those at all levels of society. Available health care solutions have vastly improved over the last 100 years or so, but those most likely to benefit have been those who can afford it. Part of improving the lives of those who are impoverished is providing greater health care access to those who lack it.

Even taking the most selfish viewpoint, epidemics of infectious disease never before seen occur every few years, always with a new name that threatens to be the scourge that kills us all. Most of these diseases originate in poor, highly populated areas with inadequate health care. So ensuring health care for the most disadvantaged is part of the effort to ensure the health of everyone.

The difference between the US model of healthcare and that of Europe and Japan can be traced to their differing models of democracy. The US model emphasizes the rugged individualism that served people on the frontier who were continually confronting new dangers as they moved west. This type of individual believes her or himself self-sufficient, not needing help from anyone. This is an illusion that is shattered by the reality of needing help from others, which happens to everyone at some point.[122] The models of some older societies reflect the view that acknowledging our interdependence leads to more effective health care systems.

RELIGION

The founding principle of most religions is the dignity of the human spirit. Followers at first are attracted by the insights and humanity of their leaders. Later this leads to concepts about those insights and conflicting ideas about how to put them into practice. Then some followers resort to rigidity and intolerance of those who don't follow the same practices that they do. This is why new religious leaders – with renewed insights – have appeared periodically to remind us that religion really is about a connection to a force beyond ourselves.

Religions – at their best – remind us of the ever-present nature of the divine. At their worst, religions turn the insights of their founders into weapons against those who don't think as they do.

In Hinduism, the world's oldest religion that still is practiced, there is a recognition of the unity of all people and things, expressed via an endless pantheon of gods. In Judaism there is recognition of the One God whose approval depends on following traditional commands. In Christianity, there is forgiveness of sins based on faith in God's representative. In Buddhism, there is a goal of unity with God based on meditation and contemplation. In Islam, there is a chance to gain access to Allah based on leading a good life. All offer different paths to salvation for the believer, but salvation – even if aimed at a future life – only can be understood and worked on in this life.

The right to hold one's religious views is a basic tenet of democracy. That includes the right not to have religious views – or any views – imposed on us. Those who do not respect the beliefs or views of others exist in all major religions and have been at the root of many wars, from the Crusades right up to the present wars in the Mideast. The pledge of democracy is to allow all to hold their views as long as they do not result in harm to others.

The tradition in the US of keeping Church and State separate goes back its the founders. Thomas Jefferson wrote of "a wall of separation between Church and State,"[123] and James Madison explained: "Every new and successful example therefore of a perfect separation between ecclesiastical and civil matters, is of importance. . . . Religion & Govt. will both exist in greater purity, the less they are mixed together."[124]

If we look at the extremists of any religion – or the extremists of any belief system such as atheism, for example – we see an intolerance that has little to do with an actual religion or belief system and more to do with the narrow views of the individual.

When we attack people for their beliefs we show the same disregard for them that we fear for ourselves. If we assume that any religion is violent we are condemning the vast majority of those of that religion who are not. By branding people as terrorists because of their religion we can cause resentment that may justify violence in their minds. If we believe ourselves more tolerant than religious extremists we need to become models for the tolerance we espouse.

Religions are not violent but people – and their beliefs – can be. The texts of every religion can be used to justify tolerance or intolerance. Many people choose their beliefs and then back them by the use of religious texts. Countless Hindus and Muslims have been killed in religious wars on the Indian subcontinent because they choose to use their beliefs to back an "us" vs. "them" mentality. In the Hebrew Bible it says "You shall love your neighbor as yourself,"[125] but intolerance can be justified by the Biblical stories of the Israelites destroying Jericho and other cities on their journey out of Egypt (see Chapter I). In the Christian Bible, Jesus preaches forgiveness: "For if you forgive men their trespasses, your heavenly Father also will forgive you; but if you do not forgive men their trespasses, neither will your Father forgive your trespasses."[126] But another quote can and has been used to justify violence: "I have not come to bring peace, but a sword."[127] There also is a history of Buddhist wars of intolerance in Burma. The Qur'an teaches: "We shall always find treachery in others, so pardon them and turn away: surely Allah loves those who are good to others."[128] But a minority of Muslims seeks revenge for wrongs they believe were inflicted on them by Western nations and participate in a policy of Jihad (which actually means struggle), and then use the Qur'an to justify their hatred: "I will cast terror into the hearts of those who disbelieve. Therefore strike off their heads and strike off every fingertip of them."[129]

Those who believe that all religion is dangerous also can be just as intolerant. Atheists, like those of any other belief system, can espouse views equally extreme to those of any religious fanatic. Richard Dawkins, once considered a great evolutionary biologist, is now known mainly as a shrill voice in the darkness of extreme atheist intolerance.[130] On the other hand, Sam Harris, a spokesman for atheism in a number of books such as *The End of Faith* (2005), and *Freewill* (2012), recently made an effort to have a dialogue with a Muslim leader as recorded in *Islam and the Future of Tolerance, a Dialogue* (2015).

Some believe that science and religion not only are compatible, but represent two views of the truth. Francis Collins is an American physicist and geneticist and was leader of the project that successful mapped the human genome. He now is Director of the US National Institutes of Health. In his book *The Language of God* (2006), he states his view that: "The principles of faith are, in fact, complementary with the principles of science."[131] He asks the following regarding morality: "In all areas of human knowledge. . . each party attempts to appeal to an unstated higher standard. This standard is the Moral Law. But is this sense of right and wrong an intrinsic quality of being human, or just a consequence of cultural traditions?" Regarding God: "If God exists, then He must be outside the natural world, and therefore the tools of science are not the right ones to learn about Him."[132] In other words, for Collins, God cannot be known by the workings of the universe, but only from the workings of our minds.

Many great scientists have written or spoken of God, although their definition of God may not always be identical to those who consider themselves religious. Newton never considered that his discoveries contradicted his belief in God. For Einstein: "To sense that behind anything that can be experienced there is something that our minds cannot grasp, whose beauty and sublimity reaches us only indirectly: this is religiousness. In this sense, and in this sense only, I am a devoutly religious man."[133] As for Stephen Hawking: "If we discover a complete theory, it should in time be understandable by everyone, not just by a few scientists. Then we shall all, philosophers, scientists and just ordinary people, be able to take part in the discussion of the question of why it is that we and the universe exist. If we find the answer to that, it would be the ultimate triumph of human reason – for then we should know the mind of God."[134]

Carl Jung held a different view of religion from Sigmund Freud, who considered it an illusion. Jung considered religion an opportunity to retain one's individuality: "The individual who is not anchored in God can offer no resistance on his own resources to the physical and moral blandishments of the world."[135]

Once, religion was seen as the route not only to salvation, but to truth. Over time, as we have learned to observe the world more closely, dependence on religion for understanding the world no longer is important for many of us. Scientific discovery is an ongoing process that seems continually to be getting closer to explaining the mysteries of existence, and yet always comes up short. Perhaps science always will be unable to answer some questions about the universe, such as why it exists.

At the point where we acknowledge the limits of scientific inquiry and arrive at a sense of wonder as we contemplate the universe around us – at did Newton, Einstein, and Hawking – we will appreciate that there always will be much that remains beyond our understanding.

Whether religious or not, we can evoke that part of us that holds inflexible standards for others and ourselves, or that which acts based on toleration and our common humanity. This is how we can bring the insights of the founders of the great religions into our lives.

SCIENCE AND INNOVATION

Science has transformed the way we live, but has it altered our most basic nature? We can reach for the stars, but do we know ourselves?

From the time we discovered that rocks can be used as hammers to the moment we stood on the moon, we have been curious creatures that have, unlike others, been able to progress based on an ability to pass on knowledge to others across generations. At first we no doubt used grunts or gestures to communicate, but the evolution of our species took off when we discovered how to use symbols and words to convey ideas.

At some point, both as individuals and as a species, cooperation became a key value. That ability would be impossible without language and symbols, such as the ones we use in mathematics, but it also would not happen without the basic cooperative behavior rooted in our genes. Thus cooperation, as well as competition, is a part of our makeup.

Michael Tomasello, at the Max Plank Institute for Evolutionary Anthropology in Leipzig, Germany, is a pioneer in the study of human interaction. He has published a number of books on his discoveries made while observing young children learn social skills. In *Why We Cooperate* (2009) he provides the crux of his theories that are based on years of research:

> *Unlike their nearest great-ape relatives. . . humans have spread out all over the globe. . . . Human artifacts and behavioral practices become more complex over time. An individual invents an artifact . . . and others are quick to learn* [use of a spear for example]. *To date, no animal species other than humans has been observed to have cultural behaviors that accumulate modifications and so ratchet up in complexity over time. . . . We may refer to the underlying psychological processes that make these unique forms of cooperation possible as "shared intentionality."* [136]

He goes on to show how helping behavior can be seen in infants. For example, if an adult drops a spoon during an experiment, the young child will try to help. This behavior is universal. Apes, among other species, do not have this ability.[137] Then children at about the age of three, with a maturing sense of self as they develop more of a sense of separateness, become less willing to share. But at this age they are more able to incorporate social norms about behavior, such as knowing that they are to hang up their coat when they enter a room. Some children also become enforcers of social norms and behaviors. Slightly older children begin to incorporate the idea of "we" – meaning they understand that there are behaviors that humans, or those in their group, automatically perform. Thus social norms become universal. Empathy – the ability to identify with another's situation, and altruism – concern about another's welfare, are among those norms.[138]

Ben Bergen, in *Louder than Words,* takes this principle one step further. He discusses the way that we impart meaning to concepts as they surge through our minds.[139] This is not easy to study. If I use the word "patriotism" in our conversation is there a place in your body where you actually experience the meaning of that word? This gets into how we experience knowledge and how we know what really is important from all the stimulation we receive every day.

In his MRI studies, Bergen has confirmed that when we see or hear a description, for example, of someone running through the woods, we actually have an experience of running in our legs. Thus a good story teller can engage us in a way that not only is mental, but physical.[140] Bergen also discusses the concept of *mirror neurons,* our experience of empathy when, for example, we see someone laughing or crying.[141] Toward the end of the book he asks: "What is it to communicate successfully? . . . All that's needed is a sufficient degree of commensurability between a speaker's intent and a hearer's interpretation."[142]

So what does this all have to do with the progress of science and civilization? If an ape comes up with a great new idea such as how to use a stick to eat termites (this behavior has been observed), he may be able to show his friend how to enjoy this great gourmet treat, and his friend may even copy the behavior. But that's where the communication ends. If I make a similar discovery, and I communicate it by symbols or words, it may become a part of my culture and be remembered for generations. And why should I care to even communicate my discovery? Because – unlike apes – I am a part of the cultural *we*; my natural altruism revels in the discovery and I want to share it. That is the way that you and I build civilizations. Sorry if you don't actually like termites.

In Chapter 1 we traced much of the history of science so we don't need to do this here. However, I think it important to spend a little more space on how science progresses and, as is rarely discussed, in many ways it's personal. In our segment on education we discussed how teaching and learning, at their best, are conveyed in a way that evokes excitement. This happens not only in that part of people that we call their minds, but as mentioned above, the most effective communication and understanding actually are experienced in one's body.

Michio Kaku, a modern popularizer of scientific ideas, quotes Einstein discussing his early life in *Einstein's Cosmos* (2004): "Einstein would bitterly nurse the scars left by the authoritarian methods of his day: 'It is, in fact, nothing short of a miracle that the modern methods of instruction have not yet entirely strangled the holy curiosity of inquiry; for this delicate little plant, aside from stimulation, stands in need of freedom.' "[143] We then learn of the excitement that Einstein felt upon making his greatest discoveries: " 'The solution came to me suddenly with the thought that our concepts and laws of space and time can only claim validity insofar as they stand in a clear relation to our experiences.' "[144] Kaku succinctly describes the essence of General Relativity: "In a Newtonian world, gravity waves cannot exist, since the 'force' of gravity acts instantaneously throughout the universe. . . . But in general relativity…gravity waves have to exist, as vibrations of the gravitational field cannot exceed the speed of light."[145] And: "As Planck once said, 'Science cannot solve the ultimate mystery of Nature. And it is because in the last analysis we ourselves are part of the mystery we are trying to solve.' "[146] Putting it all in perspective: "Thus, our moon revolves around the earth, the earth revolves around the sun, and the sun revolves around a black hole."[147] Einstein's early education shut him down mentally and physically, but making his greatest discoveries excited and engaged his entire being.

In *The Double Helix* (1968), James Watson describes his discovery, along with four others, of DNA, the basic building block of life.[148] This won three of them a Nobel Prize in 1962. In his book, he discusses the rigorous process of creating one scientific model after another in collaboration with those on his team at Cambridge. He describes the interplay between common sense and advanced scientific theory – intuition and insight – that, with luck, leads to the progress of knowledge. He and his colleagues batted about a number of models and ultimately had to create a unique one once it became evident that the structure of DNA was likely to be irregular.[149] He describes the interpersonal difficulties and anger between various researchers who were, after all, only human. He discusses the "vitality of the English intellectual life" which provides an atmosphere in which scientific progress can flourish (Newton also had been at Cambridge).[150]

The above only are two examples of the way that scientists pursue a deeper understanding of our universe and of ourselves.

But we might consider that starting in the sixteenth century, when scientific inquiry began to replace the dogma of the Church, civilization's advances seem to have primarily taken place in the West, where innovation and scientific inquiry usually were encouraged en route to establishing greater democracy.

A fear of challenging elements of Church dogma as the teaching that the Earth was at the center of the universe quashed the ability of Copernicus to publish his theories until he at last did so on his deathbed in 1543. The Inquisition still had a chilling effect on Galileo when he confirmed these theories with his telescope nearly a century later. But the hold of the Church on the floodgates of scientific inquiry had begun to loosen by that time, and by the mid 1600s a torrent of discovery followed. Once the heavy hand of censorship was lifted, the natural curiosity of the human mind, which craves creating and sharing new discoveries, went into full bloom. We changed our world, which in turn changed the way we live.

Amongst the discoveries of that period were the laws of planetary motion by Kepler (1609-19), the discovery of the circulation of the blood by Harvey (1628), Boyle's gas laws (1662), Hooke's discovery of the cell (1665), Newton's discovery that light is made of a spectrum of colors (1672), the use of calculus by Leibniz (1675), the microscope by van Leeuwenhoek (1675), the first measurement of the speed of light by Romer (1676), and the universal laws of gravitation by Newton (1687).

The list continues into the 1700s with the discovery of oxygen (Priestly), a listing of the planets (Messier), the conservation of mass (Lavoisier), and into the 1800s with atomic theory (Dalton), electricity (Ohm), the conservation of energy (Joule), evolution (Darwin), germ theory (Pasteur), and genetics (Mendel).

The charming classic, *Great Inventors and their Inventions* (1918), profiles sixteen discoveries that changed the world from

Watt's design of the steam engine in 1777 to the 1909 invention of the wireless telegraph by Marconi. All sixteen were creations of Western democracies.

As the human creative impulse freed itself from censorship in the 1600s a flood of discovery followed that changed the world. But this largely happened in nations that took interest in – or at least did not block – human progress. For much of the rest of the world at that time and since, the emphasis was on conformity to the pre-established views of governments that were more interested in retaining control over their residents than in promoting their welfare. But now the people of those countries are able to take advantage of technology that developed elsewhere, and as fellow human beings sharing our earth, this only is right.

Now back to the second part of the question with which we started this section.

THE HUMAN MIND

For the ancient Greeks – as they sought to understand both the outer world and the inner – all knowledge was considered part of philosophy. Since then we have altered our outer world via an astounding cascade of discoveries that leaves it nearly unrecognizable. Socrates, perhaps the most legendary of the Greeks, famously claimed: "the unexamined life is not worth living."[151] Socrates was on trial for his life in the Athenian Senate when he made this bold statement. We have done an impressive job of ignoring his admonition for nearly 2,500 years.

While perhaps unaware of it, we all have a philosophy – or philosophies – by which we guide our lives. If we believe that people are basically good, we express that in our interactions to create an atmosphere of trust and cooperation. If we think people are bad or selfish they become the "other" in our minds and we are convinced we must avoid or compete with them. The real challenge is to become aware of our beliefs. Do we just follow them automatically or do they really serve us? There is no real philosophy – or magic pill – that always works to understand people or the world. But when we pay attention we see that every person and situation is different.

In democracies we tend to think of ourselves as free. But what is freedom? Rudolph Steiner was a philosopher with a huge following in Germany in the late 1800s and early 1900s. He started the Waldorf Schools that still are popular today. He believed that nature is our best teacher and encouraged people to get in sync with the rhythms found in nature and themselves. In his *Philosophy of Freedom*, first published in 1894, he claimed that we tend to create ideals that always are beyond our reach: "we seem born to dissatisfaction." He expressed concern about what he saw as two sides of human nature that rarely are in harmony: "Mind and Matter . . . Thought and Appearance." All we know of the world is our inner concepts: "We can find Nature outside of us only if we first learn to know her within us." [152] He taught that the key to morality is to be found by looking inside of ourselves: "We meet with a special kind of these moral principles when the law is not proclaimed to us by an external authority, but comes from our own selves. . . . The name for this voice is conscience." [153] To Steiner, freedom is acting in accord with this inner sense of morality. But the difficulty comes when we try to codify our morality into concepts and laws. [154]

Carl Jung was a Viennese psychiatrist who championed awareness – and also respect – for the inner life of each individual. In *Man and His Symbols* (1961), Jung tells us that we retain many of the basic instincts from our earliest times; that our moods and emotions often are governed by inner impulses of which we may not be aware. He discusses the seductive myths of political systems that promise a heaven on earth and always are bound to disappoint. It is our beliefs and convictions that give life meaning, yet reality rarely can live up to the ideal that we hold in our minds.[155] Our myths and stories always have been a part of our minds and cultures and have given meaning to life, but modern living largely has destroyed our emphasis on meaning as people struggle to meet their material needs each day: "His moral and spiritual tradition has disintegrated, and he now is paying the price for this break-up in world-wide disorientation and dissociation.... As scientific understanding has grown, so our world has become dehumanized.... The surface of our world seems to be cleansed of all superstitious and irrational elements."[156] Our inner, irrational self needs acknowledgment or it may break through and express itself in harmful ways.

Jung was writing at a time when one totalitarian regime (the Nazis) had attempted to conquer the world in the name of "purity" and another (the Soviets) dominated Eastern Europe in the name of a utopian mirage. The appeal of both was a perfect world that its founders had sold to a gullible population. Jung's insistence on the acknowledgement of the complexities of the human being – as opposed to an illusion of perfection – was a move in the direction of sanity.

Moving up to our own time, in *Thinking Fast and Slow* (2011), psychologist Daniel Kahneman, like Aristotle, Steiner and Jung, points to two aspects of the human mind, based on his research, that have evolved to add efficiency to our lives: "System 1 operates automatically and quickly, with little or no effort and no sense of voluntary control.... System 2 allocates attention to the effortful mental activities that demand it, including complex computations." We have limits to our attention span that cause failure if we try to go beyond them. It wouldn't work for us to be continually paying attention to our every act, so acting automatically usually is beneficial.[157] Hearing a message repeatedly works its way into System 1 and creates a belief system of which people may be unaware: "A reliable way to make people believe in falsehoods is frequent repetition." But, putting people in a good mood helps them to relax and improves learning.[158] Even though we think of ourselves as rational, we tend to believe that which confirms what we already think we know.[159] Perhaps most importantly for our everyday functioning, we tend to put people into categories of being all good or all bad regardless of evidence that they have mixed qualities.[160] Causality – the idea that one event causes another – is wired into our belief system whether supported by evidence or not.[161] And as mentioned previously in these pages: "The world in our heads is not a precise replica of reality; our expectations about the frequency of events are distorted by the prevalence and emotional intensity of the messages to which we are exposed."[162] Similarly to Jung: "Regret and blame are both evoked by comparison to a norm."[163] Thus we automatically categorize each of our experiences as positive or negative.[164]

In *The Power of Habit,* Charles Duhigg also tells us that much of our daily routine is based on habits of which we are largely unaware: "And though each habit means relatively little on its own, over time, the meals we order, what we say to our kids at night, whether we save or spend, how often we exercise, and the way we organize our thoughts and work routines have enormous impacts on our health, productivity, financial security, and happiness."[165] The development of willpower, another habit, can be instrumental in overcoming routines that interfere with our real preferences: "Dozens of studies show that willpower is the single most important keystone habit for individual success."[166] But willpower can be developed: "Willpower isn't just a skill. It's a muscle, like the muscles in your arms or legs, and it gets tired as it works harder, so there's less power left over for other things."[167]

Our habits ultimately are the result of the way we see the world: ". . . your habits are what you choose them to be. . . . The way that we habitually think of our surroundings and ourselves create [sic] the worlds that each of us inhabit."[168]

In *The Righteous Mind*, Jonathan Haidt claims that nearly all people hold an ideal of right and wrong in their minds: "If you ask kids about actions that hurt other people, such as a girl who pushes a boy off a swing. . . . Nearly all kids say that this is wrong."[169] Yet in our actual behaviors we often do what is most comfortable without thinking about right and wrong. After we commit ourselves to action we will find reasons to justify what we just have done. It is common to put aside what we once thought was moral to participate in behavior that we have been taught, even if it is cruel and harmful to others, as long as it seems that the group will approve.[170] Our reactions – and thus our actions – often are automatic: "Affective reactions are so tightly integrated with perception that we find ourselves liking or disliking something [or someone] the instant we notice it, sometimes even before we know what it is."[171] But our interactions with others – for better or worse – often are what shape our moral behavior: "The main way that we change our minds on moral issues is by interacting with other people."[172] Looking at the world of politics: "Liberals score higher on measures of. . . openness to new experience. "Conservatives. . . prefer to stick with what's tried and true."[173] Regarding cooperation: "We trust and cooperate more readily with people who look and sound like us."[174] And on a lack of open-mindedness after we identify with a political party: "Once people join a political team, they get ensnared in its moral matrix. . . . It's difficult to convince them they are wrong if you argue from outside the matrix.[175]

Whether aware of it or note, we continually are guided by our ideals. Democracy is an ideal. Communism is an ideal. Religions teach ideals. We hold ideals about marriage and families – and even of ourselves – and the reality often falls short. We become disillusioned when our world – or others – do not meet the ideals we have set, and we often want to punish those we consider responsible.

In *Utopian Thought in the Western World*, Frank and Fritzie Manuel trace how ideals have shaped our history. They discuss the ideal city of Plato in his *Republic,* the Christian/Judaic belief that we have come from an ideal garden and that some will return there, and Thomas More's distant island as portrayed in his *Utopia*. There are those who consider utopians hopeless dreamers, but utopian writers often have captured the aspirations of their times: "Paradoxically, the great utopians have been great realists. They have an extraordinary comprehension of the time and place in which they are writing and deliver themselves of penetrating reflections on socioeconomic, economic, or emotional conditions of their moment in history. They have discovered truths that other men have only vaguely sensed or have refused to recognize."[176] Many leaders are utopians because of their ability to invoke a vision that appeals to their contemporaries.

Utopian thought, as expressed in ideals that often attract followers to a world that is yet to come, is needed to guide civilization forward. It is the vision that allows us to work together toward a common cause, and the starting point for many countries that consider themselves democratic. But when not aware of how we compare our world with the ideals we have set we tend to curse our fate and those around us. When we are able to move beyond our ideals to recognize the individuality of ourselves and those around us we also get to experience the uniqueness of who we are.

To make democracy work, we need to temper our ideals with reality. The founders of American Revolution encompassed the ideal of freedom in their writings. Part of the vision of those revolutionaries was to rid themselves of what they considered tyranny. As difficult as that was, it was the easy part. Those who wrote the Declaration of Independence – and later the US Constitution – were followers of the Enlightenment authors who espoused human dignity. The real challenge was how to translate that concept into laws for themselves and posterity.

The US Constitution is very short for what it tries to accomplish. It turns a vision of human dignity into law as best could be done for its time. For those who believe in this vision, the way it is expressed in our lives – between individuals, on a national scale, and on an international scale – is continually being rethought.

As individuals, and as nations, we are guided by ideals that we try to keep in our minds as we move forward into new territory that often is uncharted. In democracy the ideal is moving toward greater equality and respect for people. But there remains within us, perhaps except for the smallest children, a conflict between our ideals and our lived reality. The real world often fails to cooperate with our good intentions. This is why our ideals – and how they are to be lived – must be worked out with others on an ongoing basis. We may believe in bringing the principle of greater dignity into our own lives and those of others, but the way we make that principle a reality in the world in cooperation with others always will be different than anything we might have imagined.

VIOLENCE AND WAR

Humanity has a violent past. Dividing people into "us" and "them" probably is set in our genes because at some point it helped some of "us" to survive. Wars go back to competition for limited resources and territory as far back as we can see.[177] Recent archeological finds have unearthed the skulls of early victims of mass attacks 10,000 years ago.[178] The unification of Egypt took place about 5,000 years ago due to the forces of one conquering king.

Since World War II there has been a series of wars in numerous locations around the world, usually involving a large power and a small one. These include two in Vietnam against France and then the US, two in Afghanistan against the Soviets and then the US, a civil war in Algeria against France, an Iran-Iraq War, three Israeli wars against their neighbors, an Indian-Pakistan war, the Korean war, a war in the Congo, plus numerous civil wars and revolutions.

Many wars have been in response to what the large powers consider the attempts of "insurgents," or revolutionary forces, to overthrow an established government. But the thirteen colonies that started a revolution against Britain also were considered insurgents by many. Choosing one side regardless of its rights record often results in the opposite of what we intend. Thus our guiding principle always must be supporting human rights. After revolutionaries establish new governments they can be just as intolerant and oppressive as those they replace. Rather than stubbornly staying with one side we must be on the side of human dignity.

In his book *In the Crossfire,* Ngo Van describes his role in the fight to free Vietnam of French domination. In 1936, he was captured, imprisoned and tortured in Saigon.[179] There were numerous attempts to overthrow colonialism in his country throughout the Twentieth Century. When Vietnam threw off the French, Ngo Van barely escaped while many of his friends were imprisoned or killed by the nationalist Communist freedom fighter Ho Chi Minh. Another war in South Vietnam was lost decisively when the US was forced to withdraw in 1975. That same Vietnam now is considered a friend of Western nations. But its current government also is oppressive to its people.[180]

The Soviet-Afghan war lasted for ten years starting in 1979 and killed over one million people. The US, including its CIA, helped to arm the insurgents (Mujahideen) against the occupying Soviets, but after they were forced out the insurgency group used US weapons to rule the country. After a period of civil war, the Taliban, fundamentalists who were an outgrowth of the Mujahideen, took over and imposed strict conservative Islamic law. Organizers of subsequent attacks on the US, including the World Trade Center attack of 2001, were veterans of the Afghan war.[181]

In the 1960s through 1980s, the US supported brutal dictators against insurgents in El Salvador, Nicaragua, and Guatemala from army bases in Honduras and Costa Rica for fear of a "Communist" takeover in those countries. The Castro regime established itself in Cuba in 1959 despite the best efforts of the US to support the Batista dictatorship (see Chapter II).[182]

For most of the last half of the twentieth century one of the key motivators of American foreign policy was containing what it considered Communist takeovers in many parts of the world. Nearly all of these efforts failed as the US tried to sustain brutal dictatorships that sacrificed millions of lives.[183] The US, like many large nations, made decisive moves to support or overthrow regimes based on ideology, failing to acknowledge the humanity of those they purported to help.

To correct what they see as failures of justice, some have resorted to terrorism to restore order in a world that they believe has lost its values. Jessica Stern, in her book *Terror in the Name of God* (2004) courageously interviewed known terrorists of various backgrounds and religions. She spoke to many who have killed – or would kill – for their causes. She was able to get them to talk because they welcomed a chance to have their ideas publicized, and she interviewed them in a spirit of empathy for them as human beings, which is not the same as sympathy for their causes. She tells us that terrorists all have one thing in common:

"They have lost the ability to empathize with their victims." Terrorists have a common motive: "Religious terrorism is about purifying the world. The way forward is clear: kill or be killed. Kill and be rewarded in heaven. Kill and the Messiah will come. It is about seeing the world in black and white. About projecting one's fears and inadequacies on the Other."[184]

She interviews Terry Noble. He had been member of a violent cult that firebombed a synagogue and a church that had accepted homosexuals. His group conspired to assassinate federal officials and stockpiled cyanide with the aim of poisoning major city water supplies. They hoped to bring down the US "Zion occupied" government and replace it with a Christian one. They wanted to rid the world of blacks, Jews, and all other sinners to bring on the Apocalypse and return of the Messiah. According to Noble: "All those who refused the word of the Lord. They were the enemy. And so they would have to die. . . . We wanted peace, but if purging had to precede peace, then let the purge begin."

Her general assessment of those who join terrorist organizations: "Once inside an organization whose goals include killing, ordinary people can commit seemingly demonic acts. . . . Cult members become two people: the self they were and a new, morally disengaged killer self. . . . Because the true faith is purportedly in jeopardy, emergency conditions prevail, and the killing of innocents becomes, in their view, religiously and morally permissible."[185] Regarding the intent of terrorists: "First, terrorism is aimed at non-combatants. . . . Second, terrorists use violence for dramatic purpose: instilling fear in the target audience is often more important than the physical result."[186] Terrorism is about "dehumanizing our enemies, putting innocent civilians at risk. It is an approach we should be sure to avoid if we aim to succeed in counteracting them. . . . Although we see them as evil, religious terrorists know themselves to be perfectly good. To be crystal clear about one's identity, to know one's group is superior to all others, to make purity one's motto and perfection of the world one's life work – this is a kind of bliss. . . . Participants in the Crusades, the Inquisition, and the kamikaze suicide-bombing raids all understood the appeal of purifying the world through murder."[187]

Stern then goes on to describe terrorists from other religious backgrounds. "Ramzi bin al-Shibh, a mastermind of the September 11 attacks, describes violence as 'the tax' that Muslims must pay 'for gaining authority on earth.' He says that 'it is imperative to pay a price for heaven.' The moral 'obligation of jihad' is equally as important as the duties of prayer and charity."[188] "Jewish extremist Avigdor Eskin invoked an ancient mystical prayer to bring about the death of Israeli Prime Minister Rabin. . . . He wanted Rabin to die because he was giving away 'Jewish' territory to Muslims."[189]

Regarding the leaders of terrorist cults: "The leader has to be a psychologist. He has to have a gift for knowing what people need, what they want, what is missing from their lives."[190] An organization like Hamas combines terrorism with genuine charitable work. "The most important element of Hamas' success is its social welfare activities."[191] "How does Hamas identify a likely candidate? . . . Young, often a teenager, he is mentally immature, there is pressure on him to work, he can't find a job, he has no options, and there is no social safety net to help him. . . life has no meaning but pain. . . marriage is not an option."[192]

More on Jewish terrorists: "In 1990, a messianic group known as the Temple Mount Faithful announced its intention to lay a 4.5-ton cornerstone at the site where the ancient Jewish temples once stood. . . . The group's ultimate goal is to destroy the Muslim holy sites and build a third Temple. . . . The group's presence near the site incited the deadliest riots in Jerusalem since the city was taken over by the Israeli army almost a quarter of a century earlier. The movement has attracted a number of messianic individuals and groups – both Christians and Jews. Among them is Yoel Lerner, an MIT trained mathematician and linguist who was imprisoned for a variety of terrorist plots, including a plan to blow up the Dome of the Rock to make room for the new Temple." [193]

But there are voices of sanity in Israel: "Michael Ben Yair, Israel's Attorney General in the Rabin government, describes the current situation: 'The Six Day War (1967) was forced on us; but the war's seventh day. . . continues to this day and is the product of our choice. We enthusiastically chose to become a colonial society, ignoring international treaties, expropriating lands. . . . Since the signing of the Oslo accords in 1993, official Israeli government policy has been that no new settlements will be built. . . . [but] The government allows existing settlements to expand, sometimes into new neighborhoods."[194]

Stern describes what she considers the essence of terrorism:

All the terrorist groups examined in the book believe – or at least started out believing – that they are creating a more perfect world . . . all of them describe themselves as responding to a spiritual calling, and many report a kind of spiritual high or addiction related to its fulfillment. . . . My interviews suggest that people join religious terrorist groups partly to transform themselves and to simplify life. What seems to happen is that they enter a kind of trance, where the world is divided neatly between good and evil, victim and oppressor. . . . There is no room for the other side's point of view. . . . They persuade themselves that any action – even a heinous crime – is justified. They know they are right, not just politically, but morally. Unless we understand the appeal of participating in extremist groups and the seduction of finding one's identity in opposition to the Other, we will not get far in our attempts to stop terrorism. . . . The terrorism we are fighting is a seductive idea, not a military target.[195]

Those we call terrorists are heroes to some. So what is it that makes one group of fighters terrorists and another heroes? We might claim that the difference is that real heroes are those that fight for liberty, but those we call terrorists also make that claim.

One possible answer is that for those who believe in democracy war is a last resort. The essence of democracy is respect for others and their beliefs which is expressed in ongoing dialogue. Going to war only is considered when there is a clear threat and no choice – after every other means of resolving issues is exhausted. Even then, in the countries that consider themselves democratic, the decision must be made after discussion of the alternatives by a legislative body, not by the limited vision of only one leader.

This is the kind of debate that only can happen where the opinions of all are honored, if not necessarily followed. Democratic debate lends itself to actions that maximize respect for people to the extent possible. The act of participation in a discussion where there is genuine dialogue instructs us how to be more respectful toward others. And if we agree on a plan that might work to reduce violence rather than going to war, we must ask: "Are we willing to try it?" and "What must we do to put our idea into action?"

For those countries that consider themselves democracies, a decision to go to war must be based on the same essential questions that we always must consider: "What kind of world do we want to live in?" and "Are our actions moving us toward, or further from, that kind of world?"

No one is immune to feelings of hate. If children start out as loving, how do they learn to hate? If they start as innocent, how do they grow into terrorists? When they are treated with respect they are more likely to learn to be respectful toward others. If children are taught that that all infractions are to be punished – that forgiveness is weakness – they are more likely to believe that it is their role to punish others. The belief that people easily can be categorized as good or bad is the most undemocratic of ideas.

But changing our thinking and acting are difficult. Within us we each have a possibility for blame and revenge. This is our personal "persistence of the past." Yet the human mind also is capable of moving forward toward identifying and creating the world in which we want to live. This is an ongoing process and takes patience. There may be no ultimate point of arrival. Yet there can be great satisfaction in working toward our goal.

Those who are under leaders who speak of liberation but practice tyranny eventually will overthrow those leaders. To avoid spreading violence and tyranny, we can begin to bring respect for human dignity into our homes, schools, organizations, governments, and relations with those in other parts of the world. We can wait for others to take the first step – or we can begin.

The question we need to continually ask our children and ourselves is: does violence and war make the world a better or worse place, and if worse, what is the alternative?

INTERNATIONAL RELATIONS

Before the end of World War II, forty-four countries met in Bretton Woods New Hampshire at the charming old Mount Washington Hotel in the White Mountains to establish rules for the post war economy. One of their main goals was to avoid the mistakes of the victorious Allies of World War I who, through draconian reparations on Germany, contributed to creating a monster bent on revenge.

They established the World Bank and International Monetary Fund to provide loans for the vast rebuilding project that soon would be needed. All agreed to avoid a return to the protection-ism that had contributed to a deepening of the Great Depression between the wars and that ultimately protected no one. The World

Bank, also set up at that time, would make loans and regulate exchange rates based on the gold standard. The Bretton Woods system, however, began to stumble in 1947 due to a post-war economic slump. The US stepped in to provide rebuilding funds for Europe and Japan. The Marshall Plan provided $17 billion in grants to Western Europe. This, plus investments in NATO and the Korean War, made the dollar the world's dominant currency.[196]

The United Nations was established in San Francisco in 1945 when fifty countries met to replace the League of Nations. The "big five" – the United States, Britain, the Soviet Union, China and France – had veto power as Security Council members, which tended to weaken the ability of the UN to make decisive decisions. The Security Council did have the power to recommend to the General Assembly that they sever diplomatic relations with specific nations, apply economic sanctions, or even go to war. It also set up a commission (UNESCO) to help the development of economically backwards nations. The UN moved to its new headquarters in New York City in 1950.[197] It became the scene of many acrimonious debates, often between the US and the Soviet Union, particularly during the Cuban Missile Crisis of 1962, when the US confronted the buildup of missiles in Cuba. After a few days of tension that many feared would end in World War III, Russian supply ships turned back.

The European Economic Community worked out trade rules beginning in 1957 to encourage free trade and establish institutions that would function independently to create a more united Europe. This led to unprecedented economic growth and prosperity for the region. Many of the methods used to stimulate the economy were based on the principles of John Maynard Keynes (see THE ECONOMY, above).[198]

Other trade agreements were put in place over the years, including GATT (General Agreement on Tariffs and Trade, 1948) that included 23 nations, which eventually was replaced by the WTO (World Trade Organization, 1995), and NAFTA (North American Free Trade Agreement, 1994). Now it appears that TPP (Trans Pacific Partnership) will be put into place. The purpose of trade agreements is to eliminate or lessen tariffs between countries and create a more robust economy for participants. However, the effects of some of these agreements, according to critics, are that they protect manufacturers and make workers compete for wages internationally, which shifts manufacturing jobs across borders. What is clear is that manufacturing firms – accompanied by jobs – have been moving to where they can find cheaper labor.[199] If manufacturers can move their operations and then ship items back to their own countries to minimize expense, it clearly will cost jobs in the original country, and in many cases cause workers to work for low – and sometimes subsistence – wages. The amount that consumers can spend is reduced along with their wages.

Safety and environmental rules also are easy to avoid by moving to countries desperate for jobs. Trade cannot be eliminated, but the guarantees of workers' rights to safety and a decent salary would go a long way toward winning wider approval for these agreements.

A major issue facing all nations in an era of globalization is how each country can maintain its own identity and values while benefiting from the advantages of international trade. Every country has contributions to make that are unique to its own culture and traditions. This is true in the areas of produce, manufactured products, art and crafts, clothing, music, and technology. The issue is how to develop and market what each nation does best. Countries can support each other in ways that move toward greater economic and cultural independence for all. But making these agreements work requires recognizing the economic needs of people at all levels of society. To work for all, international trade agreements must not be based only on increasing trade, but must take into account the effects of trade on the people of the nations involved.

Hillary Clinton was US Senator from New York from 2001 to 2009, and Secretary of State from 2009 to 2013. In her book *Hard Choices* (2014), she discusses her determination to meet with leaders around the world to establish connections so that smaller countries don't feel ignored by the US. To get to know those countries better she would need to meet with local as well as national leaders.

Clinton describes the difficulty of standing up for the human rights of dissidents – in China for example – while trying to improve working relations with countries with which the US has a fundamental disagreement. On Russia for example: "Should the United States stop negotiating on arms control because we objected to Russia's aggression in Georgia?"[200]

She expresses her basic support for trade agreements, such as the Trans-Pacific Partnership (which she later withdrew). She believes that other trade agreements that were worked out on her watch were worthwhile, such as the Pacific Alliance that included Canada, Mexico, Columbia, Peru and Chile, but expresses her concern that "economic inequality in Latin America was still among the worst in the world." Yet she offers no clear cure for inequality.

She discusses her vote to back the 2003 invasion of Iraq based on false evidence which she now "deeply regrets." She describes her role in sending a surge of 30,000 troops to Afghanistan in 2010 when it appeared that the country was going to be overwhelmed by the Taliban. She expresses support for a two-state solution "that ensures dignity, justice, and security for all Palestinians and Israelis."[201]

She states her concern about countries like Egypt being able to sustain a democratic government: "Functioning democracies require the rule of law, an independent judiciary, a free press and civil society, respect for human rights, minority rights, and accountable governance. In a country like Egypt, with a long history of authoritarian rule, it would take strong, inclusive leadership and sustained effort from across society, as well as international support, to put these building blocks of democracy in place. No one should expect them to appear overnight."[202]

Regarding the Syrian refuge crisis: "The crisis began in early 2011, when Syrian citizens, inspired in part by the successful peaceful protests in Tunisia and Egypt, took to the streets to demonstrate against the authoritarian regime of Bashar Al-Assad. . . . It was a lopsided fight. [As of early 2014, estimates put the total killed at more than 150,000]. . . . Despite an international outcry over the violence in Syria, Russia and China vetoed a modest resolution at the U.N. Security Council. . . that would have condemned Assad's human rights abuses. . . . The United States and our partners steadily ratcheted up sanctions on the Assad regime. We froze their assets, imposed travel bans, and restricted trade. The Syrian economy was in free fall. But with Russia and Iran bankrolling Assad's war effort, the fighting continued unabated."[203]

About trade: "For too long we'd seen companies closing factories and leaving the United States because they could do business more cheaply in foreign countries where they didn't have to pay workers a living wage or abide by U.S. rules on pollution. Using diplomacy and trade negotiations to raise standards abroad could help change that calculus."[204]

She warns about the US keeping its policies in line with its mission: "If we. . . let our policies diverge too far from our ideals, our influence will wane and our country will cease to be what Abraham Lincoln called 'the last best hope on earth.' "[205]

On women as champions for human rights: "When women participate in peace processes, they tend to focus discussion on issues like human rights, justice, national reconciliation, and economic renewal that are critical to making peace. They generally build coalitions across ethnic and sectarian lines and are more likely to speak up for other marginalized groups."[206]

She expresses concern about the falling purchasing power for most people: "In the end, our strength abroad depends on our resolve and resilience at home. Citizens and leaders alike have choices to make about the country we want to live in and leave to the next generation. Middle class incomes have been declining for more than a decade, and poverty has increased as almost all the benefits of growth have gone to those at the very top."[207] Yet again she offers no solution for the problem of inequality.

International relations are interpersonal relations on a larger scale. In relating to those of other nations, we might ask ourselves: "What is our intent?" Do we want to use people or nations to serve our purposes while ignoring their desires and needs? Do we want to impose our ideals on others – no matter how noble – while suppressing their own values? Do we want to play the role of bully without considering the possible resentments and consequences that may result?

A hundred years ago Western countries thought they were doing other nations a favor by imposing their values and customs. In the meantime they didn't mind stripping those nations of resources to benefit themselves. When we try to impose our concept of democracy on others who haven't asked for it we usually end up with more resentment than thanks. Sometimes that resentment turns to violence. This is because people – no matter how democratic their aspirations – want to be allowed to act in the ways to which they have become accustomed. But regardless of customs or cultures, people still seek recognition for themselves as human beings.

Those who act violently against others – or against nations

– often condone their actions by stating that they are victims of unjust treatment. They believe that others have refused to respect their dignity and therefore they are justified in retaliating. Resentment and violence can feed into an endless chain until someone – or some nation – steps outside the cycle and decides to do things differently. This chain can be broken by initiating dialogue that recognizes the humanity of those who believe themselves to be victims. The best intervention – other than killing people and perpetuating the chain of hate among the survivors – is listening to people so that they know they are heard. This often is done after wars, so why not before they start? Violence may be justified for self-defense after all alternatives are exhausted, but at some point we nearly always return to dialogue with those we once considered our enemies.

And here we might ask ourselves: "Are we willing to do what it takes to move our world in the direction of ending the chain of violence?" If the answer is yes, then we might ask whether we are willing to substitute sacrificing billions of dollars and millions of lives to violent confrontations and instead engage others toward common understanding. Using violence to convince others that we are right clearly never has worked and is unlikely ever to work.

If we support the essence of democracy we must begin to approach others from a stance of respect. We must interact with regard for their human dignity regardless of differences in views – even their view of democracy. The root of democracy is, essentially, the message of our common humanity.

If, in my approach to you, I express a belief in my superiority or that of my lifestyle, I already will have contributed to a gap in our ability to communicate. But if I approach you with a sense of humility, I am creating the possibility of a connection between our minds and beings.

In *Power and Governance in a Partially Globalized World*

(2002), Robert Keohane emphasizes the need for understanding other people and nations – and their views – rather than imposing our own perspective, particularly by the US, the world's only remaining superpower:

Americans, in particular, could combine a praiseworthy resolve to stop terrorism with reflection about the role of the United States in the world. They could try to understand more about world politics, to become both less arrogant toward other cultures and political systems, and more resolved to play a positive role in improving the often horrible conditions of life that contribute to support for terrorism and other types of violence. . . . Such an orientation will require more openness toward information. . . even, or especially, information that makes us uncomfortable, such as information about the negative views of American policy held by many people in the world, and not only in the Middle East. . . . We face a moral imperative to understand world politics better. Better understanding should enable people to design better policies and institutions, although it is no guarantee of such improvements. Better institutions would enable ordinary human beings to live the lives of their own choosing, free from fear. Under such conditions, people could devise their own ways to love and respect other people and to value the natural world on which we all depend.[208]

The best way to develop this way of interacting is by practice – in our homes, schools and every other situation in which we have the potential to encounter conflict. When we show respect for others, no matter how strongly we may disagree with their views, we honor the individuals holding those views. We set an example for creating the respect that we want from others. Our actions convey our point more strongly than our words. Of course those who espouse murder to express their views must be removed from society, but there also are many who express extreme views because they have given up hope of being heard.

Such people exist within every nation, and they are not limited to those of any one race or religion.

All successful relationships are based on trust and respect. This applies to our families, our neighbors, our cities, our states and successful relationships between nations. Trust is based on understanding – or at least an attempt at understanding.

Human beings are much more alike than different. The main question is: "Shall we use the behavior of violent persons as examples for our actions, or shall we appeal to a higher standard in our interactions with others?"

POLITICS AND GOVERNMENT

The word "democracy" comes from the word "democratia," or popular government, and is attributed to Aristotle according to the *Oxford Dictionary of the English Language*.

In his *Politics*, Aristotle tells us:

Experience teaches us that every state is an association, and that every association is formed with some good end in view, for an apparent good is the spring of all human activity. Consequently, the state or political association, which is supreme and all-embracing, must aim at the sovereign good.[209]

Like many of the Enlightenment authors two thousand years later (see Chapter I), he believed that the purpose of the state is to create the greatest amount of good for the most people. His idea of equality:

It is not so much the property as the desires of men that need equalizing, and that cannot be done unless the laws provide a satisfactory education.[210] *... But the most powerful factor ... contributing to the stability of constitutions, but one which is nowadays universally neglected,* *is the education of citizens in the spirit of the constitution under which they live. In extreme democracies. . . everyone lives as he pleases. . . . But this is an altogether unsatisfactory conception of liberty.*[211]

A complete education that includes instruction in how to be a good citizen is essential for democracy. Democracy doesn't mean being free to do anything you want. Regarding how to choose leaders, Aristotle writes:

Nor is it desirable that men should offer themselves for election; the worthiest should be obliged to take office whether they like it or not. In any case they should be chosen. . . on the basis of their personal life and conduct.[212]

We should choose leaders who show us what it is to be exemplary citizens by the way they live their lives. As for the purpose of democracy:

The idea underlying the democratic type of government is liberty, one form of which provides that all citizens shall rule and be ruled in turn. The democratic notion of justice is that all should enjoy numerical rather than proportionate equality on the basis of merit.[213]

Real liberty and justice include the view that each person is just as valuable as every other. Regarding inequality:

A true democrat should make it his business to see that there is not excessive poverty among the masses. Gentlemen of feeling and good sense may also help the poor to make a start in some occupation, each of them adopting a group and allowing its members a grant for that purpose.[214]

To be strong, democracy must help those in poverty gain skills to move closer to the point where all are on an equal footing.

Conservative and Liberal Values

Ideas about what enables a state to best serve its people go back to ancient times. Yet we often hear a debate in England, the US and other countries about whether conservative or liberal values are the best to guide us. One might say that the 2,400-year-old perspective of Aristotle, who insisted that our views must be honed by science and dialogue, are as conservative as one can get, yet many present-day conservatives still might find this idea radical. How we label our views is not as important as using respectful dialogue to move toward democratic solutions to our issues.

Edmund Burke was a Member of Parliament in the late 1700s and a founder of modern conservative ideology. Burke was in favor of the American Revolution but was appalled by the excesses of the French Revolution. Even though reason may provide guidance for people to act, Burke believed that the role of reason is limited: "People cannot reason themselves into a good society, for a good society is rooted not merely in reason but in the sentiments and the emotions."[215] When looking across the Channel into the mass destruction of the French Revolution, he noted: "The present case. . . is not a revolution in government. It is not the victory of party over party. It is a destruction and decomposition of the whole society."[216] Burke believed that conservatism demands a realistic – not romantic – view of human nature, but that society must recognize the social needs and grievances of its people, and must be able to change with the times while maintaining its basic principles: "A state without the means of some change is without the means of its conservation."[217] He also believed that leaders must be humble in their roles as public servants: "The modesty of a leader must extend not simply to respect for the social order but to the limits of his own powers."[218]

In 1832, thirty-five years after Burke's death, Benjamin Disraeli, head of the Conservative government, said: "I am a Conservative to preserve all that is good in our constitution, a Radical to remove all that is bad."[219] Thus the tradition continued in England of a conservatism that combined a belief in the essence of democratic government with a need for it to move forward to meet the ongoing needs of society.

What is considered conservatism today in the US has little to do with traditional conservative values. Many conservative leaders express views that purport to contain forward looking values, but fail to identify any real path forward.

Paul Ryan is the current Speaker of the House of Representatives in the US. He is a gentle, soft spoken man who appears sincere and thoughtful. In his book *The Way Forward, Renewing the American Idea*, Ryan describes growing up in a small Wisconsin town where people know and care for one another. He writes eloquently about "The American Idea:"

. . . A way of life made possible by our commitment to the principles of freedom and equality are rooted in our respect for every person's natural rights. . . . What's missing is fresh thinking, good solutions, and real leadership. . . . One path. . . is a government-centered approach. Along this path, the federal government continues to expand, attempting to meet our every need with outdated policies that put the state in the center of our lives. . . . The second puts society, not government, at the center of American life.[220]

So far so good – limit big government and put people at the center of American life. Probably no one wants to have government for its own sake – it must justify its existence and expense.

He expresses concern about the demise of the auto industry in Detroit, not far from where he grew up:

The decline of Detroit is a 60-year-old story of how a city that was once the envy of the world slowly eroded before our eyes. . . in part because of a bad economy – a cycle of spending, borrowing and taxing until the bottom fell out. . . . . Many city government positions came with generous retirement and health-care benefits, the results of concessions made to public-sector unions over the years.[221]

Where did the "bad economy" come from? Ryan doesn't say. He seems to believe that government is to blame for having given benefits to workers.

Life isn't just defined by what we can do as individuals, but also by what we can do together. Society functions through institutions that operate in the space between the individual and the state. . . . Government is not the ultimate or supreme social institution: rather it is the enabler of other institutions. It exists to keep us safe, to enforce uniform laws, to enable free and open exchange, to ensure fair competition in the marketplace, to promote economic growth.[222]

And what are these institutions that government is supposed to enable, and how to do that? He doesn't say.

Empower Americans in every possible way. . . help the poor by reforming welfare so they can move up the ladder and out of poverty.[223]

Again, how to do that? Does he plan to create job training plans? Ryan is critical of Newt Gingrich in his stance against Bill Clinton in 1998:

It was a good lesson: You can't simply run against your opponent: you have to stand for something.[224]

Again, to stand for what?

Our country was founded on the principles of free enterprise, limited government, individual freedom, and a strong national defense. . . .

The President's true failure was that he was pulling us away from all of that.[225]

This points to why we need to learn more history. He omits that the US was founded on the principle of people working together to identify and move toward common goals.

What do we think the government ought to do? Today, there is widespread agreement that the government should provide some measure of health and retirement security. It should maintain a robust safety net, particularly for those who are unable to help themselves, and help able-bodied Americans who have fallen on hard times. . . . It must encourage economic growth by supporting free enterprise and the talents and ingenuity of our citizenry. It must protect the space where civil society thrives. . . provide for the national defense and implement a foreign policy that defends America's interests and values internationally.[226]

A little compassionate conservatism here. But should the government intervene if giant companies dominate the economy to the detriment of small companies and competition?

The bottom line is that when you tax something, you get less of it. So when we tax prosperity and success, we get less of each – and we need more of both so that we can get the economy working for everyone again.[227]

If we don't tax prosperity and success, shall we then tax only the poor?

Multigenerational poverty is a growing crisis for our country – and a lot of what we're doing is making it worse. . . . Our policies aren't creating opportunity or giving people the ability to climb the ladder into the middle class.[228]

Everyone agrees, but how do we fix it?

In 2013 Ryan and House Republicans proposed The SKILLS Act, HR 803 that basically takes money away from jobs training programs under the guise of creating them. Instead it gives block grants to states to do as they please and takes away control of the funds from local officials most familiar with the job needs in their areas. This is typical of funding proposals in other areas – such as health care – that try to reduce budgets by setting pre-set amounts that don't respond to actual needs.

Ryan's summary is one with which I totally agree:

A common vision allows us to move forward together in service to our shared goals. In the end, we share the same objective: we want a leaner, smarter government. We want to recover our founding principles. We want to restore prosperity, opportunity, and security. We want to free the engines of moral reform and heal our culture. We want to ensure that our nation remains a symbol of all the blessings that can be secured only through a commitment to liberty and the rule of law.[229]

Again there is no idea here about how to make that vision happen. Yet other than the idea that people should care for one another, Ryan suggests no actual "way forward" in his book. What he claims to be the way forward actually is a repeat of clichés from the past.

Moving to the other end of the political spectrum of US politics, Bill Clinton became President in 1993. His book, *My Life,* also contains a charming coming of age story. His campaign motto during the economic slowdown was: "It's the economy stupid!" He raised taxes, put more money into circulation, and cut the deficit. The economy improved tremendously under his presidency.[230] He also brokered a peace agreement between Israel and the Palestinians and helped to resolve the ancient feud between Catholics and Protestants in Northern Ireland.[231] But his book is more remarkable for what it omits that what it includes. Regarding Monica Lewinsky, with whom he admitted having an affair, he states: "I was unsure of exactly what the curious definition of sexual relations meant."[232] His Welfare to Work Bill (1996) actually caused many mothers to quit their jobs for lack of child care.[233] He never mentions the Gramm-Leach-Bliley Act of 1999 that he signed, which de-regulated the financial markets, leading to the biggest economic downturn since the Depression. And then, of course, he famously admitted smoking marijuana but insisted that he "never inhaled." He instead discusses youthful indiscretions around alcohol.

In almost every Western country, administrations shift between conservative and liberal leadership every few years (see Chapter II). This is not because one side of the political discussion suddenly has the answers. The more likely reason is that political parties usually only see and present a piece of the whole with which they personally or politically identify. When that piece of the puzzle no longer works to solve problems, people tend to think that another piece may provide a better option. When that fails the cycle repeats.

Despite the warning of George Washington at his inaugural address (see Chapter I), political parties have proliferated across the globe. But political parties and their leaders must reach across space and time — to those of different views and to history — to best serve those who put them in power. The tenets of democracy never can be contained in one person or party. We can be blinded by the right or the left.

E.J. Dionne, an American political commentator, sums up his thoughts on transcending the conservative/liberal divide in *Our Divided Political Heart* (2012). The basic tenets of the American system of government go back to its beginnings: "In the American system, private initiative and public enterprise complement each other."[234] Learning to honestly assess one's country's strengths and weaknesses should be a part of our education: "Giving students an accurate account of the country's shortcomings as well as its triumphs will not endanger anyone's patriotism. On the contrary, doing so is just as likely to show how acknowledging and correcting mistakes is an American long suit."[235] Historically, the views of historians have varied to fit the current political climate. In FDR's time, the US emphasized shared values and working together. More recently: "our public language about who we are and what we believe emphasizes liberty, individual rights, freedom of conscience, and personal autonomy."[236] He shows a deep respect for conservatism: "Conservatism has always made its greatest contributions as a corrective force that seeks to preserve the best of what we have."[237] And about the essence of democracy: "In a democracy, government should be seen less as an entity that issues commands than as a forum where citizens debate the future of their community and nation. . . . Democratic self-government, if it is functioning properly, is simply the expression of the will of the community."[238] About the founding of the US: "our forebears were not revolting *against* taxes or government as such. On the contrary, they were making a revolution *for* self-government. . . . Note that the signers [of the Declaration of Independence] wanted to pass laws, not repeal them, and they began by speaking of 'the public good,' not about individuals." [239]

Real conservatism in a democracy seeks to preserve the essential freedom of the individual. As history and the radicals who founded the US government have shown, that only can happen when there is a government that guarantees the maximum amount freedom compatible with justice. This is the promise of the constitutions of all nations that have them (see Chapter II). But the reality of how freedoms are protected expands with our definition of "We the People." When my freedom conflicts with yours, we need to work together to create a system that protects and respects us both. Conservatism based only on rigid concepts of right and wrong, on the "persistence of the past," will bring our ideas – and us – to extinction. Rigid ideas and actions by those who consider themselves conservatives or liberals that ignore the larger purpose of democracy only perpetuate the "us" versus "them" worldview that has caused most of the world's ills.

Once officials in a democracy are elected to office, they have a responsibility to "preserve and protect" (from the Presidential Oath in the US Constitution) the laws they were elected to enforce, and serve all the people whose lives are affected by those laws. But sometimes, at best, due to a lack of commitment or, at worst, willful neglect, those sworn to protect us suspend the rights of some in an alleged effort to preserve the rights of the majority.

In *Lords of Secrecy* (2015), Scott Horton describes how the CIA destroyed evidence of possibly illegal interrogation techniques used on prisoners from the US wars in Afghanistan and Iraq. Senator Dianne Feinstein, a member of the Senate Foreign Relations Committee, was a supporter of the CIA in the "war on terrorism." In her role to provide oversight of the use of torture by the CIA, she discovered that much of the evidence of its treatment of prisoners was missing. Originally these tactics had been authorized by Vice President Dick Cheney. The CIA, in fact, set out to intentionally sabotage the Senate's investigation. CIA leadership was concerned that exposure of illegal activities on its part could lead to prosecution.[240]

President Obama stated that he was "absolutely committed" to releasing the full report on the interrogations investigation, but only released a redacted summary.[241] To stay one step ahead of the Senate, the CIA launched their own search of the computers of Senators. In a speech on the Senate floor on March 10, 2014, Feinstein complained: "I have grave concern that the CIA's search might well have violated the separation of powers embodied in the United States Constitution."[242]

In 2011, President Obama decided to attack and overthrow the dictator of Libya, Muammar Gaddafi. The move was supported by the President's staff, including Secretary of State Hillary Clinton and UN Ambassador Susan Rice. There was no speech to the American people justifying the need for the attack, nor congressional debate and approval, as is required when going into war. The US Justice Department supported the attack under the guise of it not qualifying under what the framers of the US Constitution meant by "war." During the first Gulf War (1990-91) President Bush had engaged in extensive consultation with the US Congress, although Secretary of Defense Dick Cheney insisted that no Congressional approval was required. Nevertheless, President Bush asked for a vote on whether to attack to remove Iraq from Kuwait. Again, in 2003, the second President Bush, despite a huge national outcry, asked for Congressional approval to invade Iraq directly, which again was granted.[243]

According to the US Constitution, war-making powers are vested in Congress as are all laws, with the role of the Executive Branch under the President being to execute those laws. In an era of great secrecy, where the public is given less information about the process that leads to war, the distinction between making laws and the execution of laws can become less clear. The question we should be asking is: "Is it up to the President to make law as well as to enforce it?" If that is the case, the powers of Congress are greatly diminished.[244]

This brings us to a larger question. In a democracy should we simply vote for leaders and hope that they follow the Constitution and protect our rights? In ancient Athens, the representatives of "the people," though only a small percent of the population, voted directly for or against going to war, as did the people of

Sparta and other Greek city-states. Thus they took full responsibility for the consequences of their decisions, which at that time could result in the ruin of their city, with men being slain and women and children forced into slavery (see Chapter I).

The consequences for our times are not nearly as dour, but our democracies are new inventions, having been around just over 200 years. The Greek civilizations lasted nearly two thousand years – from the Minoans to Alexander, and that of the Egyptians three thousand years. Surely they thought that their civilizations would last forever, and they nearly did by our standards. Yet the modern overturn of the current seats of ancient civilizations such as Iraq and Libya – along with the chaos that followed – were easily accomplished by the advanced military might of modern nations.

In the funeral oration attributed to Pericles by Thucydides a high standard was set for democracies, although that standard rarely was kept even by Athens itself:

Instead of looking on discussion as a stumbling-block in the way of action, we think it an indispensable preliminary to any wise action at all. [245]

Who then, is the ultimate arbiter of the freedoms guaranteed by the constitutions of democracies? The United States currently is the leading world democracy. It has created one of the most vibrant economies on earth. Yet the abuses of those who are charged with enforcing laws for our benefit have caused alarm even among those in Congress whose role is to make the laws. And not long ago, under Tony Blair, Britain went to war with the US in Iraq and, as it was later discovered, a secret arrangement to participate in that war had already been made during a meeting between Blair and George W. Bush (see Chapter II).

There always will be sharp disagreement over significant issues such as going to war. But to make decisions that avoid these discussions violates the tenets of democracy. Discussions that take place in the context of what best serves the greatest number of people forces them to be framed in the context of democracy. It brings daylight to what decision-makers might prefer to hide in an effort to avoid scrutiny for their actions.

We should therefore choose our leaders carefully and hold those responsible who take actions that jeopardize our democracies. We do not follow the Athenian example of executing or sending into exile those leaders who failed to uphold their constitution, but as citizens we do have a right to vote and remove those who fail to respect human rights according to the laws they have been given to enforce.

If there was any one underlying theme to all we have covered here it would be respect – respect for the uniqueness and potential of every human being. Respect is a foundation of democracy. Human respect is the basis of the constitutions of nearly all democracies, but that principle is not always taken seriously. This brings us to a realization that it is not a written constitution that is the real foundation of democracy. It is rather a commitment to recognizing the validity of every human being on an ongoing basis. But as we have discussed, this principle is easy to state and believe, but bringing in into our actions is the great human challenge.

To work, real democracy must be practiced at all levels – the family, school, organization and government – by those who believe in it. Real democracy includes an ongoing and respectful discussion to identify our priorities and how best to work toward them together. We cannot expect leaders – or any of us – to become good at democratic methods when only trained to do what we are told and taught what to think. To work best, the practice of democracy must begin in one's youth and then be brought into every part of our personal and political lives. Practice may not make democracy perfect, but it at least will make it possible.

Guide to voting in a democracy

People often think that democracy is just about voting, but voting also happens in countries where democracy is a sham – in places where leaders don't have an interest in serving the public or perhaps even a concept of how to do so. True democracy is about responsibility on the part of all members of a society to understand and commit themselves to actions that move toward greater respect for every human being.

Leadership in democracies is based on the principle of ongoing elections and periodic leadership change where the rule of law, not an individual, is sovereign. Therefore everyone who aspires to office – or who seeks reelection – is a candidate whose qualifications and performance must be periodically evaluated.

If we want to preserve democracy we must do more than just vote. We have to pay attention to what candidates do as well as say. We must notice whether they really are committed to democratic principles. This means spending time examining individuals and their records. Party affiliations or labels such as conservative or liberal mean little.

Recently there has been a trend in Europe and the US for support of popular candidates outside the main political parties. Political parties provide stability, but often become entrenched and fail to respond to changing needs. New parties come into play to address people who consider their views or needs neglected. This happened with the Republican Party in the US in 1860 to prevent the spread of slavery[246] and the Labour party in Britain in the late 1800s in response to poor working conditions.[247] Thus candidates for office should be considered for what they are likely to contribute to improve democracy rather than their party affiliations.

Here are some questions we might ask about those who

would be our leaders:

1. Has the candidate shown an ability to work with others for the common good?
2. Does the candidate consistently show respect for people of all backgrounds?
3. Does the candidate's record show a commitment to the principles of democracy, that is, doing what is best for the greatest number of people?
4. Does the candidate only present complaints, or present a clear picture of realistic objectives and how to work together to achieve them?
5. Does the candidate listen to people or only is interested in foisting opinions on others?
6. Is the candidate talking down to people, or respecting their intelligence?
7. Does the candidate encourage people to think for themselves, or tell them what to think?
8. Does the candidate put out contradictory messages, depending on who he or she wants to impress?

Ultimately the future of democracy rests on our willingness and ability to have the most important conversation, which is a dialogue with others about how best to bring its benefits to the greatest number of people.

SUMMARY AND POSSIBLE LESSONS

We can bring democracy more fully into every human situation, including our families, schools, organizations, and nations. Each best serves our needs when we strive to extend dignity and respect to every human being. We also can bring democracy more fully into our interpersonal interactions as we develop the art of listening to each other.

Preparation for active involvement in democracy starts in childhood. To have a positive effect on our lives and interactions, democracy must be practiced in the home and school in addition to being taught. Families that are run democratically welcome the input of each member; they encourage children to clarify and express their views. Schools prepare students to become responsible participants in democracy by honoring their ability to come to their own conclusions, especially ideas about what makes a just world.

Organizations are most effective when all members are encouraged to give input and work as a team to identify and move toward common goals. And in governments that best serve their people, representatives openly discuss what is best for the vast majority as they clarify and work toward long-term objectives with popular input.

We divide the way we view and understand our world into realms: ethics, economics, the environment, religion, science, psychology, history, politics, and many more. But no area into which we categorize our world and universe is free of values. In addition to being tools to aid our understanding, each area has the potential to contribute to – or detract from – the practice of democracy.

Ethics, for example, is about the effects of our interactions on others. As individuals – and as a nation or race – if we practice respect for those we see as being different from us, rather than putting them into a category of "the other," we are more likely to live in a world where we together identify and progress toward common goals. Economics can be used to benefit a segment of the population or the people as a whole, and must be combined with ethics to identify what works best for all. A study of our environment is needed to determine which actions toward our planet will best sustain it and the human race. Our religions express deep-seated beliefs about the nature of human beings – whether we are many groups who must remain divided or one humanity who see ourselves as a united whole. The benefits of science can be extended to only a segment of the population or expanded to more people, especially in the area of health care. Psychology can promote the idea of human beings as separate entities or emphasize our common hopes and aspirations. We can see history as a series of destructive trends to avoid, or use it to identify and work toward new directions that move us in the direction of a better future. Politicians can cater to the needs of a privileged constituency or address the needs of the vast majority.

Thus each area into which we divide our world has the potential to contribute to greater human dignity. This is best done in situations that are democratic – that recognize the essential equality of every human being and encourage each of us to contribute to the creation of the type of world in which we want to live. In democracy at its best we identify and work together toward our most essential common goals. In situations that are autocratic or authoritarian the views and interests of some are imposed and those of others are ignored, which leads to resentment, discontent, and eventual rebellion.

We always must ask whether the way we treat others – both as individuals and nations – incites them to be resentful or respectful toward us. Humility on our part is likely to accomplish more than assuming that our values are superior to those of others. Self-defense, of course, may be justified when we are attacked. But if we want to move toward a just world we should hold ourselves and our leaders accountable to the rules of common decency and law – both nationally and internationally.

On April 30, 2016, I attended the commencement ceremony at Shimer College in Chicago. The keynote speaker was Dennis H.

Holtschneider, president of DePaul University. He reminded his audience about a phrase originated by the abolitionist Theodore Parker before the US Civil War, later used by Martin Luther King, Jr. and Barack Obama:

> *I do not pretend to understand the moral universe, the arc is a long one, my eye reaches but little ways. I cannot calculate the curve. . . . But from what I see I am sure it bends towards justice.*

Rev. Holtschneider ended his talk with two questions: "Will you be just?" and "Will you work for justice?"

The arc of justice does not have a will of its own. It will curve in the direction we guide it, hopefully to bring justice more fully into our lives and institutions. Those who support democratic values and human dignity believe in justice, but the meaning and practice of justice need to be continually adjusted to fit the reality of a changing world.

Democracy assumes justice, yet leaders can assure people via rhetoric and written constitutions that their intent is democratic as they move toward autocracy, oligarchy or other forms that do not reflect what is best for the vast majority. This is why a continual conversation is required at all levels of society – in our homes, schools, organizations, and governments – to ensure that the ever-changing form, but never-changing essence of democracy is maintained.

We all carry within us a vision of a just society. We all want justice for ourselves and those close to us. In the Introduction we began our conversation with the idea of trust – how we each started out in a mode of trust for those around us, how our trust often was betrayed, and how, with effort, we might restore trust between ourselves and others. When justice is seen as revenge it leads to endless repercussions and never rests. But when we begin to reestablish trust by recognizing the intrinsic value of others regardless of what we see as the differences between us, we can renew a sense of justice between and amongst us.

We can begin the conversation about the forms that democracy should take as we build it into our institutions and then rebuild them as needed. We may not need to tear down existing institutions, but they will need an infusion of democracy over time based on the continual insights that we gain together. The easy part is describing what we don't want or like. The real challenge is deciding what to replace it with.

We can bring democracy into our interactions every day of our lives by providing the respect for others that we want for ourselves. The conversation that we need to move democracy forward can happen everywhere that people interact.

Here are some questions to get us started:

1. What kind of world – or relationship, family, organization, nation – do we want for ourselves that is compatible with human dignity and justice?[248]
2. What does that actually look like in the real world?
3. What specific steps can we take together to move toward that vision?

We will need to repeat these questions periodically as we adjust our democracies to a continually changing world.

My suggestion?

Start the conversation.

Endnotes

1   *Albert Einstein, Philosopher-Scientist,* Page 13.
2   *Enlightening Symbols,* Page 7
3   *Enlightening Symbols,* Page 169
4   "Debate over *Homo naledi* continues." Science News, May 14, 2016
5   *The Second Bill of Rights,* Pages 45-51
6   "Hence the result of the discussion, as far as I'm concerned, is that I know nothing; for when I don't know what justice is I'll hardly know whether it is a kind of virtue or not, or whether a person who has it is happy or unhappy." *The Republic,* Section 354
7   *Aftershock,* Page 5
8   "...the adult's sense of his own ego cannot have been the same from the beginning. It must have undergone a development, which naturally cannot be demonstrated, but which admits of reconstruction with a fair degree of probability." *Civilization and its Discontents,* Pages 11-12
9   "By thus relying on preconceived notions the prejudiced frame of mind creates a rigidity which can become uncomfortable; but it has the advantage of permitting the projection of everything that feels alien within one's own heart unto some vague enemy outside..." *Childhood and Society,* Page 416
10 "There is and can be no self-knowledge base on theoretical assumptions, for the object of self-knowledge is the individual..." *The Undiscovered Self,* Page 8
11 *The Bullying Antidote,* Pages 76-77
12 *The Bullying Antidote,* Pages 255-64
13 *Politics,* Section 1337a
14 *In Defense of a Liberal Education,* Pages 40-44
15 "Medieval children had largely learned by living, eating and sleeping with their elders, all of whose activities they observed first hand. They were not isolated or protected from the adult world. Only boys from higher society attended school, and they did so in all-purpose, all-age groups. One of the earliest instances of a school being divided into classes was recorded at St. Paul's School in London in 1519. With age-grouping, and the extension of schooling, came a great increase in imposed discipline. Christian morality, codes of conduct, and humiliating punishments were imposed from above. Schoolboys were the first to be introduced to a prolonged and graduated progression toward adulthood. Girls, sometime married as early as thirteen, were much more likely to miss out." *Europe,* Pages 514-15
16 *The Birth of Europe,* Pages 36 and 99
17 *The Fortunes of Africa,* Pages 205, 519-20 and 594
18 *Contemporary China,* Pages 38-40
19 "Weak and wasteful schools hold Brazil back," The Economist, December 9, 2010
20 *The Oxford History of the American People,* Pages 70-71
21 *The Oxford History of the American People,* Pages 423, 486 and 531-33
22 *In Defense of a Liberal Education,* Pages 47-52
23 Quoted in *Autobiography of William O. Douglas, The Court Years, 1939-1975.* Page 109
24 *Excellent Sheep,* Page 13
25 *Excellent Sheep,* Page 25
26 *Excellent Sheep,* Page 60
27 *The Test,* Page 3
28 *The Test,* Page 14

29   *The Test*, Page 16
30   "After years of alleged bullying, an Ohio teen killed herself. Is her school district responsible?" Washington Post, May 23, 2016
31   *A Theory of Justice*, Pages 3-4
32   *A Theory of Justice*, Pages 6-7
33   *A Theory of Justice*, Pages 10-15
34   *The Idea of Justice*, Page viii
35   *The Idea of Justice*, Page xiii
36   *The Idea of Justice*, Page 17
37   *The Idea of Justice*, Page 2
38   *The Idea of Justice*, Page 184
39   *The Idea of Justice*, Page 276
40   *The Moral Consequences of Economic Growth*, Page 78
41   *The Moral Consequences of Economic Growth*, Page 148
42   *The Moral Consequences of Economic Growth*, Page 170
43   *The Moral Consequences of Economic Growth*, Page 177
44   *The Moral Consequences of Economic Growth*, Page 193
45   *The Moral Consequences of Economic Growth*, Page 194
46   *The Moral Consequences of Economic Growth*, Pages 273-79
47   *The Moral Consequences of Economic Growth*, Page 300
48   *The Moral Consequences of Economic Growth*, Page 307
49   *The Moral Consequences of Economic Growth*, Page 330
50   *The Moral Consequences of Economic Growth*, Page 333
51   *The Moral Consequences of Economic Growth*, Page 411
52   *The Moral Consequences of Economic Growth*, Page 422
53   *A Fighting Chance.* Page 41
54   *A Fighting Chance.* Page 72
55   *A Fighting Chance* Pages 89-90
56   *A Fighting Chance* Pages 112-13
57   *A Fighting Chance* Page 250
58   *The Jurisprudence of John Marshall*, Page 187
59   *The Autobiography of William O. Douglas, The Court Years, 1939-1975*, Page 43
60   *The Autobiography of William O. Douglas*, Page 111
61   *The Autobiography of William O. Douglas*, Page 115
62   *The Autobiography of William O. Douglas*, Page 134
63   *A Matter of Interpretation*, Page 47
64   *Active Liberty*, Page 11
65   "World Population Populations and Incarceration Rates," Business Insider, January 14, 2014
66   "The Price of Prisons: What Incarceration Costs Taxpayers," Vera Institute of Justice, February 4, 2012
67   "Education vs. Prison Costs," CNN Money, undated
68   *It's About Time: America's Imprisonment Binge*, Pages 23 and 166-67
69   *"...money is a matter of belief, even faith; belief in the person paying us; belief in the person issuing the money." The Ascent of Money, Page 29*
70   *Inflation Rate in Brazil averaged 373.82 percent from 1980 until 2016, reaching an all time high of 6821.31 percent in April of 1990 and a record low of 1.65 percent in December of 1998. Inflation Rate in Brazil is reported by the Instituto Brasiliero de Geografia e Estantistica (IBGE).*
71   *"...[on] Mesopotamian clay tablets...the transcriptions recorded...were repayments of* commodities that had been loaned..." *The Ascent of Money*, Page 30

72   *The Wealth of Nations,* Book V, Chapter I, Part II
73   Mark 14:7, *The New Oxford Annotated Bible*, Page 1234
74   *This Time Is Different*, Page 254
75   *Aftershock*, Page 12
76   *Capital in the Twenty-first Century, Page 1*
77   Using the online US Inflation Calendar.
78   "Income inequality in the U.S. by state, metropolitan area, and county," Economic
     Policy Institute, June 16, 2016
79   *Capital in the Twenty-first Century,* Page 297
80   *Capital in the Twenty-first Century*, Page 416
81   *Aftershock*, Page 2
82   *Aftershock*, Pages 3-5
83   *Aftershock*, Page 7
84   *The General Theory of Employment, Interest, and Money,* Page 248
85   *Aftershock,* Page 75
86   *Infectious Greed*, Page 207
87   *Greenspan's Bubbles,* Page 3
88   *The Moral Consequences of Economic Growth,* Page 411
89   "The interesting thing that happened when Kansas cut taxes and California hiked
     them," Washington Post, June 17, 2016.
90   *The Politics of International Economic Relations*, Page 7
91   *The Politics of International Economic Relations,* Pages 9 and 94
92   *Aftershock*, Page 117
93   *Energy Revolution*, Page 15
94   *Energy Revolution*, Page 2
95   *Energy Revolution*, Page 176
96   *Plan B 4.0*, Page 131
97   *The Boom*, Pages 30-31
98   *Energy Revolution*, Page 27
99   "Clean-Energy Jobs Surpass Oil Drilling for the First Time in US," Bloomberg,
     May 25, 2016.
100 *Plan 4.0*, Page 216-221
101 *Earth Odyssey*, Page 46
102 *Water 4.0.*, Page 183
103 *Water 4.0.*, Page 188
104 *Water 4.0.*, Pages 227 and 234-37
105 *Water 4.0.*, Page 250
106 *The Healing of America*, Pages 67-68
107 *The Healing of America*, Pages 48-51
108 *The Healing of America*, Pages 103-16
109 *The Healing of America*, Pages 83-86
110 "Privatization and its discontents – the evolving Chinese health care system,"
     New England Journal of Medicine, September 15, 2005
111 *Contemporary China*, Pages 38-39
112 *Russia,* Page 104
113 "Russian Health Care is Dying a Slow Death," Moscow Times, April 16, 2015
114 *Russia*, Pages 271-77
115 *Is Inequality Bad for Our Health?* Page 3
116 *Is Inequality Bad for Our Health?* Page 5
117 *Is Inequality Bad for Our Health?* Page 9
118 *Is Inequality Bad for Our Health?* Page 15

119 *Is Inequality Bad for Our Health?* Page 25
120 *Is Inequality Bad for Our Health?* Page 26
121 *Is Inequality Bad for Our Health?* Page 33
122 "The emergency of the Self-Made Men...and their great success in the new American democracy have a lot to do with what it is that defines a 'real' man." *Manhood in America*, Page 17.
123 Letter to the Danbury Baptist Association, 1802
124 Letter to Edward Livingston, 1822
125 Leviticus 19:18, *The New Oxford Annotated Bible*
126 Matthew 6:14, *The New Oxford Annotated Bible*
127 Matthew 10:34, *The New Oxford Annotated Bible*
128 *The Qur'an*, 5:17
129 *The Qur'an*, 8:12
130 "Richard Dawkins draws criticism for 'clock boy' Ahmed Mohamed tweets," CNN, November 25, 2015
131 *The Language of God, Page* 3
132 *The Language of God, Page* 30
133 From a 1930 essay entitled: "What I Believe."
134 *A Brief History of Time*, Page 193
135 *The Undiscovered Self*, Page 23
136 *Why We Cooperate*, Pages IX to XIII
137 *Why We Cooperate*, Pages 12-15
138 *Why We Cooperate*, Pages 29-42
139 *Louder than Words*, Page 6
140 *Louder than Words*, Page 16
141 *Louder than Words*, Page 76
142 *Louder than Words*, Page 259
143 *Einstein's Cosmos*, Page 35
144 *Einstein's Cosmos*, Page 62
145 *Einstein's Cosmos, Page* 142
146 *Einstein's Cosmos* 205
147 *Einstein's Cosmos, Page* 218
148 *The Double Helix*, Page 4
149 *The Double Helix*, Page 52
150 *The Double Helix*, Page 64
151 *Plato: Complete Works, the Apology, 38a*
152 *The Philosophy of Freedom*, Pages 26-30
153 *The Philosophy of Freedom*, Page 104
154 *The Philosophy of Freedom*, Pages 109 and 129
155 *Man and His Symbols*, Pages 83-85
156 *Man and His Symbols*, Pages 94-95
157 *Thinking Fast and Slow, Pages* 20-25
158 *Thinking Fast and Slow, Pages* 50-52
159 *Thinking Fast and Slow, Page* 81
160 *Thinking Fast and Slow, Page* 82
161 *Thinking Fast and Slow, Page* 115
162 *Thinking Fast and* Slow, Page 138
163 *Thinking Fast and Slow*, Page 347
164 *Thinking Fast and* Slow, Page 393
165 *The Power of Habit*, Page XVI
166 *The Power of Habit,* Page 131

167   *The Power of Habit,* Page 135
168   *The Power of Habit,* Page 273
169   *The Righteous Mind*, Page 11
170   *The Righteous Mind*, Pages 50-56
171   *The Righteous Mind*, Page 65
172   *The Righteous Mind*, Page 79
173   *The Righteous Mind*, Page 172
174   *The Righteous Mind*, Page 244
175   *The Righteous Mind*, Page 365
176   *Utopian Thought in the Western World,* Page 28
177   *The Origins of Political Order*, Page 23
178   "A study of ancient Japanese bones might challenge our ideas about human nature," Washington Post, April 1, 2016
179   *In the Crossfire*, Page 3
180   "Vietnam's human rights record remains dire in all areas. The Communist Party maintains a monopoly on political power and allows no challenge to its leadership. Basic rights, including freedom of speech, opinion, press, association, and religion, are restricted. Rights activists and bloggers face harassment, intimidation, physical assault, and imprisonment. Farmers continue to lose land to development projects without adequate compensation, and workers are not allowed to form independent unions. The police use torture and beatings to extract confessions. The criminal justice system lacks independence. State-run drug rehabilitation centers exploit detainees as laborers making goods for local markets and export. Nevertheless, increasing numbers of bloggers and activists have called publicly for democracy and greater freedoms." From the website of Human Rights Watch, 2016.
181   *A History of the Middle East*, Pages 428-29
182   *The Penguin History of Latin America*, Pages 326 and 353
183   "In Argentina, mothers of 'disappeared" protest Obama's marking of 1976 coup," The Guardian, March 23, 2016
184   *Terror in the Name of God*, Page ix
185   *Terror in the Name of God*, Pages xv-xvi
186   *Terror in the Name of God*, Page xx
187   *Terror in the Name of God*, Page xxviii
188   *Terror in the Name of God*, Page 4
189   *Terror in the Name of God*, Page 7
190   *Terror in the Name of God*, Page 31
191   *Terror in the Name of God*, Page 41
192   *Terror in the Name of God*, Page 50
193   *Terror in the Name of God*, Pages 85-86
194   *Terror in the Name of God*, Page 103
195   *Terror in the Name of God*, Pages 281-83
196   *The Politics of International Economic Relations*, Pages 14-17
197   *The Oxford History of the American People,* Pages 1054-55
198   *Contemporary Europe*, Pages 34-35
199   *The Future of Success,* Pages 79-80
200   *Hard Choices*, Page 230
201   *Hard Choices*, Page 311
202   *Hard Choices,* Page 345
203   *Hard Choices*, Pages 448-49 and 460
204   *Hard Choices*, Page 517

205 *Hard Choices*, Page 566
206 *Hard Choices,* Page 571
207 *Hard Choices,* Page 594
208 *Power and Governance in a Partially Globalized World*, Pages 17-18
209 *Politics*, 1252a
210 *Politics*, 1266b
211 *Politics*, 1310a
212 *Politics*, 1271a
213 *Politics*, 1317a
214 *Politics*, 1320a and b
215 *Edmund Burke – The First Conservative,* Page 29
216 *Edmund Burke – The First Conservative,* Page 159
217 *Edmund Burke – The First Conservative,* Page 205
218 *Edmund Burke – The First Conservative*, Page 231
219 Speech at High Wycombe, England (27 November 1832); published in *Selected Speeches of the Late Right Honourable the Earl of Beaconsfield*, ed. T. E. Kebbel (1882), Volume 1, Page 8.
220 *The Way Forward,* Page x
221 *The Way Forward,* Page 23
222 *The Way Forward,* Page 28
223 *The Way Forward,* Page 57
224 *The Way Forward,* Page 72
225 *The Way Forward,* Page 125
226 *The Way Forward,* Page 172
227 *The Way Forward,* Page 188
228 *The Way Forward,* Page 214
229 *The Way Forward,* Page 258
230 *My Life,* Pages 495-96
231 *My Life,* Page 579
232 *My Life*, Page 773
233 *My Life*, Page 720
234 *Our Divided Political Heart,* Page 7
235 *Our Divided Political Heart,* Page 56
236 *Our Divided Political Heart,* Page 71
237 *Our Divided Political Heart,* Page 122
238 *Our Divided Political Heart,* Page 258
239 *Our Divided Political Heart,* Page 266
240 *Lords of Secrecy*, Pages 1-3
241 *Lords of Secrecy*, Page 7
242 *Lords of Secrecy*, Pages 7-10
243 *Lords of Secrecy*, Pages 14-16
244 *Lords of Secrecy*, Page 18
245 Quoted in *Lords of Secrecy*, Page 33
246 *Team of Rivals,* Page 9
247 *The Oxford History of Britain,* Page 571
248 "We the People of the United States, in Order to form a more perfect Union, establish Justice, insure domestic Tranquility, provide for the common defence, promote the general Welfare, and secure the Blessings of Liberty to ourselves and our Posterity, do ordain and establish this Constitution for the United States of America." Preamble to the US Constitution, 1787 in *America's Constitution, a Biography*, Page 479

REFERENCES

Active Liberty: Interpreting our Democratic Constitution. Stephen Breyer. 2005, Knopf.

Africa Uncorked: Travels in Extreme Wine Territory. John and Erica Platter. 2002. Kyle Cathie Limited.

Aftershock. Robert B. Reich. 2010, 2013. Vintage.

On Aggression. Konrad Lorenz. 1963, 1966. Harcourt.

Aias. Sophocles. 2011, 2012. Harper Perennial.

Albert Einstein, Philosopher-Scientist. Edited by Paul Arthur Schilpp. 1949. Tudor Publishing Company

American Exceptionalism: A Double-Edged Sword. Seymour Martin Lipset. 1996, 1997. Norton.

America's Constitution: A Biography. Akhil Reed Amar. 2005. Random House.

Angler: The Cheney Vice Presidency. Barton Gellman. 2008. The Penguin Press.

Arthurian Romances. Chretien de Troyes. [1914] 1968. Everyman's Library.

The Ascent of Money: A Financial History of the World. Neal Ferguson. 2008. Penguin.

The Audacity of Hope: Thoughts on Reclaiming the American Dream.

Barack Obama. 2006. Crown.

The Autobiography of William O. Douglas, the Court Years, 1939-1975. 1980. Random House.

Between the World and Me. Ta-Nehisi Coates. 2015. Spiegel and Grau.

The Birth of Europe. Jacques le Goff. 2005, 2007. Blackwell.

The Boom. Russell Gold. 2014. Simon and Schuster.

A Brief History of France. Cecil Jenkins. 2011. Running Press.

The Bullying Antidote. Louise Hart and Kristen Caven. 2013. Hazelden.

Capital in the Twenty-First Century. Thomas Piketty. 2013, 2014. Belknap/Harvard.

Childhood and Society. Erik H. Erikson. [1950]. 1986. Norton.

China, a History. John Keay. 2008, 2009. Basic Books.

Christendom. Roland H. Bainton. 1964, 1966. American Heritage Publishing.

The Civil War. Harry Hansen. 1961. Mentor.

Civilization and Its Discontents. Sigmund Freud. [1930]2011. Martino Publishing.

Common Sense. Thomas Paine. [1776] 2015. Penguin.

A Concise History of Japan. Brett L. Walker. 2015. Cambridge University Press.

Constitutions of the World. Robert L. Maddex. 1995,1996, 2014. Routledge.

Contemporary China. François Godement. 2016. Rowman and Littlefield.

The Communist Manifesto. Karl Marx and Friedrich Engels. [1848] 1998. Signet.

Contemporary Europe. 2000, 2012. Edited by Richard Sakwa and Anne Stevens. Palgrave Macmillan.

Creating a Culture of Revolution. Deborah Pearl. 2015. Slavica Press.

Critique of Pure Reason. Immanuel Kant. [1781] 1966. Anchor.

In the Crossfire. Ngo Van. Ken Knabb and Helene Fleury editors. 2010. AK Press.

The Cultural Origins of Human Cognition. Michael Tomasello. 1999, 2000. Harvard University Press.

Day of Reckoning: The Consequences of American Economic Policy. Benjamin M. Friedman. 1988, 1989. Vintage Books.

The Dance Macabre of Women. Edited by Ann Tukey Harrison. 1994. Kent State University Press.

In Defense of a Liberal Education. Fareed Zakaria. 2015. Norton.

Democracy: A History. John Dunn. 2005. Atlantic Monthly Press.

Democracy in America. Alexis de Tocqueville. [1835] 1994. Everyman's Library.

The Discourses. Niccolò Machiavelli. [1516] 1998. Penguin.

The Double Helix. James D. Watson. 1968. Atheneum.

Earth Odyssey: Around the World in Search of our Environmental Future. Mark Hertsgaard. 1998. Broadway Books.

Edmund Burke - The First Conservative. Jesse Norman. 2013. Basic Books.

Eichmann in Jerusalem, a Report on the Banality of Evil. Hannah Arendt. 1963, 2006. Penguin.

Einstein's Cosmos. Michio Kaku. 2004, 2005. Norton.

To End All Wars. Adam Hochschild. 2011, 2012. Mariner Books.

The End of Karma: Hope and Fury among India's Young. Somini Sengupta. 2016. W.W. Norton.

Energy Revolution: The Physics and the Promise of Efficient Technology. Mara Prentiss. 2015. Belknap/Harvard.

Enlightening Symbols: A Short History of Mathematical Notation and its Hidden Powers. Joseph Mazur. 2014. Princeton University Press.

An Essay Concerning Human Understanding. John Locke. [1690] 1997, 2004. Penguin Classics.

Europe: A History. Norman Davies. 1996, 1998. Harper Collins.

Europe before Rome. T. Douglas Price. 2013. Oxford University Press.

Excellent Sheep, The Miseducation of the American Elite and the Way to a Meaningful Life. William Deresiewicz. 2014. Free Press.

The Fall of the Third Republic. William L. Shirer. 1969. Simon and Schuster.

A Fighting Chance. Elizabeth Warren. 2014. Metropolitan.

The Fortunes of Africa. Martin Meredith. 2014. Simon and Schuster.

Founding Brothers. Joseph J. Ellis. 2001. Knopf.

1491: New Revelations of the Americas before Columbus. Charles C. Mann. 2005, 2011. Vintage.

Franklin and Winston. Jon Meacham. 2003. Random House.

Freefall: America, Free Markets, and the Sinking of the World Economy. Joseph Stiglitz, 2010. Norton.

The Future of Success. Robert B. Reich. 2000. Knopf.

Gargantua and Pantagruel. Francois Rabelais. 1990. Norton.

The General Theory of Employment, Interest, and Money. John Maynard Keynes. [1935] 1964. Harcourt.

Great Inventors and their Inventions. Frank B. Bachman. 1918. American Book Company.

Greenspan's Bubble: The Age of Ignorance at the Federal Reserve. William A. Fleckenstein with Frederick Sheehan. 2008. McGraw Hill.

Guns, Germs and Steel. Jared Diamond. 1997, 1999. Norton.

Hard Choices. Hillary Clinton. 2014. Simon and Schuster.

Haut-Brion. Asa Briggs. 1994. Faber and Faber.

The Healing of America. T.R. Reid. 2009. Penguin.

High Price. Carl Hart. 2013. Harper Collins.

A History of Egypt. Jason Thompson. 2008, 2009. Anchor.

A History of the Global Stock Market. B. Mark Smith. 2003, 2004. University of Chicago Press.

A History of the Middle East. Peter Mansfield. Revised and updated by Nicolas Pelham. 1991, 2013.

The Human Condition. Hannah Arendt. 1958, 1998. University of Chicago Press.

The Idea of Justice. Amartya Sen. 2009. Belknap/Harvard.

An Indigenous Peoples' History of the United States. Roxanne Dunbar-Ortiz. 2014. Beacon Press.

Is Inequality Bad for our Health? Norman Daniels, Bruce Kennedy, and Ichiro Kawachi. 2000. Beacon Press.

Infectious Greed: How Deceit and Risk Corrupted the Financial Markets. Frank Partnoy. 2003. Holt.

The Inferno. Dante Alighieri. [1308-20] 1954, 2001. Signet.

Inferno: The World at War, 1939-45. Max Hastings. 2011, 2012. Vintage.

Jean-Jacques Rousseau, Restless Genius. Leo Damrosch. 2005. Houghton Mifflin.

John Dewey and the Promise of America. Progressive Education Booklet No. 14. 1939.

The Jurisprudence of John Marshal. Robert Kenneth Faulkner. 1968. Princeton University Press.

The Landmark Thucydides. Thucydides and Robert B. Strassler. 1998. Touchstone.

The Language of God. Francis Collins. 2006. Free Press.

On Liberty. John Stuart Mill. [1859] 2002. Dover.

Long Walk to Freedom. Nelson Mandela. 1995. Little, Brown and Company

Lords of Secrecy. Scott Horton. 2015. Nation Books.

Louder than Words. Benjamin K. Bergen, 2014, Basic Books.

Man and His Symbols, Carl G. Jung, 1961, Doubleday.

The Man without a Face: The Unlikely Rise of Vladimir Putin. Masha Gessen. 2012. Riverhead Books.

Manhood in America. Michael Kimmel. 1996. Free Press.

A Matter of Interpretation: Federal Courts and the Law. Antonin
  Scalia. 1997. Princeton University Press.
The Metaphysics of Morals. Immanuel Kant. [1797] 1996, 2000.
  Cambridge University Press.
The Moral Consequences of Economic Growth. Benjamin M. Friedman.
  2005. Vintage.
My Life. Bill Clinton. 2004. Knopf
Napa: The Story of an American Eden. James Conway. 1990.
  Houghton Mifflin
Natural Law and Natural Rights. John Finnis. *[1980] 2002.* Oxford
  University Press.
The New Oxford Annotated Bible. 1962, 1973. Oxford University
  Press.
The Origin of Species. Charles Darwin. [1859] 2003. Signet Classics.
The Origins and History of Consciousness. Erich Neumann. 1954.
  1973. Bollingen.
The Origins of Political Order. Francis Fukuyama. 2011, 2012.
  Farrar, Straus, and Giroux.
Our Divided Political Heart. E.J. Dionne Jr. 2012. Bloomsbury.
The Oxford History of the American People. Samuel Eliot Morison.
  1965. Oxford University Press.
The Oxford History of Britain. Kenneth O. Morgan, editor. 1984,
  2010. Oxford University Press.
The Oxford Illustrated History of Prehistoric Europe. Barry Cunliffe.
  2001. Oxford University Press.
Passions: The Wines and Travels of Thomas Jefferson. James M.
  Gabler. 1996. Bacchus Press.
The Penguin History of Latin America. Edwin Williamson. 1992,
  2009. Penguin.
Philosophical Dictionary. Voltaire. [1764] 1972, 2004. Thomas
  Besterman, Editor and Translator. Penguin Classics. 351
Philosophies of India. Heinrich Zimmer. 1951, 1974. Bollingen

Series/Princeton.

The Philosophy of Freedom. Rudolf Steiner. [1894] 2011. Reprint of 1916 translation.

Plan B 4.0: Mobilizing to Save Civilization. Lester R. Brown. 2009. W.W. Norton.

Plato, Complete Works. 1997. Edited by John M. Cooper. Hackett.

Politics and the Athenian Constitution. Aristotle. 1959, 1961. Everyman's Library.

The Politics of International Economic Relations. Joan E. Spero and Jeffrey A. Hart. 2003. Thomson Wadsworth.

Power and Governance in a Partially Globalized World. Robert Keohane. 2002. Routledge.

The Power of Habit. Charles Duhigg. 2012. Random House.

The Prince. Niccolo Machiavelli. [1513] 1981. Bantam Classics.

Quantum. Einstein, Bohr and the Great Debate about the Nature of Reality. Manjit Kumar. 2008. Norton.

The Qur'an, A new translation by M.A.S. Abdel Haleem, 2004, 2010. Oxford World's Classics.

A Rage for Order. Robert F. Worth. 2016. Farrar, Straus, and Giroux.

Relativity and Common Sense, Herman Bondi. 1962, 1980. Dover.

The Renaissance. Walter Pater. [1873] 1959. Mentor.

The Republic of Plato. 1997. Hackett Press.

The Righteous Mind. Jonathan Haidt. 2012, 2013. Vintage Books.

Russia. Jonathan Dimbleby. 2008. BBC Books.

Russia, a History. Gregory L. Freeze. 1997, 2009. Oxford University Press.

The Second Bill of Rights. Cass R. Sunstein. 2004. Basic Books.

1776. David McCullough. 2005, 2006. Simon and Schuster.

The Social Contract. John Jacques Rousseau. [1762] 1974. Penguin.

The Spirit of Democracy. Larry Diamond. 2008. Henry Holt and Company.

SPQR. Mary Beard. 2015. Liveright.

Summa Theologiae. Thomas Aquinas. [1265-74] 1964, 1969. Doubleday Image Book.

Team of Rivals. Doris Kearns Goodwin. 2005, 2006. Simon and Schuster.

Tear Down This Myth. Will Bunch. 2009. Free Press.

Terror in the Name of God. Jessica Stern. 2004. Ecco Publishers.

The Test. Anya Kamenetz. 2015. Public Affairs.

A Theory of Justice. John Rawls. 1971, 1999. Belknap/Harvard.

Thinking Fast and Slow. Daniel Kahneman. 2011. Farrar, Strauss, and Giroux.

This Time is Different. Carmen H. Reinhart and Kenneth S. Rogoff. 2009. Princeton University Press.

Three Germanies: West Germany, East Germany and the Berlin Republic. Michael Gehler. 2011. Reaktion Books Ltd.

In an Uncertain World. Robert E. Rubin. 2003. Random House.

The Undiscovered Self. Carl Jung. 1957, 2006. Signet.

Utopia. Thomas More. [1516] 2015. Privately printed.

Utopian Thought in the Western World. Frank E. Manuel and Fritzie P. Manuel. 1979. Belknap/Harvard.

Wall Street, a History. Charles R. Geisst. 1997, 2012. Oxford University Press.

Walking the Bible. Bruce Feiler. 2001, 2014. William Morrow Publishing.

Water 4.0. David Sedlak. 2014. Yale University Press.

The Warmth of Other Suns: The Epic Story of America's Great Migration. Isabel Wilkerson. 2010, 2011. Vintage.

The Way Forward. Paul Ryan. 2014. Hachette Book Group.

The Wealth of Nations. Adam Smith. [1776]. 2004. Barnes and Noble.

Western Civilization, the Struggle for Empire to Europe in the Modern World. William L. Langer, General Editor. 1968. Harper and Row.

Why We Cooperate. Michael Tomasello. 2009. MIT Press.

Wine. Andre Domine. 2000, 2001. Konemann Press.

Wine and War. Don and Petie Kladstrup. 2001. Broadway Books.

The Years of Lyndon Johnson: the Passage of Power. Robert A. Caro. 2012. Willam A. Knopf.

You are under Arrest for Masterminding the Egyptian Revolution. Ahmed Salah with Alex Mayyasi. 2016. Spark Publication.

Index

The typestyle used throughout this book is
Granjon, except for *The World of Wine* boxes
which are set in Papyrus.

CPSIA information can be obtained
at www.ICGtesting.com
Printed in the USA
FSOW01n0619260816
24199FS